Ally No More

ALLY
NO
MORE

*Erdoğan's New
Turkish Caliphate
and the Rising Jihadist
Threat to the West*

Center for Security Policy Press

For more information about this book, visit
SECUREFREEDOM.ORG

*Ally No More: Erdoğan's New Turkish Caliphate
and the Rising Jihadist Threat to the West*
is published in the United States
by the Center for Security Policy Press,
a division of the Center for Security Policy.

ISBN-13: 9781717071675
ISBN-10: 1717071678

The Center for Security Policy
Washington, D.C.
Phone: 202-835-9077
Email: info@SecureFreedom.org
For more information, visit SecureFreedom.org

Book design by Bravura Books

Contents

FOREWORD

The ancient land of Turkey is at one of those pivotal points in history when change is occurring at a pace almost too fast to monitor comprehensively, let alone analyze with confidence. During most of the 20th Century, the world, and especially the West, became accustomed to a post-Ottoman Empire Turkey that was making strides toward modernization under a succession of administrations committed to the formula for secular governance of a Muslim country laid out by the Turkish Republic's founder, Mustafa Kemal Ataturk. And, when it became necessary from time to time to correct regime deviations from the path laid down by Ataturk, the Turkish Army would step in.

Beneath the surface, however, Turkey's deeply conservative Islamic masses seethed with discontent at the loss of their Ottoman caliphate and relegation of Islam to the mosques. Figures like Syed Nursi drew Muslim students to secretive "study circles," where Islam's totalitarian political, military and legal system known as Sharia and the jihad it commands were inculcated into generations of willing young students. The jihadist Sunni cleric, Fethullah Gülen was one of those who, having studied under Nursi, set up his own networks to the same end. By the time a young Recep Tayyip Erdoğan emerged from an Imam Hatip Islamic school in the early 1970s, both he and legions among his age cohort were ready to jettison Ataturk's secular agenda and bring Turkey back to Islam.

The repercussions and future implications of this phenomenon is the focus of a series of splendid essays contained in this, the Center for Security Policy Press' newest offering. *Ally No More: Erdoğan's New Turkish Caliphate and the Rising Jihadist Threat to the West* documents the momentous shift that is now taking place in a Turkey ruled by President Erdoğan and his Justice and Development Party (AKP).

Drawing on the combined insights and scholarship of ten authors, the book comprehensively explores an array of topics that convey just how dramatically things have changed in and with Turkey, a once-trusted NATO ally—and the extent to which they are likely, all other things being equal, to change still more and *for the worse* in the period ahead.

Although a plethora of other recent publications have been devoted to Erdoğan personally, various aspects of Turkish society, or to Turkey's expanding regional aggression, by drawing on such a wealth of expertise, this book offers a comprehensive assessment of where the Sharia-supremacist regime in Ankara is now, and where it appears to be headed.

In particular, as its title makes plain, such developments are of such a momentous character that long-held attitudes toward Turkey must be adapted to the new reality: A course-correction is urgently required in the relationship between the United States and her other NATO allies on the one hand and Turkey on the other.

No honest observer of Middle East events can ignore the intensifying and increasingly brazen hostility of Erdoğan's policies, both domestic and foreign, toward America and other Western nations, including notably the Jewish State. At home, he rules ever-more as a tyrant, trampling Turkey's constitution and jailing thousands of his supposed enemies. Abroad, alarm is rising over regime rhetoric that threatens Cyprus, Greece, Israel, the Balkans, and France, even as the Turkish military has been rolling over Syrian battlefields, seizing territory from Kurdish militias long allied with and supported by the United States.

Meanwhile, Erdoğan and his top officials speak openly of engaging in "jihad" and a revival of the Ottoman Empire under the rule of a new Islamic caliph. Increasingly, the Turkish president and his admirers at home and abroad explicitly describe him as assuming that role.

Yet, senior American military and national security officials continue to cling to an image of Turkey as a reliable NATO ally. They have, it seems, yet to face up to the nature, let alone the magnitude of Turkey's Islamist transformation and, with it, much of the familiar landscape of the Middle East.

It is absolutely imperative that the U.S. leadership recognize and address the new paradigm. The Middle East Forum's Daniel Pipes takes on this challenge directly in his chapter of *NATO's Turkey Challenge*. He helpfully includes a list of possible measures Turkey's erstwhile NATO partners could—and soon must—take in the face of Erdoğan's apparent determination to destabilize the entire region.

Other highlights of *Ally No More* include: An analysis by long-time Pentagon duty expert and Middle East scholar Harold Rhode that concludes Erdoğan's entire *raison d'etre* seems to be the destruction of Ataturk's legacy and the re-orienting of Turkey's government and society away from the Western community of nations, characterized by re-Islamization and a power struggle for domination of the Islamic *umma*. Turkish writer Uzay Bulut and Center for Security Policy (CSP) Senior Fellow Deborah Weiss describe the sharp deterioration in measures of liberal democracy, including education and freedom of speech. Financial analyst and essayist David Goldman examines the difficult economic and demographic challenges facing Turkey in the near future. And Turkish columnist Burak Bekdil's chapter on upcoming elections cites these and other key societal data that may indicate a more difficult electoral campaign for Erdoğan than generally thought.

Were Turkey's destabilizing activities confined to the Middle East, it would be bad enough. But the effects of the Erdoğan agenda are being felt well beyond the immediate region. As CSP's Executive Vice President, Christopher Hull, explains in his chapter, Turkey's already large and growing diaspora population in Western Europe portends deep societal disruption in Germany and elsewhere. Similarly, a pair of authors who have chosen to remain unidentified and CSP Vice President for Research and Analysis Clare Lopez arrive at a similar conclusion in their separate contributions: The malevolent handiwork of the two erstwhile partners in jihad, Recep Tayyip Erdoğan and Fethullah Gülen, has not been confined to Turkey. Notably, the Gülen Movement has been assiduously working to replicate in the United States the extensive network of schools and business connections that were used to re-Islamize Turkey. Today, Gülen's influence operations are able to exploit a sizeable infrastructure here in the form of some 160 K-12 charter schools, four universities and dozens of cultural centers.

Perhaps the most disturbing chapter of the book, however, is the one written by Center for Security Policy staff concerning the direct collaboration now increasingly evident between Erdoğan's jihadist AKP regime in Ankara and subversive elements inside the United States. This is the practical effect of the Turks' many years of support for Hamas and the Muslim Brotherhood and its relatively recent, and ominous, embrace of the U.S. Council of Muslim Organizations (USCMO), a toxic political organization established by the Brotherhood in this country.

With the 2016 opening of the massive Diyanet Center of America in Lanham, Maryland—an event at which President Erdoğan officiated, the government of Turkey secured what amounts to a hub for seditious operations on U.S. territory mounted in collaboration with the Muslim Brotherhood elements engaged in the stealthy, subversive mission they have dubbed "Civilization Jihad." Interestingly, notwithstanding the appearances of a bitter split between Erdoğan and Gülen, senior U.S. Brotherhood officials, specifically from the Council on American Islamic Relations (CAIR), continue to collaborate openly with identifiable Gülen groups, such as the Atlantic Institute.

The publication of *Ally No More* could scarcely be more timely. We hope that this book will serve its intended purpose of alerting U.S. national security practitioners, both inside and outside of government, to the rising threat of an aggressive, expansionist jihad state still nominally doing business as a NATO ally. The unavoidable truth is that Turkey's leadership appears bent on inexorably returning to the days of the Ottoman Caliphate, with all the alarming consequences for its own minority Kurds as well as others—including our vital interests—both near and far.

For the United States, the dangers posed by a putative NATO ally openly collaborating on American soil with an insurgent jihadist Muslim Brotherhood are especially worrying. These trends must be recognized and confronted, both expeditiously and effectively. To that end, it is our hope that this volume—with its path-breaking chapters addressing Turkey's worrying political and geostrategic evolution, its sponsorship of and alliance with the Muslim Brotherhood, Ankara's unravelling relationship with the Western alliance and the attendant dangers for U.S. national security of all these dynamics—will serve to sound the alarm: The Turkish government of Recep Tayyip Erdoğan is no longer an ally and we must adopt *at a minimum* the sorts of corrective actions identified herein to address that reality.

Frank J. Gaffney, Jr.
President
Center for Security Policy
9 April 2018

CHAPTER 1

How to Understand Erdoğan & His Neo-Ottoman Strategy to Destroy Ataturk's Turkey

• BY HAROLD RHODE

Whither Turkey? That question has been asked for many years, even before Erdoğan made his appearance on the political scene in Turkey. To be sure, Mustafa Kemal Ataturk, who in the early 1920s founded the Secular Republic of Turkey, did his utmost to re-orient Turkey's political affiliation from being a—possibly "the"—most important power in the Muslim world to being a member of the Western community of nations.

He changed the script in which the language was written from a modified form of the Arabic script, to the Latin script, making it much easier for Turks to learn to read and write, but also at the same time cutting them off from their Islamic past. It is therefore not surprising that most Turks today having grown up with the Latin script, deep inside see the Arabic script which their ancestors used to write Turkish as foreign, and at times, even threatening.

Ataturk tried to relegate Islam to the realm of the private—*i.e.*, the basis for ethnics and morals—as long as they didn't conflict with Western values. Islam was no longer to the basis of the political identity of the state, as it had been under the Ottoman Empire.

But could Ataturk succeed in reorienting Turkey's identity? His mission was a revolutionary one—to say the least. Is it even possible to change people's identity so quickly? What happened in reality is that many people began to mouth Ataturk's dictums, but history shows us that sayings aren't easily assimilated when they represent such a radical reinterpretation of how people see themselves.

Up until the end of World War I, the Ottoman Empire's basic *raison d'être* was the propagation and expansion of (Sunni) Islam. Sunni Islam was the basis of identity for the vast majority of the people living in that Empire. But until the last few years of the Empire's existence, its ruler—the Ottoman sultan - sold himself to the Sunni Muslims of the world as their Caliph. That meant that he was the ruler not only the subjects of his Empire, but as the true ruler of all the Muslims—even non-Sunnis - no matter where they lived in the world. The traditional Islamic identity does not recognize political borders. Many Sunni Muslims, wherever they lived in the world, looked to him as their spiritual and even political ruler, even if they lived in far-away places such as today's northwestern China or Central Asia. Non-Muslims—including the Christians, Jews and Alevis—*i.e.*, Turks and Kurds who followed a form of Islam much closer to Shiism—and who were living in the Ottoman Empire, were second class citizens, and never could reach the highest levels of the Empire because they weren't Sunni Muslims.

The Ottoman identity was therefore what we in the West would say was religious in nature, and in conflict with the Western idea that borders form the basis of group/national identity. Until the European Union (EU)'s promotion of a European identity, which only started in the late 20th century, the borders of countries—from the Western point of view—were almost sacrosanct.

It is that Western identity that Ataturk tried to inculcate into the people of the Republic of Turkey, which Ataturk founded on the embers of the defeated Ottoman Empire after World War I.

Most of the citizens of Ataturk's newly founded Republic of Turkey had great difficulty assimilating Ataturk's view of the world. In the early 1940s - less than ten years after Ataturk's death - the great Turkish poet Ak Sakal summarized this problem beautifully. "Turkey", he wrote, "is like a ship the crew of which is sailing full speed ahead towards the West, while the people of the country are sailing the boat full speed ahead towards the East—*i.e.*, in the traditional Islamic direction—*i.e.*, in the opposite direction.

The ruling "secular establishment" knew this. Their descendants almost "worshipped" Ataturk. Oddly enough, Ataturk was in many ways similar to the Muslim prophet Muhammad, who tried to forge a new identity among his Arabian followers. After their prophet died, many of Muhammad's followers tried to re-assume their traditional pre-Islamic identities. After Ataturk died, many citizens in his Republic tried to do the same—in this case reverting to the Islam as the basis for their identity. But the army—the guarantor of the survival of Ataturk's secular Republic— prevented them from doing so. This struggle between Ataturkism and the traditional Turkish Muslim identity continued until Erdoğan entered the political scene. It is he who managed to destroy the secular basis both of Turkish society, and to emasculate the Turkish army and make it kowtow to his political will. Into this life and death struggle for the soul of modern Turkey was born Turkey's future leader,

Recep Tayyip Erdoğan. Erdoğan grew up in a devout traditional family in Istanbul, which loathed what the secular establishment had imposed on the Turks and Turkey, and who waited for the opportunity to put right all of the wrongs which Ataturk and his cohorts had imposed on the people of Turkey.

Erdoğan appealed to the very essence of the Turkish soul. His message was simple. Let us stop trying to be what we aren't and return to our traditional way of understanding ourselves and the world. In truth, even many of the passionate secularists, when you scratched their surfaces, deep down understand themselves in eastern—*i.e.*, Muslim—terms, even if they cloaked themselves in Western garb and mouthed Western platitudes about who they were.

For example, some of Turkey's political and military leaders often privately lamented the fact that Ataturk did not force his countrymen to abandon Islam altogether, and make them become Christians. Leaving aside the utter impossibility of his being able to do this, the question arises as to why these passionate Ataturkists could even come up with such an idea.

From thousands of hours of conversations with Turks in their native language, it seems clear that they hated the fact that deep inside, these secular Turks still saw themselves culturally first and foremost as Muslims. How can we come to that conclusion? The following examples illustrate their mindset:

After the 1974 Greek-Turkish war in Cyprus, the Americans eventually imposed what was called "the 7 to 10 ratio" for military aid to both of America's NATO allies—Greece and Turkey. Greece, because of its small size, received 7/10 of whatever aid Turkey, with its far greater population and territorial size, received. Even though the Turks were happy to receive the aid, they felt that because of their vast territory which also shared a border with the Soviet enemy, that they deserved much more. In many discussions with Turkey's political and military elite, both constantly complained that America always favored Greece because the Greeks were Christian and the Turks were Muslim. From a Western perspective, this the religious identity of either was irrelevant. But from a Muslim perspective, this is paramount. There is an Islamic dictum attributed to the Muslim prophet, Unbelief—*i.e.*, the non-Muslims—is one nation (in Arabic *"al-Kufr millatun wahida."*[*] Meaning that from a Muslim perspective, there are only two nations in the world—the Muslim nation and the non-Muslim nation. That means that all Muslims are brothers to each other and all non-Muslims are brothers to each

---

[*] For more on this hadith, see https://www.gatestoneinstitute.org/2572/brotherhood-in-islam

other. The differences the non-Muslims have which each other, therefore are irrelevant. Greek, Americans, Orthodox Christians, Protestants, Catholics, and Jews, are all one people. Opposed to them are the Muslims, be they Shiite, Sunni, Turk, Arab, Persian, etc.

As a result, from this perspective, the Turks who are Muslims, and the Americans who are Christians, when push comes to shove, can never be on the same side. Greeks, Americans, Jews, and Israel, on the other hand, also form one nation, and are united against the Muslims. Even "secular" Muslims learned this from the time they were little. Their culture made this clear to them. By this logic, Turks and Americans could never be permanent friends or brothers, because they belong to different worlds. By this definition, the Turkish identity is based more on religious identity rather than ethnicity or national origin.

What Does It Mean to be a Turk Today in Turkey?

So what does it mean to be a Turk today in Turkey? It has two meanings: 1) an ethnic Turk living in Turkey; and 2) a non-ethnic Muslim citizen of Turkey—whether ethnically Turkish, Kurdish, or of some other Muslim-origin ethnic groups like 19th Caucasian immigrants to Anatolia, and the huge migration of southeastern Muslim Europeans who left their ancient homelands when the 19th century southeastern countries of Bulgaria, Albania, Greece, Serbia, Bosnia, and Macedonia eventually came into existence.

As such, non-Muslims who have lived in what is Turkey today since time immemorial like the Jews, and various Christian group like the Armenians and Greeks, are essentially outsiders, meaning guests in their ancient homeland.

This, then, is the Turkey and the ethnic, religious, and philosophical background of the country that Kemal Ataturk created, and over which President Recep Tayyip Erdoğan rules today.

Erdoğan's domestic and international goals can best be understood in terms of the framework explained above.

Erdoğan was a protégé of the Turkish fundamentalist Prime Minister Necmettin Erbakan who, as a result of a political bargain, was the Prime Minister of Turkey in 1996-1997. Erbakan made no secret of his goal of having Turkey revert to its pre-Republican identity—*i.e.*, Sunni Islam was to be the basis of identity for the state. He did his utmost to quickly re-Islamify government and society. But his secular enemies—most notably the Ataturkist military—pressured him to resign, because he was so blatantly violating Turkey's secular Constitution. Thereafter, Turkey's Constitutional court banned him from participating in politics.

Erdoğan and his colleagues, passionate supporters of Erbakan, then spent long hours analyzing why the secular establishment had succeeded in blocking Turkey's return to its true Muslim roots. Among the most important lessons they learned was that Erbakan's mistake was to move too quickly on re-Islamification. They devised a plan which they hoped would circumvent the military and delude the West into believing that Erdoğan was loyal to Turkey's secular and democratic constitution. But those who had studied the history of the Ottoman Empire and modern Turkey could see exactly what he was doing, if they chose to.

Sadly, that did not include most of the American political and some in the academic establishment which was obsessed with finding "moderate Muslims" with whom we could deal, and upon whom we could rely to make sure Turkey continued to be a reliable ally to NATO and the West. Regarding what "moderate Islam" is, had we chosen to, all we had to do was to listen to Erdoğan on this issue, who repeated over and over that "there is no moderate Islam. There is only Islam. The term "moderate Islam" is ugly and offensive."[†] Why didn't this set off alarm bells in Western capitals?

To anyone who would listen, Erdoğan had already made his plan for Turkey clear, long before he entered national politics. He did not lie, but he did dissimulate. He had been mayor of Istanbul from 1994-1998, during which time he did his best to address the city's chronic issues, keeping his re-Islamification agenda in the background, hoping to lull and pacify potential secular domestic opponents and Western governments into thinking he really wasn't a hard-core jihadi. Sadly, most opponents took the bait, which enabled him to strengthen his political base and sideline potential opponents.[‡]

Even before he entered Turkish national politics, Western political establishments just chose to ignore what he was saying. And more importantly, it seems that Western leaders—especially the Americans - seemed to have not understood that by meeting with committed Turkish

---

[†] There are voluminous citations on the net where Erdoğan makes this point. One, for example, from 2007 is as follows: The Term "Moderate Islam" Is Ugly And Offensive; There Is No Moderate Islam; Islam Is Islam."
http://www.thememriblog.org/turkey/blog_personal/en/2595.htm

[‡] For Erdoğan's views on the role of Islam in government before he became Prime Minister, see: https://www.turkeyanalyst.org/publications/turkey-analyst-articles/item/578-ticking-clocks-erdo%C4%9Fan-and-turkeys-constitutional-referendum.html

Islamic leaders—Erbakan and Erdoğan, and their likes—before they became major political leaders—means in Turkish eyes that the American government conferred upon them the international political legitimacy these Turkish fundamentalists so deeply craved.

Strange as it might seem to Western ears, from a Turkish cultural perspective,these meetings between American leaders and these Turkish Islamic leaders "proved" to the Turkish secular establishment that America wanted these devout Muslims to replace the Turkish Ataturkist secular government. That is because throughout the Middle East—which of course includes Turkey—the fact that a meeting takes place means more than what was said at the meeting.

Erdoğan's Role as He Understands It

Erdoğan's goal from the beginning was nothing more than to return Turkey to its proper place within the world order—as **the** major Sunni power in the world, and possibly—or should we say probably—reestablishing the Sunni caliphate in Istanbul.

Let's examine a few issues which demonstrate clearly who Erdoğan is and what he wants to accomplish. It should be eminently clear from our examination of these issues that Erdoğan's world view and ours are incompatible.

Erdoğan uses the words he knows we want to hear—democracy, freedom, human rights, etc., and then distorts them in ways his Turkish audience intuitively understands. We either willfully ignore what he means, or simply don't understand the ramifications of what he is saying.

In 1997, then as mayor of Istanbul, Erdoğan said: "Democracy is not the goal. It is a means to an end."[1] At another time, Erdoğan said: "Democracy is like a train. You get on the train and when you reach your stop, you get off.[2] Both were recorded—see the footnotes below—and are available on YouTube. How much clearer did Erdoğan need to be to prove to the world what his intentions were? But as Erdoğan only speaks Turkish, and few Western officials know that language, it would not be surprising if he believed he could get away with saying what he wanted without us knowing or possibly understanding what he was conveying to his people.

What he said about democracy sounds different from how we in the West understand democracy. That should have been a warning to us, but we refused to address it, because, as our diplomats often said: "it might negatively affect Turkish-U.S. relations." Western leaders chose to ignore this, much to their detriment, even though they had ample evidence to substantiate it.

Those few Western political advisors who do know Turkish, and who did try to get our leaders to see Erdoğan as he saw himself, failed to convince our superiors. This certainly wasn't for lack of evidence. These two above-mentioned examples regarding Erdoğan's view of democracy are simply the tip of the iceberg demonstrating that the only difference between Erbakan—Erdoğan's mentor—and Erdoğan and his cohorts, is the speed at which they wanted to take Turkey back to its role as the leader of political Islam.

Why didn't our leaders listen? One American leader privately lamented: "I fear that some, possibly many of us do understand the ramifications of what Erdoğan is saying. But if we admit this, we will have to change completely our foreign policy towards the Muslim world, something we are not now prepared to do."

The Search for 'Moderate Muslim' Leaders

Washington's political establishment simply refused to read the writing on the wall. This stems from our obsession in finding "moderate Muslims" with whom we decided we could work. What is moderate Islam? It's our deciding that anyone willing to talk with us and use the words we so long to hear—democracy, freedom, etc.—is a moderate. But as Erdoğan reminded us (see above), Islam is Islam. There is no moderate Islam.

Western leaders desperately wanted to find "moderate Muslims." Western diplomacy is based on finding people we can deal with in other countries and civilizations and over the long haul to find ways to prevent war and political unrest. Throughout the Muslim world, our establishment did its utmost to find political and public opinion leaders who could help us pursue this goal. On the surface, this is clearly an admirable pursuit. But is it realistic? Is Islam looking for ways to co-exist with the West, or are its adherents looking for ways to spread Islam throughout the world?

Erdoğan brilliantly understood what he was up against. So, when dealing with Western leaders, he brought his own translators who made sure they translated what he meant rather than exactly what he said.[3] He most definitely was on guard not to say anything which might raise red flags with his Western counterparts. He knew he had to lull them into believing that he was the "moderate Muslim leader" they were looking for. He clearly knew that if he revealed his true intentions before he neutered his military and destroyed his political opponents, he feared that America and other Western countries might look the other way if these Ataturkist anti-Islamic leaders tried to restore Turkey's secular and Western-oriented government.

As for "moderate Islam", Erdoğan repeatedly said: "Islam is Islam. There is no moderate Islam. In fact, he mocked the concept of "moderate Islam. His exact words, in a speech he gave in 2007, were "The Term "Moderate Islam" Is Ugly And Offensive; There Is No Moderate Islam; Islam Is Islam"[4]

What are the ramifications of Erdoğan's statements on democracy and on Islam? Anyone who has studied the history of Islam and its principles realizes that there can never be a permanent peace between the Muslim and the non-Muslim world. There can at best be truces, when the Muslims realize they are weak and wait to regroup so that they can again continue their campaign to bring Islam to the entire world.[5]

Muslims have been in retreat since the Christians defeated the Turks at Vienna on September 11, 1683. Even so, examining their abundant literature in Arabic, Persian, and Turkish, they licked their wounds and believed that eventually they would retake their lost lands, and continue their campaign by whatever means necessary to make the entire world Muslim—of course, Allah willing.

Seen in this context, it is obvious where Erdoğan is headed. What we don't know is whether he sees himself as a modern-day Ottoman Sultan, or does he hope to be the leader not only of what was the territory of the Ottoman Empire, but also, the entire Muslim world.

Erdoğan & the Muslim Brotherhood

Erdoğan is a strong supporter of the Muslim Brotherhood, an organization founded in 1928 in Egypt. This organization at least theoretically believes that all Muslims are brothers and that the differences between Muslims are irrelevant. The Islamic State (IS) (formerly known as ISIS) and other hard-core jihadist organizations like HAMAS and al-Qa'ida are either offshoots or branches of the Muslim Brotherhood. It is therefore obvious why Erdoğan so strongly supports HAMAS and looked the other way as fighters and arms of IS, flowed via Turkey into northern Iraq and Syria. Erdoğan denied he was helping IS. But Turkish journalists exposed this and were then promptly arrested.[6]

In 2012, when the Muslim Brotherhood took over in Egypt, Erdoğan rushed to Egypt to address the Egyptian Parliament, lavishing praise on Egypt's then new President Mohamed Morsi. Erdoğan warned the Egyptians not to move too quickly on imposing a full implementation of Islam and Islamic Law. Erdoğan advised the Egyptian Brotherhood ruler to go slowly, lest they suffer the same fate that Erdoğan's mentor suffered in 1998. Erdoğan in fact even suggested that they adopt a secular constitution so as not to provoke a coup against them.[7] The Egyptian Brotherhood was furious that Erdoğan called for secularism and did not heed his advice on moving too quickly.[8] But Erdoğan proved right. The Brotherhood moved very quickly to impose full, harsh Islamic law on Egypt and thereby gave the Egyptian military the excuse to overthrow the regime a year later.

Another example of Erdoğan's relationship with the Muslim Brotherhood is his close relationship with Qatar. Qatar is a staunch supporter of the Brotherhood—most specifically because the Brotherhood is now so anti-Saudi—because the Qataris hate the Saudis with a passion. The chief religious spokesman for Al-Jazeera, the Qatari TV station so popular in the Arab world, is Yusuf al-Qaradawi, the senior jurist of the Muslim Brotherhood, who has made Doha his home-away-from home now for many decades.[9]

Recep Tayyip Erdoğan vs. Fethullah Gülen

What about Erdoğan's relationship with Fethullah Gülen, once allies, but now sworn enemies? Both agree that Islam must eventually rule the world. As long as Gülen told his people to support Erdoğan, they worked almost hand in glove. Both at first were very polite and verbally accommodating to Westerners who are so easily disarmed by both leaders mouthing words like democracy, freedom, and human rights, that we so want to hear.

But just below the surface, Erdoğan and Gülen differed on important issues.

Erdoğan is more of a pan-Islamic leader, who prioritizes working across intra-Islamic sectarian differences. Gülen focuses most of his attention on the Turkic world—*i.e.*, Turkey and Central Asia, and the Chinese province of Xinjiang where the Uyghurs, a Turkic people live. Gülen is more a proponent of a Turkic Islam, and from his statements, seems to look down upon the Arabs. Erdoğan, however, sees the Arabs as brothers.

Even so, their long-term goal is the same: Bring Islam to the entire world. How do we know this? Discussions with a number of students who attended Gülenist schools in Central Asia have been revealing. When the schools' leaders believed they were among their own supporters, they often held small meetings where, believing they were among people who thought like themselves, these leaders revealed their true thoughts. They were strongly anti-American, anti-Christian, and antisemitic. But they explained that they did not believe it was wise to reveal their true thoughts to the world at that time. The Gülenists were preparing for the future.

Moreover, from each of their perspectives, they strongly disagree on which one of them should lead the fight against the world. Is this worth a fight and the huge enmity they have between themselves today? We in the West might see their long-term problems with each other as petty, but for them, it is a battle over who controls Islam. And historically, Muslims have had little compunction about killing each other when it comes to the question of who should lead Islam. We see this today in Syria and Iraq and elsewhere over and over again throughout Muslim history. From our perspective, we should wish both of them well in their war against each other, and of course not take sides. We might make temporary alliances with either, if it suits our purpose. But we must be extremely careful here. This is could be very dangerous as we seem not to understand how to use their fight to our advantage.

Erdoğan: A Turkish or a Pan-Islamic Leader?

Does Erdoğan see himself first and foremost as a Muslim leader, or a Turkish leader? Is being the Turkish leader just a means of promoting his worldwide Islamic agenda?

Erdoğan is a highly emotional man, and often blurts out exactly what he believes when he gets excited. For example, in his victory speech when he got elected for the 3rd time in 2011 as Prime of Turkey, he said: "Today, our victory here in Turkey is as important as it is in Sarajevo (the capital of Bosnia); in Izmir (Turkey) as it is in for Beirut (the capital of Lebanon), this victory is as important in Ankara (capital of Turkey) as it is in Damascus (the capital of Syria), ... in Turkey as it is in Ramallah, Jenin (the West Bank), and in Jerusalem (capital of Israel).[10]

Imagine an American Christian leader making a victory speech in which he claims that his victory is as important for other Christian countries as it is in the U.S. This would sound odd, to say the least. Sadly, the West no longer sees itself as the bastion of Christianity, and no longer feels Christian solidarity with other Christian countries. Sadly, countries like Germany which have political parties the names of which include the word "Christian" (the Christian Democratic Union and its partner the Christian Social Union), seem to be post-Christian, as their leaders have welcomed more than a million Muslim immigrants from other countries who are in the process of radically changing the social fabric of that country which had been based on Christian values.

Moreover, Erdoğan proves in this victory speech and elsewhere that Muslim solidarity is more important to him than any being the leader of a specific Muslim country. As the speech above demonstrates, Erdoğan sees himself first and foremost as a Muslim leader, and then and only then as a Turkish leader. For him, being Turkish means being Muslim. Where does that leave non-Sunni Turkish citizens? At best, second-class citizens. This explains why the Turkish Alevis[11] in Turkey—possibly 1/3 of the population of Turkey—feel so discriminated against, and why the Christians are leaving *en masse*, and why young Jews are abandoning Turkey is droves. Moreover, Erdoğan has bombed his fellow Sunni Muslim Kurds, because they resist his efforts to make them into ethnic Turks and abandon their Kurdish identity. The Islamic identity trumps any nationalist identity which can lead to separatism. He, Erdoğan demands, is their leader, and they must follow his lead. And again, listening to how he talks about the Muslims in the West Bank and Gaza Strip, it is clear that he wants them to look to him as their leader. And his deep infiltration of the Waqf institution in Jerusalem indicates the same. All of these indicate that Erdoğan sees himself more as a pan-Islamic leader than just as a Turkish leader.

After the U.S. recognized Jerusalem as Israel's capital in December 2017, Erdoğan went ballistic. In classic fashion, he threatened to break relations with Israel (as of this writing, he has not done so, because he needs relations with Israel more than the Israelis need relations with him) and spoke in the name of all Muslims saying that Jerusalem is a "red-line" for all Muslims.[12]

So Erdoğan speaks for all Muslims, or at least so he says. But many Muslim leaders say privately that they realize that Jerusalem only became holy to the Sunnis about 60 years after Muhammad died; furthermore, according to the Quran, the land of Israel was given to the Jews.[13] The reason that they say this only privately is that they fear being assassinated for saying so out loud.

Imagine a Western Christian leader reacting so strongly when people threaten to destroy or take over Rome, the center of Christianity in the eyes of Catholics and many Muslims. This sounds absurd. But Erdoğan, along with some other Muslim leaders, believe they have the right to intervene in any situation which involves Muslims in the world. This, while the Christian West remains studiously oblivious about the discrimination against Christians in the Muslim world.

Nevertheless, while Erdoğan may see himself as the leader of the Muslims, other Muslim leaders disagree. The Egyptians hate him. Egypt believes it is the center of the Muslim world because, among other things, al-

Azhar, the most important Sunni religious institution in the Sunni world, is located in Cairo. Moreover, the Saudis know they are the leaders of the Muslim world because they control Islam's two most holy cities—Mecca and Medina.

Erdoğan and the U.S.

In our obsession with finding "moderate Muslims," we chose to look the other way back in the 1990s, when Erdoğan first came onto the scene in Turkish politics. If we understood his background and understood the cultural context in which he was raised, it would have been easy to see that in Western terms, he was no "moderate." He had a deep animus for Ataturkism and all that it stood for. But he was extremely savvy and knew already how to tell us what we wanted to hear. Moreover, when he became mayor of Istanbul, many worried that he would ban alcohol and re-impose Islamic mores on the country. Erdoğan was sly; he at first temporarily put his Islamic agenda on hold, thereby giving the American establishment the ammunition it needed to argue that he supported democracy and secularism.

He was so savvy in fact and that he was able to make us believe that he supported us, while his arch-enemy—the military—was anti-American.

How did this happen? Probably the best way to demonstrate this was the Turkish Parliament's vote against letting American-led coalition forces enter Iraq from Turkish territory in 2003. We lost by three votes. Erdoğan apologized and we blamed the Turkish military for its failure. But was this true? Erdoğan controlled the Parliament and managed to get everything he wanted passed. Given the make-up of the Turkish Parliament, there was absolutely no doubt that he could have found the three votes necessary to pass the measure. Again slyly, he led us to believe that he wasn't the culprit, but discussions with several Parliamentarians show otherwise.

So, we ended up blaming our best allies in Turkey—the military - for something they did not do. And this just proved to the military that it could not rely on the U.S. to keep Turkey secular, and to protect the U.S.-Turkish relationship. This was, in short, a win-win situation for Erdoğan. We couldn't use Turkey to invade Iraq, which caused the deaths of American and coalition lives, and the Turkish military was furious with us, and now had more proof that, even though we claimed otherwise, the U.S. wanted to impose Islamic rule on Turkey.

A few years later, one of America's senior leaders visited Turkey. He met with Erdoğan and asked the Prime Minister why he was helping Iran avoid international sanctions and doing business deals with that country. Erdoğan exploded. He screamed: You worry about Iran getting nuclear weapons, but you say nothing about Israel which already has nuclear weapons. (NOTE: For Erdoğan, Iran is a Muslim country and as such Erdoğan wants Muslims also to have nuclear weapons. Israel is non-Muslim, and therefore in Erdoğan's eyes, part of the non-Muslim world which is allied against the Muslims, as explained above.) When the American leader responded: Iran threatens to destroy Israel, but Israel does not threaten to destroy anyone, Erdoğan became even further enraged.

Understanding this Turkish leader in Turkish and Islamic cultural terms, we should have had no difficulty understanding from the beginning where he was headed. Unfortunately, partially thanks to the Great Purge of instruction and training about Islam that took place in the years following 9/11 across the entirety of the U.S. government, rare is the senior official today who understands the subtleties and intricacies regarding Islam.

It was obvious to most American policy makers that they had been wrong about Erdoğan towards the end of the George W. Bush era, but by then the die was cast. We had enabled Erdoğan to neutralize his enemies in Turkey and hurt our position in the Middle East.

Later, given Obama's predilections for the viciously anti-American Muslim Brotherhood, it should have come as no surprise that he said that Erdoğan was among his most trusted friends.[14]

We should not have been surprised by Erdoğan's reaction to President Trump's call to move the U.S. the embassy to Jerusalem. As an important Muslim leader—and in his own eyes likely THE most important Muslim leader of the world—Erdoğan was enraged. After the U.N. General Assembly vote against the U.S. for recognizing Jerusalem as Israel's capital, U.S. Ambassador Nikki Haley said "we are taking names." Erdoğan reacted by screaming "you cannot buy us."[15]

Clearly, Erdoğan, long before he entered politics in the early 1990s, was no friend of the U.S., nor of the West. He deeply resented the Ataturk political establishment in Turkey. And he knew that America stood behind that establishment. But he clearly spent a lot of time figuring out how he could neutralize us, and by and large succeeded in pulling the wool over the eyes of many people in America's political establishment. In fact, he was so clever that he managed to turn that establishment against those in Washington who saw Erdoğan for what he was from the beginning. In the end, he despises both America's political establishment and those who opposed him. That internal American fight give him the time and space to consolidate his power to the point that he now has more power than any leader since the founding of the Republic of Turkey in the early 1920s.

Europe vs. Muslim Turkey

From the Turkish secularist perspective, this Western "plot" against the secularists actually started much earlier. Again, from their perspective, in the mid-1980s in West Germany, the Turks were becoming majorities in certain neighborhoods in Berlin and elsewhere. According to West German law, once the schools of an area had a significant number of students of a particular religion, they were entitled to religious instruction paid for by the government, but the government was not allowed to choose the teachers. To ensure that political Islam was not taught to Turks in German schools, Turkey sent its then ambassador to West Germany to the German authorities to ask to supply the books the Turkish government used in Turkish schools for the Turkish Muslims in Germany. The reason the Turks printed these books was because the Turkish government feared so-called *'political Islam,'* the scourge which plagues the world today—would otherwise take over Islamic instruction and overthrow Turkey's Western orientation. This was the Turkish government's attempt to rein in Islam and keep it out of politics and relegate to the private relationship between man and God.

The West Germans absolutely refused to let the Turks supply their books for religious instruction because the German law forbade the state—in this case any state—from interfering with religious instruction. The Turks explained that if the Germans did not let the Turkish government supply the books, that the jihadist foundations supported by the Libyans and Saudis would supply religious instruction, which would eventually create a Muslim fifth column in Germany. The teaching of anti-Western, anti-Christian, and antisemitic Islam, the government feared, would eventually become a major problem for the Germans and would seep back into Turkey as well.

This episode once again "proved" to Turkey's secular establishment what they feared most: that the Germans, as Christians, wanted to push Muslim Turkey out of the Western block.

But Erdoğan also doesn't always lie. He tells us exactly what he thinks and what he wants to do. We just refuse to listen.

Up to 1683, the Ottoman Empire stretched deep into the heart of Europe, and almost reached Vienna. Since its loss in 1683, it had been in steady retreat until the Empire ended between 1918-1920. As the Empire's leaders saw themselves as the vanguard of Islam, these were humiliating defeats. In Islam, any territory captured by Islam must remain under Muslim rule forever.[16] If lost, all these territories must be recaptured for Islam, and the fight to bring Islam to the rest of Europe must be resumed.

That is how Erdoğan understood his role vs. Germany and the rest of the Europe. When, in the 1960s, Germany began to bring Turkish "guest workers" to Europe, the Muslims saw in them that opportunity to resume the conquest of the "House of War,"[17] *i.e.*, from a Muslim legal point of view, the territory ruled by non-Muslims. During Erdoğan's time as Prime Minister and as President, guest workers no longer were coming to Germany. But when Muslim refugees came to Turkey from war-torn Syria, Afghanistan, Iraq, and elsewhere, on their way to Europe where they could receive all sorts of benefits as refugees, Erdoğan encouraged them to do so.

After more than approximately 1,000,000 refugees arrived in Germany in 2015, the Germans clearly had had enough. They saw their culture being overtaken by Muslims who had no desire to assimilate into German culture. German Chancellor Angela Merkel made a deal with Erdoğan whereby Germany would pay many billions of dollars to house these refugees in Turkey. So again, this was another win-win situation for Erdoğan. But Muslim refugees still continue to flow into Germany and other Western European countries as well.

This is nothing more than the resumption of Islam's war against the non-Muslim world on a large scale. But this time, the EU's Western Europeans no longer believe in their culture and in their ancestral Christian values, so they do not have the internal fortitude to stand up and fight for the values their ancestors held sacred.

Again, Erdoğan played this beautifully. So many Turks wanted to be part of the EU. There have been negotiations going on for decades. The Europeans, however, found every excuse in the book not to let the Turks in.

Erdoğan used this issue brilliantly. He told his people that he wanted to be in the European Union, knowing that Turkey would never be accepted. The Turks therefore saw that the EU was a Christian organization which did not want Muslims in it. This alienated many Turks, especially the secular ones, who saw EU membership as another way to prove their "Europeanness" and non-Islamic identity. These disillusioned secularists began realizing that the Christian West would never accept them, so they might as well retreat into their Islamic identity. It is therefore not surprising that many of these disenchanted Turks voted for Erdoğan. So again, this was another win-win situation for Turkey's strongman.

As the great Ottoman scholar Bernard Lewis has stated, if things continue as they are, then Europe will most likely have a Muslim majority by the end of this century. And if it is up to Erdoğan, that time will come sooner. Europe will then become part of the Dar al-Islam (in Islamic terms—under rule of Islamic Law).

Conclusion

Where does this leave us? Was the Ataturk period an aberration? Does Erdoğan represent the true nature of the Turkish soul? The Turkish poet Ak Sakal mentioned above believed so. From our perspective, the prognosis is not good. Given the array of forces in Turkey, it's hard to imagine a counter-coup against the forces of Islam, now running rampant in Turkey. Perhaps it is time to cut our losses and look for other allies in the region.

Turkey under Erdoğan and his ilk is clearly no longer a reliable NATO ally. Maybe it is time that we learn from the past, dig deeper into Turkish and Islamic culture, and apply what we can learn. It is time to formulate a more realistic policy based on the true nature of Turkey as demonstrated in this chapter. To be sure, the Ataturkist secular Turkey before Erdoğan's rise to power was a faithful and reliable ally. But it is not any longer.

Politics, in Turkey however, is like the mountains of southeastern Turkey—*i.e.*, high mountains with steep descents into small valleys. It is possible to imagine that as the Islamic world in general sinks further into a morass, forces within Turkey might rise and replace Turkey's current present jihadist rulers and regime.

But given Turkey's Pre-World War I 653 years of Ottoman history— where the propagation and advancement of Islam was its primary reason for existence—the present entrenchment of the Islamic forces which control Turkey, and the minuscule birthrate among secular Turks, a Western-oriented Ataturkist Turkey is more likely to be a thing of the past, rather than a reliable American ally in the future. It would be wise for our policy makers to remember this when dealing with our former Turkish allies.

HAROLD RHODE is a Distinguished Senior Fellow at the Gatestone Institute. He received his Ph.D. in Ottoman History from Columbia University in Islamic History, specializing in the history of the Turks, Arabs & Iranian peoples. He has also studied in universities in Iran, Egypt & Israel. During the First Gulf War, Dr. Rhode served as the Turkish Desk officer in the Office of the Secretary of Defense (OSD) & later on the U.S. Department of Defense's Policy Planning Staff. Dr. Rhode speaks Arabic, Turkish, Persian, Hebrew, French & some Spanish & Italian.

CHAPTER 2

Turkey's Partnership with the U.S. Muslim Brotherhood

• BY CENTER FOR SECURITY POLICY STAFF

The groundwork for what has developed into a close working relationship between Turkish President Recep Tayyip Erdoğan and the United States Council of Muslim Organizations (USCMO) began well before the March 2014 announcement of the USCMO's formation. By August 2014, a USCMO delegation led by Secretary General Oussama Jammal traveled to Ankara to meet with President Erdoğan and his Justice and Development Party (AK Party). The political climate during the 2009-2017 administration of U.S. President Barack H. Obama provided a window of opportunity for members of the USCMO to achieve the long-time Brotherhood goal of advancing the "Phases of the World Underground Movement Plan" [18] in accordance with the framework articulated by influential Muslim Brotherhood theoretician Sayyid Qutb in his seminal 1964 monograph '*Milestones*.'[19] The need as well as the opportunity to accelerate efforts towards achieving Muslim Brotherhood tactical objectives in the U.S. was recognized by Jammal well before the USCMO's First International Conference of Muslim Councils in the West held in Crystal City, Virginia, in February 2016.

The evolution of the AK Party relationship and the solidification of its ties with USCMO leadership in combination with the growing strategic role of the Turkish government's Diyanet Center of America in Lanham, Maryland should be alarming to the senior leadership of U.S. national security. Erdoğan and the AKP are now directing initiatives and programs through the Diyanet Center of America, which is a command headquarters for advancing the Muslim Brotherhood and its Civilization Jihad on U.S. soil. Unfortunately, as this monograph goes to print, U.S. President Donald J. Trump and his administration seem unaware of the paradigm shift in insurgency operations against the U.S. government led by the pro-HAMAS, hostile foreign government of Turkey in a full-fledged Islamic jihad partnership with the North American Muslim Brotherhood and USCMO.

USCMO Aligns with Turkey after Collapse of the Morsi Regime

By mid-2013, the Muslim Brotherhood experiment in governance was over in Egypt. Despite substantial, official support from the administration of U.S. President Obama, the Mohamed Morsi regime was overthrown within a year of its 2012 election. This government was then replaced by a military regime, headed by Field Marshal Abdel Fatah al-Sisi and supported by much of the Egyptian population. Even as the Brotherhood's 28-year rise to power in Egypt came asunder thanks to Morsi's calamitous rule, key leadership figures among the American Muslim Brotherhood took a major step in announcing the formation of a new political party, the first in U.S. history to be openly associated with the jihadist Muslim Brotherhood.

As a press conference was held in Washington, DC, on 12 March 2014 to announce the formation of the United States Council of Muslim Organizations,[20] USCMO Secretary General Oussama Jammal was already preparing logistics to begin tactical work for the Muslim Brotherhood with Turkish President Recep Tayyip Erdoğan. This alliance marked a strategic step forward for the Brotherhood in America. Some of its key leadership figures had now joined together to create the USCMO, but also to align with the increasingly jihadist government of Turkey that was itself in open alignment with HAMAS and the Egyptian-based Muslim Brotherhood.

The establishment of the USCMO was announced at the National Press Club, just blocks from the U.S. Capitol Building. At the podium were: Ousama Jammal, Secretary General, USCMO and past President, The Mosque Foundation; Naeem Baig, President, Islamic Circle of North America (ICNA); Nihad Awad, National Executive Director, Council on American Islamic Relations (CAIR); Mazen Mokhtar, Executive Director, Muslim American Society (MAS); Imam Mahdi Bray, National Director, American Muslim Alliance (AMA); and others associated with identified Muslim Brotherhood organizations.

Turkey and these organizations support the Cairo Declaration on Human Rights in Islam, which was issued and adopted by the Nineteenth Islamic Conference of Foreign Ministers on 5 August 1990 in Cairo, Egypt. As stated in the Cairo Declaration on Human Rights in Islam,[21] the Muslim world defines human rights exclusively in terms of shariah (Islamic Law). Note especially Articles 24 and 25 which declare as follows: *"ARTICLE 24: All the rights and freedoms stipulated in this Declaration are subject to the Islamic Shari'ah"* and *"ARTICLE 25: The Islamic Shari'ah is the only source of reference for the explanation or clarification of any of the articles of this Declaration."* As a member of the Organization of Islamic Cooperation (OIC), Turkey was an original signatory to this document that advocates for the strictest adherence to shariah and represents, in fact, an abrogation of the UN Universal Declaration on Human Rights. The USCMO-Turkey alliance attests openly to the counter-Constitutional agenda of the US. Muslim Brotherhood and an erstwhile NATO ally.

The Muslim Brotherhood agenda for the U.S. demonstrably seeks through subversive infiltration of American institutions the triumph of shariah over the U.S. Constitution. The USCMO represents the leading edge of the jihadist movement in this country even as it seeks to cloak itself in red, white, and blue—but only for the purpose of accomplishing what can aptly be described as "Star Spangled Shariah."[22]

Turkey Offers Sanctuary for Exiled Muslim Brotherhood Leaders

Fewer than three months prior to this demonstration of solidarity and leadership by the USCMO in the U.S., the interim Egyptian government and acting deputy Prime Minister Hossam Eissa, formally declared [23] on 25 December 2013 that the Muslim Brotherhood was a terrorist organization. After Morsi's regime was terminated on 3 July 2013 by a military coup d'état, the Egyptian court system in its initial verdict on 23 September 2013 [24] ordered the immediate seizure of the Brotherhood's assets, until rulings in trials of group's leaders and members in criminal courts resulted in verdicts. On 24 March 2014, just ten days following the official formation of the USCMO, 529 members of the outlawed Muslim Brotherhood were sentenced to death for murder and other offenses by an Egyptian court.[25] As Muslim Brotherhood leaders sought to escape from new Egyptian President Abdel Fatah al-Sisi's crackdown, the United Kingdom, Qatar, and Turkey became places of refuge.

While Muslim Brotherhood leadership sought answers regarding their failure in Egypt and direction for its next steps, Turkey offered sanctuary for exiled Egyptian Muslim Brotherhood leaders. In May 2014, Ahmed Yusuf, a prominent, Turkey-based[26] member of the Egyptian Muslim Brotherhood's youth section noted, "Within Ikhwan (the Brotherhood) there is deep self-criticism, and they have long meetings to discuss mistakes and what can be done in the future. The Ikhwan will learn a lot of lessons from this coup and will come out stronger."

Since President al-Sisi took over leadership of Egypt, operational elements of the International Muslim Brotherhood relocated to Turkey under the protection of President Recep Tayyip Erdoğan and the Turkish Justice and Development Party (AKP). Consequently, the AKP has taken on a leadership role in Muslim Brotherhood operations which extend to the U.S. As will be shown, the development of the USCMO's close relationship with Turkey, a foreign state actor,[27] must arouse deep concern, because the Muslim Brotherhood is operational in the U.S., jointly working in coordination with Erdoğan and AKP. These combined forces are aggressively engaged in a long-term Civilization-Jihadist process.

Turkey and USCMO Engage in Civilization-Jihadist Process

In the landmark 2008 U.S. v Holy Land Foundation, et al. HAMAS terror funding trial, a key Brotherhood document, *An Explanatory Memorandum on the General Strategic Goal for the Group in North America*[28], was entered into evidence as Government Exhibit 003-0085 3:04-CR240-G. This 1991 document, written by Mohamed Akram, a member of the Brotherhood's North American Board of Directors and a senior HAMAS (Palestinian arm of the Muslim Brotherhood) leader, described the Brotherhood's mission in the following way:

> *"The process of settlement is a 'Civilization-Jihadist Process' with all the word means. The Ikhwan [Muslim Brotherhood] must understand that their work in America is a kind of grand jihad in eliminating and destroying the Western civilization from within and "sabotaging" its miserable house by their hands and the hands of the believers, so that is eliminated and God's religion is made victorious over all other religions."[29]*

As expressed in its own words, the Muslim Brotherhood agenda for the U.S. includes the subversive infiltration of every sphere of American society and recruitment of assistance in the subversive process from unwitting Americans themselves.

The Muslim Brotherhood understood that successful execution of its plan for societal destruction from within depends on what it calls the "settlement process": "In order for Islam and its Movement" to become "a part of the homeland" in which it lives, "stable" in its land, "rooted" in the spirits and minds of people, "enabled" in the life of its society and firmly established within organizations through which the Islamic structure is to be built, the Movement must work to obtain "the keys" and tools of this "Civilization-Jihadist" project that is the responsibility of the U.S. Muslim Brotherhood.[30]

Following the formation of the USCMO and shortly after its non-publicized inaugural banquet attended by U.S. Congressmen Keith Ellison (Democrat, Minnesota, 5th District) and André Carson (Democrat, Indiana, 7th District) in June 2014, a leadership delegation of U.S. Muslim Brotherhood leaders traveled to Ankara at the invitation of the Turkish government in August 2014. It is notable that two current members of the U.S. House of Representatives are not only actively working with the Muslim Brotherhood, but also are contributors to programs held by the pro-HAMAS Turkish government-owned DCA.

Turkey Aids HAMAS' Economic and Military Infrastructure

President Erdoğan has neither concealed his support for HAMAS nor been slow to act when HAMAS has called upon AKP leadership and required his assistance. As will be shown later, USCMO senior leadership led by Secretary General Oussama Jammal and CAIR National Executive Director Nihad Awad has pledged its fidelity to Erdoğan. Despite the conviction of several former CAIR officials for various crimes related to jihad terror, CAIR officials have repeatedly refused[31] to denounce[32] HAMAS as a terrorist group.

According to the U.S. Department of State: "Foreign Terrorist Organizations (FTOs) are foreign organizations that are designated by the Secretary of State in accordance with section 219 of the Immigration and Nationality Act (INA), as amended. FTO designations play a critical role in our fight against terrorism and are an effective means of curtailing support for terrorist activities and pressuring groups to get out of the terrorism business."[33] On 8 October 1997, HAMAS received the FTO designation from the U.S. Government.

The HAMAS charter also directly ties HAMAS to the Muslim Brotherhood:

> "The Islamic Resistance Movement is one of the wings of Muslim Brotherhood in Palestine. Muslim Brotherhood Movement is a universal organization which constitutes the largest Islamic movement in modern times. It is characterized by its deep understanding, accurate comprehension and its complete embrace of all Islamic concepts of all aspects of life,

culture, creed, politics, economics, education, society, justice and judgement, the spreading of Islam, education, art, information, science of the occult and conversion to Islam."[34]

In February 2018, a large-scale HAMAS money laundering operation overseen by Zaher Jabarin in Turkey was exposed thanks to an investigation by *Sherut Habitachon Haklali* (Shabak), better known as the *Shin Bet* (Israel's internal counterespionage and counterterrorist agency).

HAMAS operatives in Turkey owned a company called IMES (a real estate and tourism firm), which, per Shin Bet, was used as "a cover for the laundering of millions of US dollars that were transferred to the Gaza Strip and various countries. An account was opened for IMES with Turkey's Akbank. The company's chairman opened another bank account under his name with Türkiye Finans Bank."[35] Additionally, Shin Bet found that "his handlers in Turkey gave him hundreds of thousands of Euros for HAMAS's military infrastructure. He hid the funds in various secret locations. A search of his home uncovered 91,000 Euros which were due to be transferred to Judea and Samaria [the West Bank]."[36]

The Shin Bet official statement declared that Turkish government officials not only looked the other way, but on occasion encouraged HAMAS's economic and military activities. The statement noted that this activity occurred "with the assistance of Turkish nationals, some of whom are close to the government. This activity relies on—inter alia—business platforms that serve HAMAS in laundering funds that are transferred to Judea and Samaria."[37]

In another plot, HAMAS commander Salah al-Arouri,[38] who had planned multiple attacks on Israeli targets, was hosted by the Turkish government in 2014. According to another HAMAS leader in December 2014, his organization was using Turkey for logistics, training and planning attacks; the same month at a high-profile party congress, HAMAS Political Bureau Chief Khaled Mashaal was hosted by Turkish Prime Minister Ahmet Davutoğlu.[39] While al-Arouri is one of the most recognized HAMAS members who found sanctuary in Istanbul, many additional senior HAMAS officials have resided there with the knowledge of the Turkish government.[40]

The FTO designation of HAMAS by the U.S. Department of State is ignored by the USCMO as it follows Erdoğan's directives. In their respective positions, Congressman Ellison (*deputy chair* of the *Democratic* National *Committee)* and Congressman Carson (member of House Permanent Select Committee on Intelligence) are actively participating in activities with the

USCMO and the DCA. Nevertheless, these members of Congress are not known to have issued any warnings to the USCMO and DCA about potential legal problems pursuant to their support for an openly pro-HAMAS hostile foreign government's operations through the DCA. Of note, Davutoğlu, who hosted HAMAS leader Mashaal in late 2014, met with key USCMO leadership in the summer of 2014.

USCMO Witnesses Turkish Democracy in Action

As illustrated on its website with full photo documentation, the USCMO stated the following regarding its relationship with President Erdoğan and AKP:

> *"The US Council of Muslim Organizations (USCMO) was invited to attend a conference by the Turkish Justice and Development Party (AK Party). The USCMO delegation also attended elections of new chairman and was able to witness Turkish democracy at work.* **The conference, considered to be an extraordinary event by members of the AK Party, was held in honor of Recep Tayyip Erdoğan, its founder and chairman, to bid him a special farewell after being elected President of Turkey.** *Mr. Ahmet Davutoğlu was elected the new chairman of the AK Party. Witnessing this fascinating democratic process was as uplifting and inspiring as feeling the shared sentiment among party members. The U.S. Council of Muslim Organizations was represented by Oussama Jammal, Secretary General; Naeem Baig, ICNA president, and Osama Abu-Irshaid, American Muslims for Palestine (AMP) National Director."*[41]

While this strategic relationship between the USCMO and a pro-HAMAS, hostile foreign state actor was yet in its nascent stage, President Erdoğan and the AKP already were calculating their next steps to benefit the Muslim Brotherhood's operations in the U.S. To any observant national security practitioner, Erdoğan's goal seemed clear: to establish the DCA as an operational hub for Turkey to direct Muslim Brotherhood influence operations against the U.S. government in collaboration with the USCMO.

Diyanet Center of America: 'A Gift for All Muslims'

Joining directly in those efforts then and now is the pro-HAMAS Turkish government, under the leadership of President Erdoğan and his AKP. As noted above, the groundwork for what is now a close working relationship with the USCMO began well before the March 2014 announcement of the USCMO's formation. But it is known that on 15 May 2013, a visiting President Erdoğan placed a ceremonial stone[42] on the 16-acre construction site that would become the Turkish DCA[43] in Lanham, Maryland.

While a USCMO delegation led by Secretary General Oussama Jammal traveled to Ankara to meet with President Erdoğan and AKP leaders in August 2014, this was preparatory for logistics to be announced at an internationally-attended Muslim Brotherhood convention in North America. And then, on 29 December 2014, in a recorded video message, Dr. Mehmet Görmez [44], President of the Presidency of Religious Affairs (Diyanet), addressed the 13th Annual MAS-ICNA (Muslim American Society-Islamic Circle of North America) Conference in Chicago, Illinois and discussed a gift for all Muslims: the Diyanet Center of America. Of note for the future of the US Muslim Brotherhood-Turkish relationship, this conference was sponsored by **the Turkish-backed American Zakat Foundation and included the first-ever attendance of a Turkish-American group**[45] at a MAS-ICNA conference.

It will be recalled that Erdoğan himself [46] officiated at the 2 April 2016 opening ceremonies [47] for the DCA, [48] located on a large 16-acre site in Lanham, Maryland. The Diyanet Center, also known as the Turkish American Cultural Center (TACC), is a wholly-owned facility of The Presidency of Religious Affairs,[49] an official state institution of the Turkish government. Likewise, the relationship between the USCMO and the Turkish government is an open one, as is their use of the DCA as a hub for joint operations. Even before the official opening of the DCA in March 2016, Turkish influence became evident when the Turkish American Cultural Society became a member of the USCMO.

Turkish American Cultural Society Joins USCMO

Shortly after Dr. Mehmet Görmez addressed the Muslim Brotherhood in December 2014 at the 13th Annual MAS-ICNA Convention in Chicago about the gift of the DCA, TACS became an official member of the USCMO in 2015. Ahmed Cetin Guzel[50] (MUSIAD USA spokesman and representative from New York) was listed as a USCMO board member [51] from 2015-2016 and described as a principal at TACS. Curiously, however, TACS no longer holds a board role within the USCMO. It seems possible that the TACS role at the USCMO may have become something of an issue following an embarrassing display in mid-April 2015 outside the Turkish embassy in Washington, DC, where a large banner was hung that read "Armenian genocide is an imperialist lie." As aptly noted on 28 April 2015 by Clifford May, President for the Foundation of the Defense of Democracies:

> "Displayed outside the Turkish embassy in Washington last week was a large banner reading, "Armenian genocide is an imperialist lie." That claim might be amusing were the subject not so dreadful. The slaughter of hundreds of thousands of Armenians in 1915 was carried out by the Ottoman Empire. It was, therefore, by definition, an imperialist crime, one regarded by most experts as the first genocide of the 20th century. The notion that some other empire (which one?) has fabricated a slander against Turkey is ludicrous. Those who came up with that slogan must assume they are addressing a clueless audience."[52]

On 19 April 2015, Secretary General Oussama Jammal issued a formal statement[53] regarding the USCMO's version of the Armenian Genocide. The "USCMO Statement on 1915 Turkish-Armenian Events" denied the evidence of this as a 'genocide' and declared:

> "As April 24 comes near, we share the pain suffered by Armenians during this period. We also believe that any acknowledgment by religious or political leaders of the tragedy that befell Armenians should be balanced, constructive and must also recognize Turkish and Muslim suffering. In this respect, characterizing the events of 1915 as genocide without proper investigation of these events by independent historians will not only jeopardize the establishment of a just memory pertaining to these events, but will also damage the efforts aimed at achieving reconciliation between Turks and Armenians."

In its conclusion, the USCMO continued to obfuscate truth regarding the slaughter of innocents: *"Muslim Americans expect our leaders to act accordingly to ensure that American-Turkish strategic relations are not damaged by a one-sided interpretation of the 1915 events."*[54]

TACS likely influenced the USCMO statement issued in April 2015. In 2016, TACS once again showed its true colors when its organization lobbied[55] Connecticut State Senator Steve Cassano (Democrat) to refrain from using the term 'genocide' in reference to the expulsion and death of Armenians in 1915 shortly before the collapse of the Ottoman Empire in 1917.

The persistence of the USCMO and its member organization TACS in denying the facts surrounding the human tragedy of the Armenian Genocide should serve as red flag warning to all lawmakers at local, state, and federal levels in the U.S. The revisionist narrative proliferated by the Muslim Brotherhood and its surrogates demonstrates an agenda that seeks to silence truth whenever it reflects badly on Islam.

It may be noted that the Organization of Islamic Cooperation (OIC) declared war against free speech in 2007 when it launched the Islamophobia Observatory in Jeddah, Saudi A Rabia. USCMO members are hard pressed to deny their support of OIC initiatives designed to criminalize any free speech which exposes the history and actual tenets of Islam. Whatever the objections from Democrat and Republican legislators in Congress because of the USCMO stance on the Armenian Genocide, they obviously did not deter the Muslim Brotherhood under the leadership of USCMO Secretary General Oussama Jammal from taking definitive steps to begin working with President Erdoğan and AKP.

USCMO Leads 1st International Conference of Muslim Councils in the West

Substantial insight may be gleaned from an excerpt taken from an interesting firsthand account[56] by AKP Member of Parliament Yasin Aktay, who clearly appreciated the leadership roles of USCMO Secretary General Oussama Jammal and CAIR National Executive Director Nihad Awad. He was in attendance at the USCMO's 1st International Conference of Muslim Councils of the West in Washington, DC, from 1-3 February 2016, held at a Crystal City, VA, hotel and published online his observations of the event. His details not only confirm the strategic relationship between the USCMO and AKP, but also acknowledge the "**connection into an opportunity, a political coalition for Turkey and the Muslim world**" as described by Aktay.

This early 2016 gathering represented an assembly of the international Muslim Brotherhood leadership to discuss strategy for addressing challenges in the West and its operational plans for the continuation of Civilization Jihad. Most striking, this event marked a strategic move by

Erdoğan to assert his leadership on the international stage and begin providing directives for the work of global Islamic Movement. Here, we see NATO "ally" Turkey spreading its influence and beginning to work with international Muslim Brotherhood leaders on an agenda aligned with the OIC that is clearly counter to the interests of other NATO members.

> *"Muslims in the US are paying greater attention than ever to political contribution. They are involved in various events in response to the rising pressures on them and to have more of a say in the US's Middle East policies and influence US policies regarding matters affecting them.* **Early last week, I attended the 1st International Conference of Muslim Councils in the West organized in Washington, DC by the US Council of Muslim Organizations (USCMO), the greatest umbrella organization for Muslims in the US.**
>
> *The aim of the conference was to gather Muslim leaders from all corners of the world, but particularly those in Western countries, share a common experience and institute a consultation mechanism to undertake the resolution of mutual problems together. A conference of such scale, which is common on the global scale, is critical for the institution of the awareness of Muslims existing as an ummah, yet is neglected.*
>
> *Over 200 leaders and representatives from Muslim communities or associations attended the conference from North and South America, the Carribeans, Australia and Europe.* **We participated in the conference with Central Decision and Administrative Board (MKYK) member Asuman Erdoğan representing the Justice and Development Party (AK Party).** *In the first part of the conference, participants from all countries made presentations on the state of Muslims in their countries and the activities of their association.*
>
> *The matters focused on were: 1. Determining and developing the strategic priorities of Muslim communities in the West; 2. Sharing ideas and developing strategies against increasing Islamophobia and anti-Muslim aggression; 3. Producing measures against the problem of violence and extremism in*

all its forms; 4. Ensuring the integration and positive contribution of Muslims to the communities in which they live; and 5. Developing ways to ensure sharing of ideas and sources to settle the new waves of refugees.

The three-day conference was promising in that it showed the level reached by Muslims living in the West in terms of developing their own political and everyday life jurisprudence. It should be noted that Turkey has a very special significance and value to everyone who attended the conference. **Even the mention of President Recep Tayyip Erdoğan's name is enough to cheer people. On the first evening of the conference, Yaşar Çolak, the head Turkey's Presidency of Religious Affairs Center in Washington, hosted the entire delegation at the center's newly built magnificent mosque and complex [Diyanet Center of America].**

<u>Even the existence of this mosque alone seems to have built a path between Turkey and the hearts of the 8 million Muslims living the US.</u> **A majority of the participants of the conference with whom we were able to meet felt the need to state that <u>they were ready for all calls to turn this connection into an opportunity, a political coalition for Turkey and the Muslim world.</u> Of course, after sharing all these good intentions, <u>they wanted us to pass on their regards and sincere love to President Erdoğan and Prime Minister Ahmet Davutoğlu.</u>**

This organization has raised promising and charismatic leaders, who attract attention in US politics with their intelligent and well-balanced behaviors. **<u>USCMO President Oussama Jammal and Council of American Islamic Relationship (CAIR) President Nihad Awad, whom I met years ago, are the ones that coordinated these activities.</u>** *They are both paving beautiful paths for the healthy political participation of American Muslims and are well-respected among US political circles.*

Our communications in the US will continue and hence, I will continue to share them."[57]

The USCMO-led 1st International Conference of Muslim Councils in the West proved to be a tremendous success as USCMO member organizations immediately began to embrace President Erdoğan's vision for the Islamic Movement after the failures and collapse of the Morsi regime. That same year, in September 2016, North American Muslim Brotherhood leadership would meet with both President Erdoğan and his senior AKP leadership. At this point, CAIR, which under Nihad Awad's direction is taking a lead role within the USCMO, would begin the groundwork needed to promote and advance the initiatives of President Erdoğan through the DCA.

CAIR Promotes and Advances Diyanet Center of America

Nihad Awad, Executive Director for CAIR, did not miss the opportunity to embrace President of Religious Affairs (Diyanet) Professor Dr. Mehmet Görmez when he was in the U.S. to inaugurate the DCA. Görmez paid a special visit in April 2016 to the CAIR National office in Washington, DC, where he received a warm reception and plaque from Muslim Brotherhood leadership representing USCMO member organizations.

While Görmez praised the work of CAIR National's role in the U.S. and around the world, he also noted in the meeting with USCMO representatives that "there are times when humanity goes through some tough phases. Today humanity is going through such a period. **There is no doubt that in these hard times it is the religion of Islam that will teach human beings peace, security, justice and the truth**." [58] Unfortunately, as we know, Islamic history is replete with countless examples where humanity has learned the hard consequences that belie the meaning of the terms 'peace', 'security', 'justice', and 'truth', because their Islamic definitions are different in legal application for Muslims versus non-Muslims.

In reply to Görmez's remarks, CAIR Executive Director Nihad Awad stressed that Turkey is viewed as source of "hope" by so many countries. He also stressed the Muslim Brotherhood's understanding of its role through the USCMO working with Turkey:

> "[T]he timing of the opening of this center is of great importance in view of the rising anti-Islamic trend in the U.S. **This facility will be the center of civilization and culture. Turkey is of great importance for us. It is a source of hope for humanity.** Turkey has become a symbol of justice. I am a Palestinian and I feel deep gratitude for what Turkey has done for the Palestinians. My Egyptian and Syrian colleagues

are also sharing these feelings. This is a sentiment that is being shared in all corners of the Ummah."[59]

Interestingly, Awad is not only acknowledging Erdoğan's Justice and Development Party; he also identifies the significant role of the Diyanet in Lanham, Maryland, purported to be a gift to America, as a place of operation for the Turkish government and Muslim Brotherhood to combat the forces of freedom that challenge Islamic supremacism. Awad's overtures praising Turkey stem also from the fact that TACS remains a USCMO member.

The close relationship between Awad's CAIR and the pro-HAMAS Turkish government by extension of the DCA is disquieting, to say the least. While CAIR declares itself a "Muslim civil rights" organization, legal evidence does not support these claims, because CAIR in fact is a HAMAS entity.[60] As USCMO members followed the counsel of Jammal and Awad focused on alignment with President Erdoğan, 2016 was a decisive year for the U.S. Muslim Brotherhood, which was not yet certain of the outcome of the presidential election in November 2016.

President Erdoğan and AKP Lead Strategic Meeting with USCMO

As reported by the pro-AKP Turkish press agency Yeni Şafak,[61] Erdoğan was in New York City for the 71st session of the United Nations General Assembly on 13 September 2016, on the sidelines of which he received a delegation of prominent Muslim Brotherhood leadership.

Those represented at this meeting with Erdoğan included the following individuals from the U.S.:

Halil Demir (Executive Director, **Zakat Foundation**)

Mazen Mokhtar (Executive Director, **Muslim American Society**)

Eliton Pashaj (Theologist & Spiritual Leader, **American-Albanian Bektashis**)

Imam Mohamed Magid (Executive Director, **All Dulles Area Muslim Society**)

Moutasem Atiya (**Al Madina Institute**)

Yaşar Çolak (President, **Diyanet Center of America**)

Ahmed Shehata (**Egyptian American Organization for Democracy & Human Rights**)

Nihad Awad (Executive Director, **Council on American-Islamic Relations**)

Oussama Jammal (Secretary General, **US Council of Muslim Organizations**)

Khalil Meek (Executive Director, **Muslim Legal Fund of America**)

Mir Masoom Ali (**Brooklyn Bangladeshi Community**)

Zahid Bukhari (President, **Islamic Circle of North America**)

Syed Moktadir (President, **All Dulles Area Muslim Center**)

Sayyid Syeed (National Director, **Islamic Society of North America**)

Behram Turan (Chairman, **TURKEN Foundation**)

Khaled Lamada (Chairman, **Islamic Relief**)

Ayman Hammous & **Lana Safah** (**Muslim American Society**)

Muhammad Tariq Rahman (Secretary General, **Islamic Circle of North America**)

Moviz Asad Siddiqi (**Islamic Circle of North America Relief**)

Sami Catovic (Director, **New Brunswick Islamic Center**)

Abdul Mawgoud Dardery (President, **Center for Egyptian-American Dialogue**)

Yasir (**Boston Muslim Community**)

Mohamed Elsanousi & **Imrana Umar** (**All Dulles Area Muslim Society**)

Mohamed Ismail (Coordinator, **Egyptians Abroad for Democracy Worldwide**)

Farrukh Raza (President, **Helping Hand for Relief and Development**)

The Turkish government and AKP delegation were represented by the following members:[62]

Veysi Kaynak, Deputy Prime Minister

Mevlüt Çavuşoğl, Minister of Foreign Affairs

Bekir Bozdağ, Minister of Justice

Fatma Betül Sayan Kaya, Minister of Family & Social Policies

Berat Albayrak, Minister of Energy & Natural Resources

Serdar Kılıç, Turkey's Ambassador to Washington, DC

Yasin Aktay, Deputy Chairman, Justice & Development Party

Ravza Kavakçı, AK Party Istanbul Deputy

Less than two months before the U.S. presidential election in November 2016, the USCMO's Muslim Brotherhood leadership gathered in New York City to meet with Erdoğan and an AKP delegation. Additionally, during this time, Nihad Awad would welcome an AKP delegation and the Turkish Ambassador to CAIR National headquarters.

According to an 8 September 2016 report from the Daily Sabah, a Turkish government delegation convened with Nihad Awad and CAIR. Serdar Kılıç, Turkey's Ambassador to Washington, DC, oversaw this meeting which included key U.S. Muslim Brotherhood representatives. The Turkish parliamentary delegation, led by AKP Deputy Chairman for Foreign Relations Mehdi Eker, included Turkish-American Inter-Parliamentary Friendship Group head Ali Sarıkaya, Turkey-EU Parliament Commission Co-Chair Ahmet Berat Çonkar and deputies Ravza Kavakçı Kan, Sena Nur Çelik and Emine Nur Günay.[63]

The purpose for this visit in advance of Erdoğan's meeting at the 71st session of the U.N. General Assembly on 13 September 2016 was to lobby members of the U.S. Congress, as Turkish government officials pressed for the extradition of Fethullah Gülen. President Tayyip Recep Erdoğan has described Gülen's extradition as a "priority, [64] because the Turkish government alleges that Gülen was behind the failed *coup d'état* attempt on 15 July 2016. Nevertheless, the U.S. government stated[65] evidence presented by Turkey was unpersuasive, while Gülen denied any role in what the AKP describes as "Turkey's July 15th."

The relationship building among Erdoğan, AKP, and the USCMO, which began long before the 2016 presidential election, was advantageous for many reasons as the Muslim Brotherhood leadership strategized its next moves and prepared for the future. As will be shown later, President Erdoğan was ready with an immediate response and plan of action to rally the USCMO and Muslims across the U.S. and around the world when President Trump began fulfilling campaign promises in the first year of his administration in 2017.

In the beginning of 2017, the DCA began collaboration with the International Institute of Islamic Thought (IIIT, a Muslim Brotherhood front group identified by the Justice Department as an unindicted co-conspirator in the 2008 Holy Land Foundation HAMAS terror funding trial), the All Dulles Area Muslim Society (ADAMS) Center (hub for Muslim Brotherhood operations in Northern Virginia), and then facilitated plans through the USCMO and Muslim Legal Fund of America (MLFA) to host seminars on how to protect the Muslim Brotherhood from potential legal prosecution in the United States.

Diyanet Center of America Signs MOU with IIIT

IIIT is a USCMO member and principal Muslim Brotherhood think tank with ties to HAMAS and Palestinian Islamic Jihad fundraising. These factors likely contributed a decision to establish a Memorandum of Understanding signed on 24 January 2017 between Dr. Yasar Colak, President of DCA and Dr. Abubaker Al-Shingieti, Executive Director of IIIT.[66] On 18 March 2017, a group of thirty imams and staff from the DCA was invited to IIIT headquarters in Herndon, Virginia and hosted by Ermin Sinanovic, Director of IIIT Research and Academic Programs.[67] It should be noted that after the establishment of its own Diyanet Islamic Research Institute and with the presence of Anadolu University on its campus, Ibn Khaldun University opened an office on 14 July 2017 on the DCA campus.[68] That President Erdoğan is collaborating with IIIT warrants carefully attention, as IIIT already has demonstrated its capacity to influence policy makers on Capitol Hill and members of the U.S. national security to the benefit of the global Islamic Movement.

Diyanet Center of America Partners with ADAMS Center

On 14 April 2017, during the 42nd Annual ICNA-MAS Convention in Baltimore, Maryland, the DCA organized and led a panel discussion focused on "Establishing a Mosque in America: Charting a Meaningful Future." Prominent speakers included Imam Mohamed Magid, Imam of ADAMS Center; Jameel W. Aalim-Johnson, President of Prince George's County Muslim Council; Nadia Hassan, a board member of KAGEM and founder of Young Leaders Institute; Dr. Zainab Chaudry, Spokeswoman and Outreach Manager for CAIR-Maryland Director, and Dr. Ahmet Aydilek, a DCA board member and Professor at University of Maryland, College Park.[69] Prior to this convention, a delegation from the DCA visited the main campus of the ADAMS Center in Sterling, Virginia in March 2017. ADAMS Center board member Mr. Robert Marro, who was joined by Imam Mohamed Magid, made a presentation about the historical background and current projects at the Center.[70]

While not an official member of the USCMO, the ADAMS Center is recognized as a Muslim Brotherhood front organization led by Executive Director Imam Mohamed Magid. He is a past President of the Islamic Society of North America (ISNA). In the 2008 trial of the Holy Land Foundation for Relief and Development, ISNA was named by the U.S. Department of Justice as one of the unindicted co-conspirators which provided financial resources to HAMAS. ADAMS Center founders include some of the most senior Muslim Brothers in the U.S. The relationship between the ADAMS Center and the increasingly influential DCA adds yet another link to the overall network, given Erdoğan's open support for HAMAS.

Diyanet Center of America Hosts Muslim Nonprofit Leadership Conference

Under the administration of U.S. President Donald J. Trump, the USCMO is especially concerned about possible legal issues, as calls were heard during the 2016 campaign urging that the 2008 Holy Land Foundation (HLF) HAMAS terror funding trial be re-opened to pursue possible cases against the more-than-200 unindicted co-conspirators named by the U.S. Department of Justice. Apparently concerned over possible vulnerability should the books of mosques, Islamic Centers, and Muslim Brotherhood front groups come under renewed official scrutiny, CAIR and other members of the USCMO therefore engaged the services of the Muslim Legal Fund of America (MLFA), itself a founding member of the USCMO.

It should come as no surprise, then, that the Muslim Non-Profit Leadership Conference[71], the first major event co-sponsored by the USCMO, Turkish American Cultural Center (TACC), and the MLFA in the Trump era (on 13 May 2017) was held at the DCA. Among the program topics were Safeguarding 501(c)3 status; Board fiduciary responsibilities; record keeping and disclosure requirements; Fundraising regulations, state registrations, unrelated business income; and Banking regulations, FDIC, DOJ, Watchlists, international charitable giving.

One of the MLFA's top legal representatives, now working openly with the U.S. Muslim Brotherhood, is U.S. Navy Lieutenant Commander (ret.) Charles Swift, formerly of the Judge Advocate General's Corps (JAG). Swift, a 1984 graduate[72] of the U.S. Naval Academy, was recognized[73] by the Muslim Brotherhood for his legal role advocating for client Salim Ahmed Hamdan[74] in the U.S. Supreme Court case Hamdan v. Rumsfield[75] 548 US 557 (2006). This role doubtless contributed to the choice of Swift as Director and Counsel for the Constitutional Law Center for Muslims in America (CLCMA), a project[76] of the Muslim Legal Fund of America[77] led by Executive Director Khahil Meek[78].

The MLFA's CLCMA project presents[79] itself as dedicated to two primary missions:

- "Challenging governmental security measures affecting Muslim communities which encroach upon the constitutional liberties guaranteed to all."

- "Protecting the rights of Muslim individuals and organizations in the United States to exercise their constitutionally and statutorily protected rights to worship."

In apparent pursuance of these missions, the MLFA continues[80] actively to seek the release from federal prison of defendants in the HLF trial, which concluded in late 2008 with a unanimous guilty verdict on all 108 counts. The MLFA also engages in lawfare, using lawsuits as an offensive means of shutting down opposition to its civilization jihad operations. For example, as noted[81] by the Thomas More Law Center in the 2009 case of Joe KAUFMAN, Appellant, v. ISLAMIC SOCIETY OF ARLINGTON, Texas, Islamic Center of Irving, DFW Islamic Educational Center, Inc., Dar Elsalam Islamic Center, Al Hedayah Islamic Center, Islamic Association of Tarrant County, and Muslim American Society of Dallas, Appellees, No. 2-09-023-CV: "The head of that organization [MLFA], **Khalil Meek, admitted on a Muslim radio show that lawsuits were being filed against Kaufman and others to set an example. Indeed, for the last several years, Muslim groups in the U.S. have engaged in the tactic of filing meritless lawsuits to silence any public discussion of Islamic terrorist threats.**"

More recently, in response to U.S. President Trump's early March 2017 revised executive order to restrict immigration from six Muslim-majority nations, the MLFA working in conjunction with the USCMO, continues referring all Muslims to its "advisory prepared by Constitutional Law Center for Muslims in America."[82] The MLFA may cloak itself in the colors of Star Spangled Shariah as a "constitutional rights organization" but Executive Director Khalil Meek still complains that "We continue to be troubled by this administration's ongoing attempts to single out Muslims for adverse actions. Such blatant discrimination is a violation of our nation's constitutional freedoms of speech, expression and religion."

Finally, it is worth taking note of the following guidance. The Assembly of Muslim Jurists of America (AMJA) represents the recognized juridical authority on Islamic Law (shariah) for the American Muslim community and U.S. Islamic legal organizations such as the MLFA. Addressing the U.S. Muslim community on 28 November 2016, shortly after Donald Trump won the U.S. presidential election, AMJA issued the following bracing statement:[83]

> *"No one could possibly be unaware of the political storm that has recently overtaken this country...For this reason, the Assembly of Muslim Jurists in America is addressing the Imams, Islamic workers and the entire Muslim community with permanent values that must be emphasized during this stage as well as a number of principles to be used in dealing with these events, what has happened as well as what is expected to happen...**Islam, with respect to its belief and legal foundations, is unalterably fixed. It does not accept any replacement for change.**" [emphasis added]*

Although the Center for Security Policy has followed the activities of the USCMO, MLFA, and AMJA, the realization of just how closely the Turkish government at the highest level is working in collusion with these Muslim Brotherhood-associated groups to thwart any legal measures that may be directed their way by the Trump administration and Department of Justice led by Attorney General Jeff Sessions still comes as something of a shock.

In the beginning of 2017, the U.S. Brotherhood and its international partners were ahead of the Trump team in foreseeing a possible renewal of legal risk and liability under this new management and began taking steps to confront it. They brought significant financial and legal resources to the fight, plus, as we now see, state-level backing from NATO member Turkey, whose pro-HAMAS stance has long been known.

But given that an official organization of the Ankara regime is now operating a large Center (with a multiplying network of supporting associated centers and mosques across this country) barely thirteen miles from the U.S. Capitol and working there in collaboration with the U.S. Muslim Brotherhood to thwart possible legal actions by the U.S. government is certainly noteworthy. As the international--as well as U.S.--Muslim Brotherhood gear up for coming confrontations, so must U.S. national security leadership as well.

NATO Ally Turkey Is Hostile Foreign Agent of Influence

The decision by President Trump on 6 December 2017 to uphold the Jerusalem Embassy Act of 1995 [84] and formally recognize Jerusalem as Israel's capital set in motion a chain of events that further exposes the deepening ties among the Muslim Brotherhood-led USCMO, our NATO "ally"

Turkey, and the overall Red-Green Axis. These events follow on an April 2017 exclusive report from Center for Security Policy, which highlighted[85] the increasingly close collaboration between President Erdoğan and the senior leadership of the U.S. Muslim Brotherhood.

Immediately following an extraordinary Organization of Islamic Cooperation (OIC) summit called[86] by President Erdoğan in Istanbul during the week of 11 December 2017, USCMO and Muslim Brotherhood organizations from around the U.S. converged on the nation's capital on Saturday, 16 December 2017 for a big demonstration on the Ellipse south of the White House. After the conclusion of afternoon Islamic prayers there, the protesters marched along Pennsylvania Avenue up to Capitol Hill. Following the lead of Erdoğan and the OIC, USCMO leadership declared Jerusalem a "red line for the Muslim world" and condemned the legitimacy and credibility of the Trump administration for the action taken by the U.S. government.

President Erdoğan Declares "Jerusalem Is Our Redline"

It was, in fact, the featured speaker from the Turkish American Steering Committee, Director Hilal Mutlu, who reiterated[87] the point made by Erdoğan as he stated, "We said before, Al-Quds [Jerusalem] is our redline." His statement is especially important because Halil is not only a first cousin of Erdoğan, but recognized by Muslims as Erdoğan's "brother" because of the closeness of that relationship.[88]

Joining directly in these efforts to send a message to President Trump and the American people was Turkey, a state actor component. The pro-HAMAS Turkish government, under the leadership of President Erdoğan and AKP, delivered a message through Hilal not only to Muslims across the U.S., but around the world. American news networks were oddly absent from this significant event outside the White House and provided no coverage of it at all.

At the 16 December demonstration (held notably while President Trump was present inside the White House), demonstrators cheered loudly when Mutlu declared, "**My President, your president, president of the ummah Recep Tayyip Erdoğan.**"[89] Demonstrators also responded boisterously at mention of Turkish President Recep Tayyip Erdoğan's defiance against a U.S. move of its embassy to Jerusalem. Responding back as Mutlu spoke[90], denouncing President Trump and calling on him to reverse his decision on Jerusalem, demonstrators shouted, "**Recep Tayyip Erdoğan, true leader of Ummah [Muslim believers]**."[91]

The Muslim Brotherhood's media messaging sequence and coordinated efforts to construct and control the narrative is emerging—and the carefully calibrated language used by the international Muslim Brotherhood leadership and its domestic affiliates here in the U.S. should serve as a warning to Western leaders.

President Erdoğan warned[92] on 5 December 2017: "Jerusalem, Mr. Trump, is a **red line** for Muslims. We will continue our fight against this with determination until the very end. And, this could go all the way to our cutting diplomatic ties with Israel."

CAIR National Executive Director Nihad Awad,[93] also speaking on 5 December 2017, but from the grounds of the U.S. White House, added: "Recognizing Jerusalem as the capital of Israel is not only morally wrong but it is against our national strategic interest in the region and in the Muslim world."

USCMO Secretary General Oussama Jammal declared,[94] "The U.S. Council of Muslim organization believes that any move on the status of Jerusalem will jeopardize peace and stability of the Middle East."

On 7 December 2017, the USCMO issued the following chilling statement:

> *"USCMO vehemently opposes President Donald Trump's unilateral and reckless declaration that the United States will recognize the Holy City of Jerusalem as the capital of Israel and denounces his order to relocate the U.S. Embassy to Jerusalem as an unwise deviation from long-standing U.S. policy...The US Council of Muslim Organizations calls upon the American people and our political leadership to reject this dangerous declaration and to begin the process of walking it back before it plunges the world deeper into intractable conflict."[95]*

In this declaration, entitled *"Statement of the US Council of Muslim Organizations on President Trump's Recognition of Jerusalem as the Capital of Israel,"* the tone of the language is both hostile and threatening, and should be taken as a serious warning. The USCMO statement is cited below in its entirety, but key language to note in the USCMO statement includes the following carefully-chosen words and phrases:

- "vehemently oppose"
- "declaration is offensive and provocative"

- "harms American interests"
- "beyond the pale"
- "lighting a fuse to an explosive conflagration . . . with slaughter and suffering,"
- "incendiary and will reap its **inflammatory** intent" (It is important to note that "inflammatory" is a term associated with "Day of Rage" messaging.)

Prior coordination in the wording of these declarations appears evident among the international Muslim Brotherhood, its U.S. affiliates, and the supporting narrative originating in Turkish media agencies. In fact, the Turkish news *Andadolu Agency* published an article that was not only directly in line with the Muslim Brotherhood but quoted from HAMAS-doing-business-as-CAIR and the American Muslims for Palestine (AMP) as sources for its 6 December 2017 report, "Trump's Jerusalem plans 'reckless and dangerous.'" Since its 2014 formation, the USCMO has routinely utilized the *Anadolu Agency* for dissemination of information to the Muslim world.

Then, at the 13 December 2017 OIC summit in Istanbul, President Erdoğan sounded a strident note when he called[96] Israel a "terror state." The following day, the OIC leadership declared that East Jerusalem is the capital of Palestine and viewed[97] the decision by President Trump to recognize Jerusalem as Israel's capital as "encouragement to Israel—the occupying power, to continue their policy of colonization, settlement, apartheid and ethnic cleansing of people of Palestine." It further warned[98]: "[We] consider that this dangerous declaration, which aims to change the legal status of the [city], is null and void and lacks any legitimacy."

Following the conclusion of the USCMO led protest and demonstration march in Washington, DC on 17 December 2017, Turkish Prime Minister Binali Yildirim followed up, discussing[99] President Trump's actions as a "miscalculation" and pointed out that "those who miscalculate on Jerusalem al-Quds in this region will eventually regret it."

Due to the strange absence of coverage by U.S. media outlets, Congressional and national security leadership, as well as the American public at large, were left uninformed about the fact that twenty-eight organizations from the across the country participated in the White House protest, which included a substantial effort to bus hundreds of protesters in from around the country including from Milwaukee, WI, Chicago, IL, St. Louis, MO, Tampa, FL, New Jersey, New York, Philadelphia, PA, Maryland, Virginia, and Washington, DC. Far-left groups like Code Pink and interfaith entities associated with the Brotherhood front group, Islamic Society of North America's "Shoulder to Shoulder" program, also stood in solidarity with the listed Islamic organizations and groups generally associated with the domestic Muslim Brotherhood.

A worldwide coalition of the Islamic Movement, that arises out of the OIC and increasingly includes allies from the anarchist, communist hard-left as well as a number of unwary faith communities, is stepping up its agenda inside the U.S. Of key significance is the financial, ideological, and physical leadership role being played by Erdoğan, AKP, and the nation state of Turkey. As the Trump administration, Congress, and U.S. Department of State move forward with plans to relocate the U.S. embassy in Israel to Jerusalem on 14 May 2018 (to coincide with the 70th anniversary of the founding of the modern State of Israel in 1948), this Red-Green Axis of opposition merits close monitoring.

President Erdoğan Regime Seeks Ummah Leadership at Home & Abroad

In the closing days of 2017, the pro-HAMAS Turkish government under the leadership of President Erdoğan and AKP dealt yet another blow to the rule of law in Turkey with a decree that legalizes vigilante action by anyone against anyone—so long as it's characterized as counterterrorism. On 24 December 2017, Erdoğan and AKP implemented Article 121 of the state of emergency decree 696[100] which states the following:

> "*Individuals, regardless of whether or not they possess an official title or whether or not they are discharging official duties, who are engaged in suppressing the attempted 15 July 2016 coup, terrorist actions or other actions that are continuations of these will be subject to the first paragraph (of Article 37 which was published in November 2016).*"

And here is what the first paragraph of Article 37[101] says:

> "*[W]ith regard to the suppression of the attempted 15 July 2016 coup, terrorist actions or other actions that are continuations of these, this decision absolves all those who make decisions or enact measures, as well as those who conduct duties with regard to all types of judicial and administrative measures and who make decisions and*

discharge duties within the framework of decisions with the force of law (KHK) that are published as part of the state of emergency, from legal, administrative, financial and penal responsibility."

In other words, the Turkish government—a supposed NATO ally—has just granted impunity to Erdoğan loyalists to take the law into their own hands when and how they see fit, to assault, injure, even kill anyone deemed a "terrorist." The decree is an open invitation to individuals, AKP paramilitary groups, and thugs claiming to be acting in response to the 2016 attempted coup to go after any and all political enemies. Who may be the targets of such incitement to violence? Christians, Jews, Kurds, and any who may be labeled "Gülenists" or traitors are left completely vulnerable by this decree.

The Turkish decree immediately followed declarations by Erdoğan (speaking to the Turkish parliament) and other OIC representatives during the United Nations General Assembly (UNGA) discussion on 21 December 2017 that Jerusalem is their "red line,"[102] followed by a lopsided vote to condemn the U.S. government and the Trump administration for daring to recognize Jerusalem as the capital of Israel. While Erdoğan rules increasingly as a despot, irony characterizes the following statement[103] from Turkish Foreign Minister Mevlut Cavusoglu, who attempts to stand on moral high ground in condemning the USG recognition of Jerusalem as Israel's capital: "This decision is an outrageous assault to all universal values...this is bullying...we will not be intimated...you can be strong, but this doesn't make you right." Once again, Erdoğan's AKP regime is stepping forward on the international stage to present itself as the leading voice of the OIC if not actual leader of the global Muslim *ummah.*

Looking back to 2014, the year that the Brotherhood's USCMO was founded in the U.S., we will recall from the USCMO's Press Release page "Witnessing Turkish Democracy in Action," how clearly the USCMO announced its partnership with Erdoğan and the Turkish AK Party, even as it now moves into a full-fledged Islamic jihad partnership with them. That partnership comes into even clearer focus if we view this relationship through the lens of the domestic Muslim Brotherhood's longstanding mission found in its Explanatory Memorandum (1991, page 4 of 18):

"The general strategic goal of the Group in America ... is the "Enablement of Islam in North America, meaning: establishing an effective and stable Islamic Movement led by

the Muslim Brotherhood which adopts Muslims' causes domestically and globally ... presents a civilization alternative, and **supports the global Islamic State wherever it is.**"

Before the close of 2017, Muslim Brotherhood leaders and supporters from around the world converged on Chicago for the 16th Annual Muslim American Society-Islamic Circle of North America convention from 28-30 December 2017. There Erdoğan and AKP energized the base and delivered a powerful message for the global Islamic Movement.

President Erdoğan Addresses 16th Annual MAS-ICNA Convention

Mehdi Eker, deputy chair of Turkey's ruling AKP, was a featured speaker who attended the MAS-ICNA convention held at the McCormick Place in Chicago. AKP was prominently featured with a booth set up for convention attendees to pick up AKP literature and meet Eker himself.[104] The highlight of the 16th Annual MAS-ICNA Convention, however, was a prerecorded video address from Erdoğan, presented on 30 December 2017. He defiantly challenged the governments of the U.S. and Israel for their actions officially recognizing Jerusalem as the capital of Israel. He further urged the audience to recognize that "The Islamic world should now become aware of its real power."[105]

Notice the Muslim Brotherhood's notorious four-finger Rabia hand sign prominently featured on Erdoğan's desktop during his prerecorded video address on 30 December 2017. The "R4BIA" finds its origins at Rabia al-Adawiya Square when a military coup (massively supported by millions of Egyptians) occurred on 3 July 2013, leading to the overthrow of Muslim Brotherhood Egyptian President Morsi.[106]

Less than two weeks after the 16th Annual MAS-ICNA Convention, USCMO members met in January 2018 with Turkish Diyanet and DCA leadership.[107] President of Religious Affairs of Turkey Professor Ali Erbas once again received the praise of USCMO Secretary General Oussama Jammal and CAIR National Executive Director Nihad Awad.

Conclusion

As with the 2015 publication of our *Star Spangled Shariah* monograph, the Center for Security Policy once again issues an alert, this time to the Trump administration, and especially its Intelligence Community, National Security Council, State Department, and Justice Department leadership: the

U.S. Muslim Brotherhood/USCMO is moving into an ever-closer jihad alliance with pro-HAMAS Erdoğan and his AKP to advance the global Islamic Movement. That relationship is brazenly pursued on American soil with the Lanham, Maryland Diyanet Center of America as its base for insurgency operations against the U.S. government, whose purpose is openly declared: to advance the establishment of a global Islamic State under rule of Islamic Law (shariah).

During a speech delivered on 24 February 2018 at an AK Party congress in the city of Kahramanmaras, Turkey, Erdoğan sent yet another foreboding message to both U.S. and Western leaders. Erdoğan saw a weeping-and-saluting 6-year-old girl dressed in a child-size military uniform. After trying unsuccessfully to comfort Amine Tiras, who was brought on the stage by Erdoğan, he told the audience: "She has the Turkish flag in her pocket. If she becomes a martyr, God willing, this flag will be draped on her." [108] This chilling statement does not signal a peaceful future between NATO Ally Turkey and the West.

The December 2017 National Security Strategy[109] of the United States boldly declared that our first "fundamental responsibility is to protect the American people, the homeland, and the American way of life." This document also speaks of defeating our jihadist enemies: the Islamic Movement, dedicated to replacement of the U.S. Constitution with shariah and represented by the Erdoğan regime, the Muslim Brotherhood, and the USCMO, is waging civilization jihad against us here in the homeland. It is time to call out, confront, and vanquish this threat.

That an official organization of the Ankara regime is now operating a large Center (with a multiplying network of supporting associated Islamic Centers and mosques across this country) barely thirteen miles from the U.S. Capitol and working there in collaboration with U.S. Muslim Brotherhood leadership (including to thwart possible legal actions against them by the U.S. government) is alarming. As the U.S. Muslim Brotherhood and the global Islamic Movement prepare for coming confrontations, so must U.S. national security leadership as well.

CHAPTER 3

Gülen and Erdoğan:
Partners on a Brotherhood Mission

• By Clare M. Lopez

As the world watches with increasing alarm, Turkey is reverting from a 20ᵗʰ century NATO ally with a determinedly secular government to an aggressive, tyrannical neo-Ottoman jihad state. While the West seems only reluctantly to be grasping this unwelcome reality, in fact the groundwork for Turkey's reversal has been long in the laying by both Turkey's current President Recep Tayyip Erdoğan and his doppelganger rival to power, the exiled Turkish cleric Fethullah Gülen. Both Erdoğan and Gülen are devout, practicing Sunni Muslims in the mold of the Muslim Brotherhood. Partners for many years in returning Turkey to its Islamic character, the two have since 2013 made a dramatic show of a power struggle split. But at deeper levels away from the glare of the public arena, Erdoğan and Gülen—and their followers and partners—remain at a minimum on parallel tracks, working steadily to advance the Islamic doctrine of the Muslim Brotherhood both in Turkey and abroad, including inside the United States of America.

This excerpt from a televised 1999 speech by Gülen to his followers illustrates how both he and Erdoğan think and operate, despite their public disputes over power:

> You must move in the arteries of the system without anyone noticing your existence until you reach all the power centers...Until the conditions are ripe, they [the followers] must continue like this. If they do something prematurely, the world will crush our heads, and Muslims will suffer everywhere, like in the yearly disasters and tragedies in Egypt...The time is not yet right. You must wait for the time when you are complete and conditions are ripe, until we can shoulder the entire world and carry it...You must wait until such time as you have gotten all the state power, until you have brought to your side all the power of the constitutional

*institutions in Turkey...Now, I have expressed my feelings and
thoughts to you all—in confidence...trusting your loyalty and
secrecy. I know that when you leave here, [just] as you discard
your empty juice boxes, you must discard the thoughts and
feelings that I expressed here.*[110]

There is long history behind the 20th-21st century Islamic revival, of course, which inspires Erdoğan, Gülen, and the entire global Islamic Movement. The Ottoman Empire had conquered and ruled huge expanses of southeastern Europe, western Asia, and northern Africa from the 14th to the early 20th century as the de facto leader of Sunni Islam. In an even larger sense, the Ottoman Sultans were the rulers of the global Muslim ummah. But following the disastrous Ottoman defeat in World War I and subsequent territorial reduction to the boundaries of today's nation state of Turkey, the multi-ethnic, multi-sectarian people of Turkey came under the control of strongman Mustafa Kemal 'Ataturk'. Having seen up close as an Army officer what modern Western societies were capable of doing to those who had not kept up in education, government, industry, or military matters, Ataturk concluded that only a forcible program of modernization and secularization could transform Turkey into a competitive peer of even the least advanced of those European countries. And for a time, he succeeded in dragging it kicking and screaming into the 20th century.

To be sure, it was no easy task that Ataturk undertook: outside of a Westernized urban elite, the majority of Turks in the early 20th century were conservative, uneducated Muslims, who lived in agrarian communities and small towns, largely isolated from the modern Western world. So, when Ataturk moved to modernize and secularize the education system, replace the Arabic alphabet used by Ottoman Turkey with the Latin alphabet, grant Turkish women civil and political rights equal to those of men (including the right to vote), ban the fez and hijab from public spaces, and restrict Islam to the mosques, along with many other civic, economic, legislative, political, and social reforms, resistance was inevitable. Besides contending with the rise of communism and fascism across Europe, Ataturk also faced the dismay of the entire Muslim world after he abolished the Ottoman Caliphate in 1924.

Concurrent with the 1928 founding of the Muslim Brotherhood jihad group in Cairo, Egypt (which was and remains dedicated to restoration of a global caliphate under rule of Islamic Law or shariah), the Islamic resistance to Ataturk's reforms inside Turkey began in the heartland, in homes and mosques across Anatolia. Some of this took the form of so-called 'reading circles' (or *dershanes*), which were popularized by Aziz Üstad Bediüzzaman Said Nursi, also spelled simply Said-i Nursî (1878-1960), who was popularly known as Bediüzzaman, an honorific meaning "wonder of the age." [111] Familiar with the thought of the Naqshbandi Sufis, Nursi helped crystalize opposition to Ataturk's modernization program by popularizing the study of his monumental *Risale-i Nur* collection of Qur'anic commentary (*tafsir*). Through the *Risale-i Nur*, Nursi hoped to bring about an Islamic revival in Turkey,[112] an objective now in fact coming to fruition in the 21st century.

Enter Fethullah Gülen

Fethullah Gülen was born in either 1938, the year that Mustafa Kemal Ataturk died—or 1941, just a few years later (there is some dispute about this). Gülen's father was an imam in a village in eastern Turkey and wanted his son to follow in his footsteps with a religious career. After a brief 5-year Islamic education, Gülen received an imam-preacher certificate and served as an imam before also beginning to teach. [113] Some of his clandestine activities, however, including organizing summer camps to teach Islam, got him in trouble with the authorities in the 1970s and he spent seven months in prison.[114] He was strongly influenced by Nursi's philosophy, especially his Sufism, and became his devoted follower. It may be said that the anti-Ataturk resistance movement that emerged in Nursi's reading circles crystalized into a program of action with Gülen.

Like Nursi, Gülen opposed the secularization of Turkish government and society and devoted much of his lifetime of preaching, teaching, and writing to restoring what he liked to call an 'Anatolian Islam' to a place of dominance in Turkish government and life. It's not that Anatolian Islam is in any way different doctrinally from the one authoritative Islam, but rather that Gülen's model for application and enforcement of shariah has followed the Muslim Brotherhood style of 'gradualism.' Gülen cultivates a benign image of tolerance and respect for others that too often fools those hoping to find in his philosophy a version of Islam that does not include jihad against non-Muslims, the harsh *Hudud* crimes and punishments, or visceral antisemitism. Gülen's 'gradualist' façade merely bespeaks a patience for achieving in the end what others rush headlong to impose.

Fethullah Gülen founded his now global *Hizmet* ("Service") organization in the 1960s to promote just such a benign, moderate image of Islam. Since then, despite having no visible organizational structure, headquarters, or official membership, *Hizmet* has expanded to include millions of followers worldwide, with an influence that extends far beyond the identifiable Gülen media outlets, schools, and think tanks that comprise it.

A quick glance back to the words of Gülen's 1999 speech, referenced at the beginning of this chapter, will remind us that Gülen's actual intentions, carefully concealed though they be, nevertheless characterize a movement whose purpose is influence and power: *"You must move in the arteries of the system without anyone noticing your existence until you reach all the power centers ..."*

A slightly deeper consideration of Gülen's own voluminous writing, much of it at his official website,[115] is well-worth reading to understand the Gülenist philosophy. As this author and Center for Security Policy (CSP) co-author Christopher Holton noted in our 2015 monograph, *"Gülen and the Gülenist Movement: Turkey's Islamic Supremacist Cult and its Contributions to the Civilization Jih*ad," that website features many dozens of his essays on topics ranging from Thought, Faith, and Sufism, to Love and Tolerance.[116] Among them, though, Gülen's 1998 book *"Prophet Mohammed as Commander"*[117] stands out as especially revealing of Gülen's views on jihad and warfare.

As the book's title suggests, Gülen is writing here about the obligatory nature of jihad in Islam, especially as waged against non-believers by Muhammad. And while he attempts (disingenuously but ultimately unsuccessfully) to couch Muhammad's motivation as one of 'compassion,' it is clear that what Gülen means by this bit of sophistry is that Muslims are obligated, you see, to fight those who refuse to acknowledge the supremacy of Allah and Muhammad—as an act of compassion. It is, as Gülen writes, *"For this reason, a Muslim's enmity toward unbelievers is, in fact in the form of pitying them."*[118] As Holton and I observed,

> *"Failing to submit to the supremacy of Islam is the very definition of 'injustice' in Islamic doctrine. Out of 'compassion' for those unbelievers, but especially to prevent them from committing further injustice, Muslims are obliged to feel enmity toward them and to fight them as enemies."*[119]

Gülen's essay goes on to explain that jihad is the central, core element of Islamic doctrine because of the Islamic obligation to establish a worldwide caliphate. Thus, any belief system, entity, person, or nation state that fails to submit to Islam is an impediment to the fulfillment of that divinely-ordained obligation and so must be destroyed.

The Gülen Networks

With this rather sobering adjustment to some of the more rose-colored portrayals of Gülen that may be found, a look at his international network of businesses, cultural centers, media platforms, schools, and supporters must now arouse some measure of concern, if not outright alarm, at the extent and continuing spread of the Gülen Movement, including inside the U.S. itself. For, even as the Turkish military intervened four times during the 20th century to preserve Ataturk's legacy, Gülen was working from within, and especially through the "Golden Generation" of graduates from his network of schools in Turkey, to undermine those modernizing social reforms. Those alumni, who ultimately numbered in the thousands, moved into the ranks of Turkish business, judiciary, media, the national police, and much of the state bureaucracy. Many have become influential, powerful, and wealthy and readily use their positions and wealth to fund and support Gülen's expanding empire. Their success in achieving a nearly-complete reversal of Ataturk's policies in Turkey is reason aplenty to take a closer look at how Gülen's highly-organized grass roots movement operates inside the U.S.

Increasingly at odds with a still-Kemalist Turkish government, Fethullah Gülen fled prosecution in Turkey and was allowed to settle in the U.S. in 1999. He has lived since then in an armed, guarded compound in Saylorsburg, PA in the Poconos Mountains. In 2008, Gülen was granted Permanent Resident status, although it does not seem that he has ever sought U.S. citizenship. He runs his sprawling U.S. and worldwide organization from the Saylorsburg compound, rarely if ever emerging from it.

The Gülen Movement empire—to date now comprising at least 155 K-12 charter schools and four universities plus myriad businesses and cultural centers in the U.S.—has come under a growing wave of criticism as allegations mount concerning murky finances, possible H1-B visa abuse, forced salary kickback schemes in some of the Gülen charter schools, fraudulent skewing of test results, and the use of all-expense-paid trips to Turkey[120] to promote a pro-Turkish, Islamic agenda while concealing the source of funding. Although there is no evidence that the Gülen K-12 charter schools in the U.S. openly teach an Islamic curriculum (touting instead a STEM—science, technology, engineering and math—program), the strong emphasis on Turkey, its culture, history, and language, provides an entry-point to the Islamic agenda that has proven so successful in corroding the once-secular policies of our erstwhile NATO ally.

The four Gülen universities in the U.S. are the North American University in Texas, the American Islamic College[121] in Illinois, the Virginia

International University[122] in Virginia, and the Respect Graduate School[123] in Pennsylvania in addition to the Gülen Institute in Houston. Of these, two—the American Islamic College and the Respect Graduate School—offer Islamic Studies degree programs, while the other two are more traditional liberal arts schools. The Gülen Institute is not a college or university, but a non-profit research organization.[124]

Of note with regard to Gülen's overall U.S. educational empire is a 2017 report from Turkey's National Intelligence Organization (MİT) that claims the Gülen Movement takes in some $500 million annually from these schools.[125] Even allowing for expected anti-Gülen bias on the part of Turkey's official intelligence agency, this is a startling figure. Those allegations find reinforcement in a 2017 study commissioned by the Turkish government. Following the 2016 coup attempt in Turkey, the Erdoğan government hired a U.S. law firm, Amsterdam & Partners, LLP, to investigate the Gülen network of charter schools in the U.S. After an extensive research effort relying on available public records, in 2017 the firm produced a massive 651-page report on the "extensive nationwide network of Gülenists, charter schools, charter management corporations, educational foundations, real estate companies, school vendors, and Gülenist cultural associations". The report documents many of the allegations made by school administrators, former students, teachers, and others about fraudulent and possibly criminal practices noted above. Unsurprisingly, the report concludes that the entire Gülen charter school network is based on fraud for the purpose of bilking the U.S. taxpayer-funded charter school system for the private profit of the Gülen Movement.[126]

Among the many other Gülen affiliates in the U.S. are some that deserve particular attention because of their prominence and role in sponsoring and paying for some of those trips to Turkey as well as a host of local Turkish cultural events. The Atlas Foundation of Louisiana, [127] the Raindrop Foundation,[128] the Niagara Foundation,[129] and the Pacifica Institute[130] are all more or less openly affiliated with the Gülen Movement. Typically targeted for cultivation and invitations are local civic leaders, Catholic and Jewish faith community leaders, journalists, state legislators, students, and university presidents, professors, and trustees.[131]

While many of these groups openly reveal their association with Gülen and the Gülenist Movement to their invitees, in at least one case involving Members of the U.S. Congress, trip funding was carefully concealed, according to a *USA Today* investigation reported on 29 October 2015. The Members duly requested appropriate approvals for their trips to Turkey from the House Ethics Committee, which then approved the trips based on allegedly falsified paperwork that concealed the Gülenist identities of the group that issued the invitations.[132] In a follow-up 2017 report, *USA Today* reported on a Center for Public Integrity study that found more than 150 state legislators who were reported to have accepted trips to Turkey at least partially subsidized by the Gülen Movement.[133]

While at least 39 states now feature the presence of some Gülen affiliate—whether a charter school or cultural center, corporate entity, other non-profit organization, or media outlet—the states of California, Georgia, New Jersey, New York, Ohio, Pennsylvania, and Texas are especially saturated with dozens of them. Texas, with a total of at least 52 Gülen charter schools and dozens of Gülen mosques, Raindrop Houses, corporations, cultural centers, and other front groups would seem to be ground zero for the U.S. Gülen Movement.

The concern with these facilities, and especially the schools, is that the Muslim Brotherhood- and jihad-oriented ideology of Fethullah Gülen is not always known or understood. Thanks to the careful shroud of ambiguity surrounding the Gülen Movement, those targeted for the Gülen Movement's influence operations often are unaware of the group's actual agenda. Most of them likely are not aware either of the widespread allegations of irregularities at the Gülen charter schools or related to the sponsored junket trips to Turkey.

As Holton and I concluded in the Center for Security Policy's 2015 monograph, "behind the carefully-cultivated façade of benign dedication to education, interfaith dialogue, peace, and tolerance lies a far more calculated agenda to promote Islam, jihad, and shariah worldwide."[134] The final sections of this chapter will look into the Gülen-Erdoğan relationship, their relentlessly-hyped feud, and some disturbing indicators from inside the U.S. that the divorce may not be quite as final as widely-portrayed.

The Gülen-Erdoğan Relationship

Turkish President Recep Tayyip Erdoğan was born in 1954 and grew up in a secular, Kemalist Turkey. His Anatolian family, however, and especially his father, Ahmet Erdoğan, were conservative and pious. The young Erdoğan was sent to the Istanbul Imam Hatip School, which set him on course for a life of Islamic activism and politics, with an outlook marked by antisemitism, nationalist pride, and hostility towards foreign, especially Western, influences.[135]

Throughout the early years of his political career, as a rising young politician, Erdoğan's conservative, pro-Islamic profile benefited from the ideological groundwork laid by the Gülen Movement, but as mayor of Istanbul from 1994-98, he won popularity by tackling many municipal problems with effective pragmatism. When Erdoğan formed the Justice and Development Party (AKP) in 2001, though, it was obviously modeled after the Egyptian Muslim Brotherhood party, the Freedom and Justice Party. Following the AKP's electoral victory in 2002, Erdoğan became Prime Minister, and Gülen and his movement threw their support behind him, marshaling their media outlets as well as an extensive following inside the Turkish judiciary and police.[136]

For a while, the partnership seemed natural and symbiotic. The Erdoğan-Gülen political alliance would last most of Erdoğan's 2003-2014 terms as Prime Minister. By 2011, however, Erdoğan and the AKP were riding high, having taken advantage of the Gülenists' intellectual assets, their media outlets, and network of supporters throughout the Turkish bureaucracy. Gülen had linked his movement to a rising political machine and likewise benefited from the relationship. After the AK Party's success in the 2011 elections, however, Erdoğan's ambitions for untrammeled rule led him to see Gülen increasingly as a rival to power. The stage was set for a very public divorce.[137]

The Gülen Movement's loss of favor with an increasingly authoritarian Erdoğan/AKP regime first became evident with a cut-off of government-awarded contracts and the sudden denial of jobs and promotions for the many Gülen followers throughout the Turkish government bureaucracy. By November 2013, tensions had escalated to the point that Erdoğan moved against one of the Gülen Movement's key sources of income and influence: the "cram schools" (called *dershanes*, like the earlier Nursi reading circles) that helped prepare high school students for the all-important university entrance exam. By shutting down the *dershanes*, Erdoğan cut off both a major funding stream for the Gülenists and their access to a large pool of potential young recruits to the movement. Subsequent corruption allegations leveled against Erdoğan and the AKP in 2013 were launched from among Gülenist allies among the judiciary, prosecutors, and police. It was open warfare after that, with Erdoğan declaring the Gülen movement a terrorist organization, arresting dozens of major Turkish editors and journalists, and shutting down their media outlets throughout the country.[138]

At the time of the July 2016 failed coup attempt in Turkey, Gülen had been living in the U.S. for many years. But that didn't stop Erdoğan and the

AKP from naming Gülen as the coup's mastermind amidst shrill demands that he be extradited to Turkey (a demand the Trump administration is unlikely to grant). A number of "confessions" from coup participants that were obviously produced under duress and a slew of expensively-produced books and other publications from the Turkish government aside, there is little credible evidence that Fethullah Gülen had anything to do with the coup, much less that he somehow directed it from his lair in the Poconos mountains. On the other hand, neighbors near Saylorsburg, PA did report fireworks going off inside the Gülen compound on the night of 15 July 2016 and also claim there was a much larger than usual volume of traffic through their little town in the days prior to the coup. For the record, Gülen's website features a detailed rebuttal to coup involvement claims.[139]

Despite Turkey's continued NATO membership, it has been at loggerheads with the U.S. on a growing list of issues, which are only exacerbated by the U.S.'s refusal to extradite Gülen. U.S. backing for Kurdish groups fighting against the Islamic State angers Turkey, which considers all Kurds to be enemies of the state, whether inside Turkey or not. Then, in June 2017, Washington, DC police leveled official charges against members of Erdoğan's security detail who were recorded on video viciously beating peaceful Kurdish demonstrators outside the Turkish embassy. The Turkish guards were allowed to depart the U.S., but Turkish rancor remained.[140] On 3 January 2018, a Turkish banker closely connected to the highest levels of the Turkish government, was convicted in a New York District Court for his role in an Iran sanctions-busting scheme involving Turkish banks. The star witness in that case was Reza Zarrab, a wealthy gold trader[141] with quadruple citizenship (from Azerbaijan, Iran, Macedonia, and Turkey) and confidant of Turkish President Erdoğan, who himself had pleaded guilty to an unspecified charge just prior to the second trial. His apparent plea deal indicates that he likely cooperated with Department of Justice prosecutors in a case that directly implicates the corrupt Turkish president in a plot to use the gold trade to help Iran evade sanctions.[142]

Jihad Operations There and Here

There is no denying that Turkey's official rhetoric is becoming increasingly aggressive and belligerent. It would be foolish to ignore it, hoping that somehow policy does not follow such rhetoric. In late January 2018, Ismail Kahraman, the Speaker of Turkey's National Assembly, called Turkey's military incursion against Syrian Kurds 'jihad.' He added, "Without jihad, there can be no progress..."[143] Just a couple weeks later, on 14 February

2018, Erdoğan himself issued a stark warning to Cyprus and Greece in the midst of a standoff over disputed gas fields in the Mediterranean Sea: "Their courage persists only until they see our army, our ships and our planes. Whatever Afrin is to us, our rights in the Aegean and Cyprus are the same."[144] Uzay Bulut (an intrepid writer of Turkish background who contributed a chapter to this book) translated more of Erdoğan's threats in a 14 February 2018 Twitter post:

> Erdoğan shouts his Ottomanist goals in the region from the rooftops: "Those who think that we've erased from our hearts the lands from which we withdrew in tears a hundred years ago are wrong....We say at every opportunity that we have, Syria, Iraq & other places in the geography [map] in our hearts are no different from our own homeland...We're struggling so that a foreign flag won't be waved anywhere where adhan [Islamic call to prayer in mosques] is recited"[145]

Erdoğan blusters while Gülen murmurs softly. But is what they believe and say and seek really all that different? The answer matters a lot because both of these ostensible antagonists are present and active inside the U.S.— and the reality is that whatever the details of their very public quarrel, they both seek exactly the same thing: the triumph of Islamic Law over the U.S. Constitution. As the Muslim Brotherhood (whose agenda claims the loyalty of both Erdoğan and Gülen) declared in its 1991 Explanatory Memorandum:[146]

> Understanding the role of the Muslim Brother in North America:
>
> The process of settlement is a "Civilization-Jihadist Process" with all the word means. The Ikhwan must understand that their work in America is a kind of grand Jihad in eliminating and destroying the Western civilization from within and "sabotaging" its miserable house by their hands and the hands of the believers so that it is eliminated and God's religion is made victorious over all other religions.[147]

The Turkish Diyanet's U.S. Network
The Turkish Islamic Center is a sprawling facility featuring a massive mosque, multipurpose center with a concert hall and sports facilities, conference halls, funeral home, guest houses, restaurant, and a traditional

Turkish bath house. Also called the Diyanet Center of America (DCA), the 16-acre project was formally opened in Lanham, MD in April 2016, with Turkish President Recep Tayyip Erdoğan in attendance for the ribbon-cutting ceremony. Administratively, the Center is the property and project of the Presidency of Religious Affairs (Diyanet), which is a Cabinet-level department of the Turkish government.[148]

It is also the hub of a vast and growing network of dozens of mosques and Islamic Centers that spans the Eastern U.S. Of even greater concern, the Diyanet is the U.S. hub of operations for the joint program of the Turkish government and the U.S. Muslim Brotherhood, including its U.S. political umbrella group, the U.S. Council of Muslim Organizations (USCMO). Both the U.S. Brotherhood and the USCMO are closely affiliated with the Erdoğan-AKP government in Turkey and use the DCA as a meeting, retreat, and training center for themselves and visiting Turkish government dignitaries from the AKP and the Diyanet.[149]

The DCA (fronting for the Turkish Government) maintains a close, strategic relationship with the Muslim Brotherhood leadership at the All Dulles Area Muslim Society (ADAMS) Center. [150] Other key U.S. Muslim Brotherhood groups likewise are closely associated with the DCA. For example, the International Institute for Islamic Thought (IIIT), named by the Justice Department an unindicted co-conspirator in the 2008 Holy Land Foundation (HLF) HAMAS terror funding trial, formalized the signing of a Memorandum of Understanding (MOU) with the DCA (aka the Turkish government) in a ceremony featured at the DCA website.[151]

It is worth quoting what the Center for Security Policy discovered about the early roots of the Turkish government relationship with the very top levels of the U.S. Muslim Brotherhood and its political umbrella group, the USCMO. As noted in an April 3, 2017 article posted at the CSP website, "*NATO Ally Turkey Working with U.S. Muslim Brotherhood,*"[152]

> *The groundwork for what is now a close working relationship began well before the March 2014 announcement of the USCMO's formation, but it is known that on 15 May 2013, a visiting President Erdoğan placed a ceremonial stone on the 16-acre construction site that would become the Turkish Diyanet Center of America in Lanham, Maryland. The following year, in August 2014, a USCMO delegation led by Secretary General Oussama Jammal traveled to Ankara to meet with President Erdoğan and AK Party leaders. And then,*

on 29 December 2014, in a recorded video message, Dr. Mehmet Görmez, President of the Presidency of Religious Affairs (Diyanet), addressed the 13th Annual MAS-ICNA (Muslim American Society-Islamic Circle of North America) Conference in Chicago, Illinois and discussed a gift for all Muslims: the Turkish Diyanet Center of America. Of note for the future of the US Muslim Brotherhood-Turkish relationship, this conference was sponsored by the Turkish-backed American Zakat Foundation and included the first-ever attendance of a Turkish-American group at a MAS-ICNA conference.

The already deep infiltration by both the U.S. Muslim Brotherhood and the Turkish government's DCA into WDC area local law enforcement units is on full display at the Center's website, which features a group photo of the Prince George County, MD Police Chief and District II Command Staff posing in front of the DCA mosque on September 8, 2017.[153] Then, on February 23, 2018, funeral prayers for slain Prince George's County police officer Corporal Mujahid Ramzziddin were held at the Diyanet Center. [154] The Council on American Islamic Relations (CAIR), one of the key front groups for HAMAS and the Muslim Brotherhood in the U.S. as identified by the Department of Justice in the HLF trial, carried condolences and an announcement of the Diyanet ceremony at its website. [155] Imam Talib Shareef of the Masjid Muhammad (often called 'The Nation's Islamic Center') was a featured speaker at the services, as he often is alongside such Muslim Brotherhood figures as Mohamed Magid of the Northern Virginia ADAMS Center and Haris Tarin of the Muslim Public Affairs Council (MPAC). Shareef was quoted infamously in 2014 when he claimed that the Islamic State was un-Islamic.[156]

A high-level delegation from the Turkish Diyanet, including its President Ali Erbas, visited the DCA in January 2018 and was presented with an award by CAIR's Executive Director, Nihad Awad.[157]

Erdoğan-Gülen: Divorced or Just Thinking About It?

Given this close and expanding relationship among the Turkish government, its U.S. Diyanet Center, and the U.S. Muslim Brotherhood, then, one would not expect to see at the same time a convivial relationship between Brotherhood representatives and the Gülen Movement. And yet, that is exactly what has been going on at surprisingly senior levels.

For example, Parvez Ahmed, elected Chairman of the Board for CAIR National in 2015 (who before that served as CAIR Chairman of the Board for Florida),[158] has a video presentation on terrorism featured at the website of the South Carolina branch of the Gülen Movement's flagship Atlantic Institute.[159] He also spoke in March 2016 on the same topic for the Atlantic Institute of Central Florida.[160] To top it all off, Ahmed serves openly on the Board of Directors of the Atlantic Institute of Jacksonville, FL, and just as openly has criticized the Erdoğan-AKP government in Turkey.[161] Ahmed is no mere CAIR groupie. He is a senior member of its national-level leadership— and yet somehow feels entirely free to not just associate, but serve, with one of the best-known of the Gülen organizations in the U.S.

Then there is the interesting figure of Murat Guzel, a wealthy Pennsylvania Turkish-American businessman and head of the Democratic National Committee's Heritage Council, who has donated hundreds of thousands of dollars to Democratic candidates from the local level to Hillary Clinton.[162] He is a Member of the Board of Directors at MÜSİAD-USA, a Muslim business association that represents Turkish companies.[163] Guzel also serves as the Treasurer of the Turkish American National Steering Committee (TASC),[164] which is a kind of umbrella group for many Turkish cultural groups across the U.S., including the Turkish American Cultural Society (TACS), a core member of the USCMO.

On the surface, Guzel would seem to be a staunch supporter of Turkish President Erdoğan; emails hacked in 2016 from the account of the Turkish energy minister (who just happens to be Erdoğan's son-in-law) include this October 19, 2014 statement by Guzel:

> "To stand by Erdoğan and do whatever we can against evil powers is not just an act of kindness but rather an Islamic obligation upon all of us..."[165]

And yet, some of Guzel's affiliations would seem to suggest the possibility of a Gülen connection, too. He has been a member of the American Turkish Chamber of Commerce (ATCOM), whose Founding Chairman and CEO, Prof. Dr. Ihsan Isik, was a former board member of the troubled Truebright Science Academy, Philadelphia, a Gülen Charter school which eventually closed. A 2014 campaign contribution to a Pennsylvania Member of Congress may be only coincidental, but the timing is nevertheless interesting. In September 2014, Guzel made a $2,600 contribution to Rep. Matt Cartwright (D-PA)[166] just weeks before Rep. Cartwright spoke on the floor of the House of Representatives to honor Fethullah Gülen.[167] Guzel had earlier donated $1,000 to Cartwright in March 2013. Rep. Cartwright subsequently returned thousands of dollars in donations from what he called "Gülenists" after a media inquiry highlighted problems with some of the donors.[168]

Let us look at one other curious connection that brought CAIR Philadelphia together at the Respect Graduate School in Bethlehem, PA, along with a group called *The Sakina Collective*[169] for a "Faith Climate Action Week 2017" in April 2017. This was not a case of one or two local CAIR chapter members attending a climate program along with some local Gülenists, but rather the Philadelphia Chapter of CAIR co-sponsoring one evening of a weeklong climate event at one of the four Gülen universities in the U.S.[170] It is difficult to imagine that the CAIR National headquarters in Washington, D.C. and its Executive Director Nihad Awad were unaware of these openly public associations between CAIR chapter leaders and known Gülen affiliates—or being aware, would not have taken steps to halt such activity, especially in the post-2016 attempted coup timeframe.

Conclusion

Both Turkish President Erdoğan and Fethullah Gülen are hard core Sunni jihadis. For a number of years, their shared commitment to the re-Islamization of Turkish government and society brought them together. Many of Gülen's thousands, if not millions, of devoted followers spread throughout Turkey's industrial, judicial, media, and police bureaucracy doubtless supported (albeit unofficially) Erdoğan's climb through the political system from mayor of Istanbul and on to Prime Minister in 2003. As we now know, even while Erdoğan and his AKP expanded their open support for HAMAS, the Palestinian branch of the Muslim Brotherhood, and began to establish a close working relationship with the USCMO (the Brotherhood's U.S. political organization), Gülen simultaneously was growing his network of businesses, charter schools, cultural societies, NGO's, and universities inside the U.S., too. Their parallel activities all converged on the same objective: empowering the Muslim Brotherhood and global Islamic Movement.

As Erdoğan amassed more and more power in Turkey, though, he no longer needed Gülen as before and began to see him as a rival. By 2013, Gülen's network in Turkey was under relentless assault and proved no match for Erdoğan's ruthless willingness to use the state instruments of power against his erstwhile partner and his followers. Whomever its organizers may have been, the attempted coup d'état against Erdoğan in 2016 provided the perfect pretext for him to seize even more sweeping powers.

Even as charges about the 2016 attempted coup d'état in Turkey continue to swirl—and likely will for years to come—it is clear that Erdoğan has shrewdly used the event to further consolidate his already authoritarian grip on power in Turkey. Tens of thousands were arrested, prosecuted, jailed, and dismissed from positions throughout the Turkish federal bureaucracy and military as well as the educational system and media. Hysterical accusations of responsibility for the coup against Gülen personally and his movement, both inside Turkey and abroad, spew forth unabated from the Erdoğan/AKP political machine.

Given this level of vitriol, it might have been expected that connections between the U.S. representatives of the Erdoğan/AKP regime and the Gülen network, such as they were, would have been severed with a finality similar to what happened in Turkey. But that is not what happened. Instead, as this chapter has documented, senior level representatives of the U.S. Muslim Brotherhood continue to associate openly at notable, publicized events with key Gülen figures and groups. In particular, we see that CAIR/HAMAS officials at the state chapter and even national level collaborate and actually serve in an official capacity with identifiable Gülen organizations.

How should we understand these developments, then, and anticipate those to come?

As I discussed in the opening paragraphs of this chapter, Erdoğan and Gülen share an Islamic outlook and commitment that transcends local power struggles. There can be only one sultan in Istanbul, but the broader dedication of both men is to Islam and the Muslim Brotherhood. Each retains the loyalty of millions of faithful Muslims who may champion different individuals to lead the global jihad movement, but who ultimately seek the same thing: a worldwide Islamic State under rule of Islamic Law (shariah).

Unless and until U.S. national security officials somehow gain an understanding of how non-violent Islamic operatives wage civilization jihad against unprepared, unwitting U.S. targets like Congressional Members and legislative representatives at every level, well-meaning faith community leaders, local law enforcement, and school administrators, but above all, senior administration figures in the Intelligence Community, National Security Council, and the White House itself, the Muslim Brotherhood will continue its unimpeded march through American society.

While it is certainly of the utmost significance that a former NATO ally is undergoing a deeply disturbing metamorphosis that increasingly places it at odds with the objectives and principles of that organization's other members (including the U.S.), its open collaboration as a hostile nation state with the Muslim Brotherhood's jihadist insurgency on the very territory of the U.S. must be considered orders of magnitude more threatening. Then add to that scenario the expanding influence operations of the Gülen Movement among U.S. businesses, civic/cultural organizations and NGOs, churches and synagogues, and above all, schools. And finally, understand that the Turkish government, the U.S. Muslim Brotherhood, and the Gülen Movement are all focused intensively on exactly the same mission—the Islamization of the United States.

What we are facing, absent the strategic vision and will to counter it, is a civilization jihad within our country that grows exponentially practically by the day. Let this chapter be an eye-opening expose that galvanizes American citizens and leadership alike to action.

CLARE M. LOPEZ is Vice President for Research & Analysis at the Center for Security Policy. A 20-year veteran of the CIA, in 2016, she was named to Senator Ted Cruz's presidential campaign national security advisory team. A member of the Citizens Commission on Benghazi from 2013-16, she was Vice President of the Intelligence Summit, Executive Director of the Iran Policy Committee from 2005-2006 & named a 2011 Lincoln Fellow at the Claremont Institute. The published author/co-author of many articles, books & papers, Ms. Lopez holds a B.A. in Communications & French from Notre Dame College of Ohio & an M.A. in International Relations from the Maxwell School, Syracuse University.

CHAPTER 4

When Thugs Fall Out: Erdoğan, Gülen, and the Turkish Lobby

"Six Stage Plot Structure"

0% 10%	25%	50%	75%	90-99% 100%
ACT I		**ACT II**	**ACT III**	

Stage I	Stage II	Stage III	Stage IV	Stage V	Stage VI
Setup	New Situation	Progress	Complications & Higher Stakes	Final Push	Aftermath

Turning Point #1 Opportunity	Turning Point #2 Change of Plans	Turning Point #3 Point of No Return	Turning Point #4 Major Setback	Turning Point #5 Climax

90's	2000	2002	2007/8	2011/12	2014/15
Early speeches and behavior	Merging under AKP	Elections AKP/domestic FG/int'l "Conservative democratization" + "Vibrant economy" = Corruption	Elections Presidency Launch of Ergenekon/Balyoz Ergenekon/Balyoz Economic crisis 2010 referendum	Elections Power struggle starts Confrontation over match-fixing leading to Hakan Fidan & exposition of Ergenekon/Balyoz	FG exploitation attempt of graft investigation similar to sham trials Current state of things

1	2	3	4	5
Who were they to start with?	How did they team up?	Was it really democratization and economic miracle, or corruption instead?	How did absolute power lead to power struggle between the two thugs?	The war goes on for the loot

The rift between Turkish president Recep Tayyip Erdoğan and the Poconos-based cleric Fethullah Gülen has deprived Erdoğan of the most sophisticated strategists in his external relations arm.

This has resulted in a bizarre and confusing competition of Turkish lobbying activities and narratives in the West. Once united in presenting a misleading vision of a "liberalizing" Turkey under the Justice and Development Party (AKP), Gülen and Erdoğan now spend phenomenal energy (and money) denouncing one another and portraying themselves as the other's victim. Americans are thus now hearing two loud and distinct lobbying voices: One represents the Gülen movement's formal and informal lobbying machine, the other Erdoğan's newly-acquired Western lawyers and professional lobbyists. Both provide excoriating accounts of the other camp's illiberalism, criminality, and dangerousness to American interests. Both are right.

Gülen and Erdoğan are often telling the truth about each other, albeit in a very selective way. We would be wise to listen to their mutual denunciations. Neither, however, is telling the whole truth—either about his own role in in the destruction of Turkish democracy or the cooperation they long enjoyed to that end. We would be terribly foolish to fail to appreciate this.

The purpose of this chapter is to help policymakers and concerned Americans recognize and make sense of the competing lobbying narratives they are now hearing about Turkey and place both of these narratives in the context of the Gülen-Erdoğan marriage and divorce.

Parallel Tracks

Both the AKP and the Gülen movement enlarge their global reach indirectly via aid and charity groups: The AKP supports groups such as the Humanitarian Relief Foundation (İHH), a Turkish NGO which works with local groups like HAMAS in the Gaza Strip; the Gülen movement supports aid organizations such as Kimse Yok Mu (the charitable arm of the Gülen *Hizmet* or 'Service' organization) . Both use a plethora of NGOs to collaborate with international NGOs and institutions, much as the Muslim Brotherhood and its extensions do.

The AKP has the luxury of using state institutions as cover for the NGOs it establishes, allowing to engage in partnerships with the state institutions in question. The Gülen movement, on the other hand, often funds Western politicians and, where needed, other international political entities to extend its international reach.

The AKP and the Gülen movement worked together and assisted each other in their international endeavors until 2012. They have since become competitors for international influence globally and for power in Turkey. But Gülenists must now pursue power in Turkey only surreptitiously, which in practice means Gülenists behave as if they're Erdoğan supporters while accusing Erdoğan loyalists as FETÖ (the Turkish government's acronym for "Fethullah [Gülen] Terrorist Organization), wherever possible, creating maximum confusion, as Erdoğan admitted when he said, "Horse and dog marks have been jumbled."

Hence, as fiercely as the parties oppose each other when competing for power, direct and open confrontation is more often than not avoided. Similarly, the two sides avoid confrontation when the other side is engaged in activities that would be of mutual benefit.

While the rift is real, Erdoğan and Gülen often continue on parallel tracks, as they share key motivations. This is evident, for example, in both parties' relationship with the Muslim Brotherhood. As viciously as the Gülenists attack Erdoğan, they seem to make no effort to hinder the AKP's collaboration with the Muslim Brotherhood, which the AKP, as the ruling party, does easily under the guise of state business. Erdoğan and the Emir of Qatar meet frequently, for example. The Gülen movement, meanwhile, keeps connected to the Brotherhood or its sympathizers via think tanks such as the Brookings Institution, academic institutions such as the London School of Economics, and various real and phony academic conferences and panels. Both use the Brotherhood's methods of social influence and engineering. While the ultimate goal of global hegemony may be the same for all three, the competition for leadership is undoubtedly a cause for direct confrontation between Erdoğan and Gülen, neither of whom will or can challenge the global power of the Muslim Brotherhood, at least for now.

The Gülen movement in the United States

Gülen left Turkey in 1999, fleeing trial on charges of attempting to overthrow the secular state. Soon afterwards, Gülenist cultural centers and non-profits began growing throughout the United States. These organizations are notably deceptive about their relationship to Gülen, deceptive about the movement, deceptive about their political and social goals, and deceptive about Gülen.

In the wake of 9/11, the Gülen movement, capitalizing upon Americans' longing for "interfaith" harmony, entered the lucrative "moderate Muslim" business. Through its cultural associations, the movement rebranded itself as a liberal, moderate, democratic force in an age of Islamic terror. This was of course absurd, as a single glance at Gülen's earlier sermons and writings would have made clear.

In unrevised editions of books from his early career, such as *Fasildan Fasila* and *Asrin Getirdigi Tereddutler*, Gülen calls the Western world the "continuous enemy of Islam." Of Christians, he writes, "[T]hey perverted and obscured their own future;" Jews, he wrote, have used "their guile and skills to breed bad blood" to threaten Islam from the beginning of time, "uniting themselves with Sassanids, Romans and crusaders." He also wrote that "The

Church, the Synagogue and Paganism form the troika that has attacked Islam persistently."[171]

Then of course there is his most infamous speech, included as testimony in his 1999 trial:

> **You must move in the arteries of the system without anyone noticing your existence until you reach all the power centers** ... *until the conditions are ripe, they [the followers] must continue like this. If they do something prematurely, the world will crush our heads, and Muslims will suffer everywhere, like in the tragedies in Algeria, like in 1982 [in] Syria ... like in the yearly disasters and tragedies in Egypt. The time is not yet right. You must wait for the time when you are complete and conditions are ripe, until we can shoulder the entire world and carry it ...* **You must wait until such time as you have gotten all the state power, until you have brought to your side all the power of the constitutional institutions** *in Turkey ... Until that time, any step taken would be too early—like breaking an egg without waiting the full forty days for it to hatch. It would be like killing the chick inside. The work to be done is [in] confronting the world. Now, I have expressed my feelings and thoughts to you all—in confidence* **... trusting your loyalty and secrecy. I know that when you leave here, [just] as you discard your empty juice boxes, you must discard the thoughts and the feelings that I expressed here.**

The Gülenists have become a formidable lobbying force in the United States. Their cultural centers organize receptions and ceremonies, handing out "dialogue" awards and honoraria to public officials who strike the movement as potentially useful to them. They organize phony academic conferences, paying university professors to talk at them, write about them, and produce books and journal articles about them. These events are often co-sponsored by public universities: American tax dollars—again—help them to enlarge their footprint, gain influence and acquire the air of legitimacy.

During the period when Erdoğan and Gülen worked hand-in-glove to destroy Turkey's democratic institutions, the movement took state and federal legislators, journalists, authors, religious leaders, university professors, community leaders, law enforcement officials, and students, in massive numbers, on subsidized trips to Turkey. They returned enthusiastically promoting Turkey as a "model" for the Muslim world.

The Gülenist Lobbying Machine in the US

For years, the Gülen machine worked to persuade Americans that Turkey was "liberalizing" when it was not. Now, they are lobbying to persuade Americans that they are the liberal alternative to Erdoğan's authoritarianism—even though the movement is plainly deeply illiberal, and they themselves were his enablers.

The movement is much larger in the United States than Americans realize. It is strategic, hierarchical, internally authoritarian, and organized. And it has grown courtesy of the US taxpayer, which funds Gülenist charter schools.

Its activities in the United States are notably deceptive and frequently criminal, as amply documented by Erdoğan's lawyers, who have patiently catalogued the movement's alleged real estate swindles, H-1 B visa fraud, and systematic patterns of highly irregular accounting practices.

The movement's efforts to gain influence in the US education system and bureaucracies, particularly in law enforcement institutions, closely—and disconcertingly—parallel its behavior in Turkey.

Through the creation of Gülen-linked lobbying bodies such as TUSKON, the Turkic-American Alliance, and the Rumi Forum, at both the federal and state level, Gülen has acquired influence in Washington and in state legislatures that Turkey's secular and liberal forces—and now, Erdoğan's hired lobbyists—find difficult to rival.[172] The lobby serves to deflect criticism from their schools' and businesses' possibly illegal and allegedly wasteful use of taxpayer funds, and to distort our view of Turkey—either by over-hyping its liberalization, when the movement was allied with Erdoğan, or, now, over-hyping its authoritarianism, since the two split.

The rift has resulted in tangible benefits to us, if we understand it properly. Erdoğan's newly-acquired lawyers have done us all a service by conducting a rigorous forensic analysis of publicly-available documents, such as tax and property records, to clearly demonstrate the movement's allegedly criminal activities in the United States. But we must understand that this account is *not* the whole truth.[173]

How Gülenists Helped Erdoğan Consolidate Power

Both lobbying camps are now trying to conceal the key part of the story: namely, that for nearly a decade, the AKP and the Gülenist movement—which Turks call the *cemaat*—were in bed together. Even Erdoğan's desperate purge has failed to separate them.

When the AKP came to power, it lacked sophisticated, educated cadres with which to staff the Turkish bureaucracy. It thus drew heavily upon the resources of the Gülen movement. The movement worked in tandem with the AKP to destroy Turkey's previously-secular institutions and provide cover for the AKP's power-grab.

This was a logical alliance: Gülen and the AKP shared key goals—promoting a larger role for religion in Turkey and a smaller role for the military and secular institutions such as the judiciary and secular civil society. They shared a vision of expanding Turkish influence abroad, particularly in the territories of the former Ottoman Empire. The movement was instrumental in promoting Turkish business interests in the Middle East, North Africa, and sub-Saharan Africa.

The *cemaat*'s assiduous penetration of the police and the judiciary allowed Erdoğan to confront the military and other key obstacles to the enlargement of his power. Erdoğan was perfectly content to use the *cemaat's* tainted evidence against suspected coup plotters to purge his own rivals. *Cemaat*-controlled media and lobbying organs generated public support for this, domestically and abroad, deflecting criticism and concern about arrests of journalists and civil society figures, the military, and the subsequent show trials. With the *cemaat's* assistance, the AKP thus systematically neutered the forces that served as a counterweight to the Party's power. In tandem with the incompetence of Turkey's opposition parties, this enabled Erdoğan to stay in power long enough to transform the internal power balance of the country.

Until recently, Gülen used his influence, and particularly his vast media empire, to support this, vigorously promoting and defending the AKP, domestically and abroad. The *cemaat* facilitated Erdoğan's acquisition of near-complete control over the media, judiciary, and the military, allowing the AKP to arrogate to itself powers that no single party had ever amassed in the history of the Republic. The stupidity of the Western commentariat and the *cemaat's* lobbying in the West explain, to a considerable degree, why the swallowing by the executive of the latter two power centers was hailed by the West as a democratic miracle and the first was largely ignored.

The *cemaat's* lobbying and public relations in the West help to explain why, for more than a decade, Americans largely believed that Turkey under the AKP was liberalizing—to such an extent that it could be promoted as a model for the rest of the so-called Islamic world—even though this was demonstrably ludicrous.

Understanding this helps us now to make sense of Erdoğan behaviour. He is not a paranoid authoritarian. He's a well-informed authoritarian. He knows better than anyone how extensive the *cemaat's* power, reach, and penetration really is: He is the one who encouraged its growth and exploited it.

It is critical that we grasp that the movement has consistently steered our relationship with Turkey in ways that have not—at all—been in our national interest or in the interests of Turkish democracy.

The AKP-Gülen Split

This divorce (more than any real change in Turkey) accounts for the West's sudden appreciation of Erdoğan's authoritarianism. Erdoğan was never a liberal, nor did Turkey "liberalize" significantly in the early years of his tenure, as the media widely suggested.

When the feud between Erdoğan and Gülen broke into the open, Americans suddenly learned things about Erdoğan that had always been true (*e.g.*, that Erdoğan is a rabid anti-Semite, that his senior ministers ascribe to the theory that enemies of Turkey are attempting to kill the prime minister by means of telekinesis, and that Turkey imprisons a staggering number of journalists). All of this could have been reported a decade before. Why wasn't it? Why did so few Westerners express concern about Turkey's human rights record, or the arrest of journalists, until Gülenists were arrested? In 2015, the Arkansas State House passed HR 1042, which calls, by name, for the release of arrested Gülenist journalists—and *only* Gülenist journalists. The list of non-Gülenist journalists who had been arrested in Turkey in the ten years before Arkansas bestirred itself with the problem of press freedom in Turkey extends for many pages. During the period of Gülenist cooperation with Erdoğan, however, the Arkansas State House passed resolutions "recognizing the friendship between the Republic of Turkey and Arizona,"[174] unaware that their Gülenist friends were busy, at the time, arresting Turkish journalists.)

Particularly after the failed coup, when the authoritarian Frankenstein they helped to build turned on them with special savagery, Gülenists reinvented themselves as "liberal dissidents." They knew whom to call to get that message into the Western media. For years, being accused of coup-loving in *Today's Zaman* was the warning that you'd be next to be arrested. This is what they had this to say of anyone who questioned these arrests: "This ongoing process is an effort to enhance democracy. Those who remain opposed to the Ergenekon investigation include the pro-Israeli Neo-Cons in the U.S."[175] These ardent apologists for the practice of arresting journalists are now the very same people appealing to the West (and to "pro-Israel neo-cons) to defend them as heroes of press freedom—ignoring Turkey's real heroes of press freedom.

For years, Turks watched the arrest and imprisonment of critics of the government. For years, the *Today's Zaman* crown told concerned Westerners why they should be in *favor* of locking up journalists, civil society activists, military officers, heads of football clubs, prominent Kurds, and anyone else who got on the movement's bad side. During the same period, the Western media and governments proclaimed Turkey was liberalizing and a model democracy for the region, even as Gülenists were locking people up by the hundreds if not thousands on charges everyone with eyes could see were fraudulent.

The US is seeking now to improve its relationship with liberal opponents of Erdoğan. As indeed we should be. But the Gülenists are not the liberal dissidents we are looking for. In a sense, we are fortunate: The Gülenists know where all the bodies are buried. They are now providing us with an extremely useful map of Erdoğan's corruption, deception, authoritarianism, and malfeasance. If we put their reporting in its proper context, it is valuable to us. The proper authorities should follow up on every lead this lobbying effort provides and investigate every claim. But we must understand that it is *not* the whole truth.

The New Lobbyists

The AKP, aware that it has suffered a tremendous loss of influence in the West, has undertaken a frantic effort to replace Gülenist lobbyists with professional American lobbyists. They have hired talented people. Robert Amsterdam's research on the Gülen movement's activities in the United States, for example, is surprisingly solid, serious, and credible. It must be taken seriously.[176] The only problem with it is that it is only half the story. It does not explain the means by which this lobby became entrenched in the United States—to wit, with Erdoğan's full support. In a sense, we are fortunate: The lawyers and lobbyists for which Erdoğan is paying are performing a public service for us. If we put their work in its proper context, it provides a valuable map of the movement's US activities. The proper authorities should follow up on every lead this lobbying effort provides and investigate every claim.

The Two Narratives

We now have two powerful lobbying narratives circulating Washington: the Gülenist version and the AKP version. Both are right in critical ways: The Gülenists are now amply and substantially documenting Erdoğan's authoritarianism; Erdoğan's lobby is correctly warning Americans about the movement's criminality, its growing US footprint, and its dangerousness. But both are also wrong, and harmful both to American and Turkish interests, insofar as both are self-exculpatory and deceptive about their own political record and agenda. Both sets of lobbying efforts should be used to gain more insight about the rival camps. But neither should guide American policy. As Kissinger said of the Iran-Iraq war, "It's a pity they can't both lose." In fact, they can. Our policy should be to encourage this.

Conclusion and Recommendations:
Reaching Out to the Rest of Turkey

Americans must realize, at long last, that there's *much* more to Turkey than Erdoğan and Gülen. We must not endeavor to back Gülen as a liberal counterweight to Erdoğan, as many Americans now seem inclined to do. He is not a liberal. He is a Sunni Muslim jihadist in the mold of the Muslim Brotherhood, just like Erdoğan. His movement is dangerous to Turkey and the United States alike.

In many ways, the Gülenists are *more* dangerous to us than Erdoğan, because the movement is so much more sophisticated than the AKP and more deeply entrenched in the West.

The Turkish public is squeezed between these two thugs. A significant part of the Turkish public is neither jihadist nor authoritarian and just wishes the two of them would stop stealing everything. We have no relationship with this part of Turkish society, because it is so disorganized and so lacking in PR savvy. Instead, we have allowed ourselves to be guided by Gülenists, who are not.

We must develop our own people-to-people relationships with the significant sector of the Turkish public who want nothing to do with either of these thugs.

We confront a considerable challenge: Americans have been oblivious to Gülen's presence on American soil, but Turks have not. Because of this, many if not all secular Turks believe Erdoğan's rise to power—with Gülen's support—was a bizarre American experiment performed on their country against their will and to no purpose save creating of Turkey a "moderate model" for more fractious Muslims.

Policymakers must understand why Turks believe this. Turks who believe this may be wrong, but they are not crazy. To condescend to Turks who perceive the United States this way or dismiss them as conspiracy-theorists is foolish: The United States *did* lend its support to both the AKP and Gülen. This is a key reason that the Turks who would naturally be our allies loathe and distrust us. We must understand this if we're to have any hope of being heard and repairing our relationship with the Turkish public.

CHAPTER 5

Erdoğan and Europe:
The Fox and the Chicken Coop

• BY CHRISTOPHER C. HULL

O n September 11, 1683, Polish King John III, a.k.a. Jan Sobieski,[177] arrived at a hill north of Vienna to break the second great siege of that city by the Ottoman Turks.[178] Within hours he led the combined forces of the Crown of the Kingdom of Poland, the Habsburg Monarchy, and the Holy Roman Empire[179] in the epochal battle at the gates of Vienna, during which Sobieski led the largest cavalry charge in world history,[180] ultimately routing a 150,000-man Ottoman army about twice the size of his own,[181] after which, according to one historian, "the Ottoman Turks ceased to be a menace to the Christian world."[182]

But times have changed.

Today, Turkish President Recep Tayyip Erdoğan is rapidly turning Turkey back into a menace to its own region as well as the West. But this time, if it does come time to cross swords with the Turks again, millions of their potential allies will already be inside the gates, in Vienna and beyond, and millions more at the ready.

The Fox: Erdoğan's Evolving Islamic State

Erdoğan's "increasingly Islamized Turkey,"[183] once a secular liberal democracy, has over the last quarter century slouched ever-more-rapidly toward Islamic authoritarianism. For instance, the Turks more than two decades ago joined other Muslim-majority countries in the now-57 member Organization for Islamic Cooperation (OIC, then known as the Organization of the Islamic Conference) in rejecting the United Nations Universal Declaration of Human Rights "on the grounds that it is inconsistent with their culture and religion."[184] In its place, the OIC crafted the Cairo Declaration on Human Rights in Islam,[185] in which according to one critic, "human rights are subordinated to Islamic law. If something is permitted in Sharia, such as stoning a woman to death for adultery or rape, it is a human right; if it is not permitted in Sharia, it is not a human right."[186]

Erdoğan himself makes no bones about his own position on Islam and human rights, and never has. Early in his career, Erdoğan remarked that democracy is like a train: once you get where you're going, you get off.[187] In 2004, Erdoğan said flat-out, "Turkey is not a country where moderate Islam prevails."[188] Granted, in that speech he also argued, "We are Muslims who have found a middle road."[189] The question at the time is where that road would lead.[190]

Now we know. Recently, Erdoğan reiterated even more clearly, "Islam cannot be either moderate or not moderate. Islam can only be one thing,"[191] criticizing Saudi Crown Prince Mohammed bin Salman's claim he would promote a "more moderate Islam" in his kingdom.[192]

But even given the Turks' role in running the Ottoman Empire that wreaked such havoc historically on Europe, a once and future Caliphate off its coasts and on its borders might worry the West less had a mass caliphate not arguably already broken through Western lines.

In part because of the illegal immigration crisis of 2015, which Erdoğan actively helped facilitate, the Muslim population of Europe had exploded to 25.8 million, 4.9% of the total population, by mid-2016, according to Pew Research Center estimates (which in some cases are dramatically lower than local sources).[193]

In Bulgaria, lying along with Greece just on the other side of the land bridge from Turkey, that percentage has according to Pew reached 11.1%, the legacy of historical Ottoman occupation.[194] In France, with the largest numbers of Muslims in Europe at 5,720,000, the percentage stands at 8.8% according to Pew, though some put the figure at 10% or above.[195] Sweden, though it has absorbed fewer Muslim immigrants, has reached 8.1% because of its smaller population, again according to Pew.[196] In Germany, with the second largest number at 4,950,000, Pew puts the percentage at 6.1%.[197]

Of course, these Muslim populations do not all originate in Turkey, nor did all illegal immigrants pass through Erdoğan's control during the recent crisis. Indeed, during the crisis, illegals poured into Europe from a plethora of places across Africa and the Middle East.

A substantial number of Turks do reside in Europe, however. More than a million of them—both ethnic Turks and Turkish citizens—lived in Germany alone as of 2008, with more than half a million in France, the UK, and Bulgaria.[198]

Moreover, Erdoğan has himself threatened on multiple occasions to single-handedly re-start the illegal immigration crisis once more. On March 18, 2016, Europe and Erdoğan agreed on a joint migration plan. According to that plan, "Ankara agreed to stop asylum seekers from crossing by sea to the Greek islands in return for three billion euros in aid to deal with the three million Syrian refugees who are living on Turkish soil." [199] (For the record, the United Nations High Commissioner for Refugees [UNHCR] puts the total number of Turkey-based refugees at 2.8 million, of which it believes 2.6 million are Syrian.[200]) In addition, the "one in, one out" agreement stipulated that Syrian refugees who reached Greece would be returned to Turkey, while Turkey-based Syrian asylum-seekers would be resettled to Europe.[201]

That's not the way it has worked out. Instead, only 1,000 immigrants have been sent back to Turkey; 3,500 have left Turkey for the EU; and 10,000 have been resettled from Greece to the rest of Europe.[202] The pact did succeed, however, at stemming the flood of illegal immigrants. Monthly sea arrivals to the EU peaked in October 2015 at 221,454, and have remained below 32,000 since March, 2016, according to UNHCR.[203]

At that point, history intervened.

On July 15, 2016, a military faction calling itself the Peace At Home Council attempted a *coup d'état* against Erdoğan's government.[204] Reports differ with respect to who in fact made up this faction. Ankara asserts feverishly that Islamic cleric and soured Erdoğan ally Fethullah Gülen drove the *coup,* and indeed many of Gülen's followers did appear to participate. However, the possibility exists that the *coup* constituted a last-gasp effort by remaining "Kemalists," that is, supporters of the founding ideology of the Republic of Turkey as instituted by Mustafa Kemal Atatürk, to halt Turkey's headlong plunge away from its country's founder, not to mention modernity and the West.

Regardless, in the chaos that followed, in which 234 died and more than 2,000 were injured according to one report,[205] Erdoğan successfully put down the *coup,* then followed with a brutal crackdown on his perceived enemies, calling the attempted putsch "a gift from God."[206]

Erdoğan's crackdown reached far, and fast. Within 72 hours, his government had detained 7,543 people, including 6,138 military officials, among them more than 100 generals and admirals, as well as 755 prosecutors and 650 civilians, and suspended 8,777 government employees, including 2,745 judges, police officers and governors of 30 of Turkey's 81 provinces.[207]

In reaction, United States (U.S.) and EU leaders issued warnings to Turkey's government to use restraint. [208] The European Commissioner leading Turkey's EU accession process charged Erdoğan appeared to be using lists drawn up in advance, "It looks at least as if something has been prepared. … The lists are available, which indicates it was prepared and to be used at a certain stage. I'm very concerned."[209]

The French foreign minister expressed the concern that, "We cannot accept a military dictatorship but we also have to be careful that the Turkish authorities do not put in place a political system which turns away from democracy."[210] A spokesperson for German Chancellor Angela Merkel warned that following through on calls to reinstate the death penalty in the wake of the *coup* "would end the country's EU accession hopes," which had begun in 2004 with the death penalty's abolition—though reluctance to admit Turkey hardly began with the *coup* attempt.[211]

Turkish officials reacted with fury, charging critics were "ignoring the fact that the parliament was hit 11 times by hijacked F-16s."[212]

Thus began—or continued—the use of refugees as pawns to pressure Europe.

According to Athanassios Drougas, an intelligence expert in Athens, "With Europe in a mess, Mr. Erdoğan feels he has a free hand in trying to blackmail the bloc using the refugee crisis as leverage."[213] By September 2016, illegal immigrants suddenly began to pour across the Adriatic from Turkey to Greece again, prompting hurried visits from EU officials.[214]

This was not the first time the West had seen this trick, and it won't be the last. Similarly, according to the Middle East Forum's Daniel Pipes, "Libya's Muammar Qaddafi turned the migrant flow on and off, thereby winning concessions from Italy in a game that anticipated what Turkey's Recep Tayyip Erdoğan now plays with Germany."[215]

Regardless, with Europe's pressure point pushed, Erdoğan's crackdown continued unabated, and foremost among the targets were Gülen and his followers.[216] Now, in spite of innumerable claims to the contrary, Gülen is no friend of the West. His movement has had to withdraw a book in which he justifies wife-beating "albeit as a last resort" in keeping with Islamic doctrine,[217] describes Christianity as ''perverted' and refers to America— where he lives, safe from deportation for now—as 'our merciless enemy.'[218] Likewise, Gülen has challenged his supporters in Turkey (at least), "You must move in the arteries of the system without anyone noticing your existence until you reach all the power centers."[219] In his 1998 book *Prophet Mohammed as Commander*, Gülen writes that "a Muslim's enmity towards unbelievers is, in fact, in the form of pitying them."[220] Finally, in *An Analysis of the Prophet's Life*, he expounds further:

[Muslim] believers should also equip themselves with the most sophisticated weaponry. Force has an important place in obtaining the desired result, so believers cannot be indifferent to it. Rather they must be much more advanced in science and technology than unbelievers so that they should not allow unbelievers to use "force" for their selfish benefit. According to Islam, "right is might"; so, in order to prevent might from being right in the hands of unbelievers and oppressors, believers must be mightier than others. [221]

That said, Gülen is in fact a U.S. person, having achieved long-sought legal permanent resident (LPR) status on October 10, 2008, and thus retains the rights of one so situated.[222] Since Erdoğan is not exactly America's buddy, either, we would do well to remember it as Ankara bellows for the U.S. to extradite Gülen to face trial.[223]

By November 2016, Turkey's president had dismissed or detained 125,000 people associated with the Gülen movement, according to one report.[224] Erdoğan's government even investigated 5,000 foster families for ties to Gülen's movement, threatening to remove children from the homes of foster parents who participated in the *coup*.[225]

Erdoğan likewise extended the repression to its Kurdish minority, which had no known ties to the *coup* attempt, arresting 11 Kurdish Members of Parliament, including both co-chairmen of the Kurdish Peoples' Democratic Party, ousting 30 Kurdish mayors from office, suspending 11,000 teachers from Kurdish regions, and shutting at least 20 Kurdish media outlets—including a children's station that dubbed cartoons such as "the Smurfs" into Kurdish.[226]

In reaction to Erdoğan's continued crackdown, European lawmakers voted to place a hold on Turkey's EU accession.[227] Luxembourg's foreign minister likened Erdoğan's handling of dismissed civil servants to methods used by the Nazis, saying the EU would eventually have to place sanctions on his regime.[228] The *Chicago Tribune* decried both his repression and the Obama Administration's "milquetoast response."[229]

Erdoğan himself railed against the critics, saying that he "could unleash a new wave of migrants on Europe if relations deteriorated further."[230] Indeed, reports at the time indicated Turkey had gathered enough boats to ship 3,000 illegal immigrants a day into Greece, saying Europe and Erdoğan had reached "the brink of war."[231]

At that point, at least, few additional illegal immigrants came.

By December 2016, Erdoğan's Turkey had more journalists imprisoned than any other country in the world, with China a distant second.[232] In fact, the Turkish government crackdown drove the global total of jailed journalists to an all-time high, according to the Committee to Protect Journalists.

Added to that total in February 2017 was a German-Turkish reporter for *Die Welt* whom Turkish authorities jailed on charges of "propaganda in support of a terrorist organization and inciting the public to violence,"[233] prompting a protest from German lawmakers[234] and ultimately Chancellor Angela Merkel herself.[235]

The journalist, Deniz Yucel, had reported on private emails obtained from Berat Albayrak, Turkey's energy minister and, perhaps more importantly, Erdoğan's son-in-law. [236] Ironically, the emails concerned "control of Turkish media groups and influencing the public by means of fake users on the messaging service Twitter."[237] Turkey had likewise detained or expelled foreign correspondents for the French website *Les Jours*, among others.[238]

Likewise, in March 2017, with no further progress on Turkey's EU accession, Turkey's EU minister again raised the question of opening the flood gates over the land bridge with Greece and Bulgaria, saying "In my opinion, the issue of the land passages should be reviewed."[239] The same month, the Deputy Prime Minister of Turkey said the EU had not kept its end of the pact, which meant that "the deal is dead."[240] Again, no additional influx arrived, indicating these plaints constituted little more than Erdoğan Syrian-rattling.

The same month, Ambassador Kaan Esener, Deputy Undersecretary for General Political Affairs of the Ministry of Foreign Affairs of Turkey, appeared before the U.N. Human Rights Council, where he discussed "the unsuccessful coup d'état in July 2016 and called upon all States to recognize the threat of the Fetullah Gülen Terrorist Organization," claiming that "Turkey had declared a state of emergency to protect its democracy, rule of law and the rights and freedoms of citizens."[241]

In April 2017, Erdoğan held a referendum to cement his control over Turkey's government. The result was close, and European observers charged both that up to 2.5 million votes could have been manipulated, and that Turkish authorities were not cooperating with efforts to investigate claims of possible election fraud.[242] Of course, election fraud goes hand-in-hand with hostage-taking. In mid-June, Erdoğan allegedly offered a German official a startling proposition: give us back two Turkish generals who'd applied for asylum in Germany, and he would return the *Die Welt* reporter.[243]

At the July 2017 one-year commemoration of the coup attempt, Erdoğan made a point of focusing heavily on religion, arguably challenging any remaining Kemalists who believe, correctly, that Turkey's republic was built upon a foundation of secularism.[244] Specifically, the celebration included a recitation of Qur'anic verses on betrayal, martyrdom and standing one's ground in front of enemies, an extended prayer by the head of the religious affairs directorate on the steps of the Turkish parliament, and Erdoğan's own explicit pledge to "cut traitors' heads off."[245]

On September 11, 2017—perhaps coincidentally 334 years to the day after Sobieski's relief of Vienna[246]—the Turkish delegation walked out of a key meeting in Poland of the Organization for Security and Cooperation in Europe (OSCE) in protest of the inclusion of a non-governmental organization (NGO) affiliated with Mr. Gülen.[247] "We must be vigilant against those who wish to infiltrate our meetings for ulterior motives," said the Turkish representative at the meeting.[248] "It is simply revolting that I will be forced to sit around the same table with a person so closely linked to those who used our own military equipment, including fighter jets and tanks, to murder 250 of our citizens, to wound over 2000 others, to bombard our parliament, and to attempt to overthrow our elected government and to assassinate our president. ... This is a betrayal to the OSCE, which we helped to establish and flourish over the decades."[249]

Now, the evidence is hardly conclusive that Mr. Gülen had anything to do with the coup attempt.[250] Indeed, the coup-plotters' statement read on the air of Turkish Radio and Television bemoaned that "The secular and democratic rule of law has been virtually eliminated,"[251] which hardly jives with Gülenist activities in Turkey to oust secularists and replace them with (Gülenist) religious Muslims.[252]

Regardless, after that outburst, Turkey continued to protest the NGO's OSCE participation, avoiding two Vienna-based follow-on meetings in November 2017, including one on the role of free media and one on access to justice.[253]

By then, Erdoğan's government had arrested at least 11 German or German-Turkish citizens over the prior year; Berlin considers them to be "political prisoners."[254] One of them, Mesale Tolu, a German citizen with Turkish roots, was imprisoned for at least five months along with her three-year-old son.[255] Ankara also began blocking visits of German parliamentarians to their country's military personnel stationed inside Turkey.[256]

Likewise, Erdoğan also pulled 40 Turkish soldiers out of a NATO exercise in November 2017 in a fit of pique over a Norwegian civilian's creation of an ersatz Erdoğan Twitter account as part of the exercise.[257] In December 2017, Erdoğan paid the first visit by a Turkish president to Greece in 65 years—and used the opportunity to lambaste his neighbor over long-simmering diplomatic, border, and other disputes, including the return of eight Turkish officers who fled to Greece during the *coup* attempt.[258]

Finally, in mid-January 2018, Erdoğan, the "bouncer at the gates of Hell," began an assault on Afrin, a Kurdish- held enclave in northern Syria, turning Turkey into "an instrument of blackmail to be wielded against the West."[259]

Going forward, UNHCR has estimated that in 2018, Turkey will continue to host the most refugees awaiting resettlement of any nation in the world—a population that numbered 2.8 million at the beginning of 2017.[260] Moreover, Turkey represents over 90% of UNHCR's projected 2018 resettlement needs in Europe.[261]

Even without Turkey or any other country flooding Europe with illegal immigrants, the future indicates that more of the same lies ahead for the Continent. Even with zero additional migration, Pew estimates the Muslim population will grow to over 35 million by 2050.[262]

In the high migration scenario—if, for instance, Erdoğan unleashes the hostile hordes he now claims he holds at bay—Pew says the figure will be more like 75 million.[263] That would leave Sweden more than 30% Muslim, with Austria and Germany just under 20%, and France, the United Kingdom and Norway at 17-18%.[264]

The reality is that, as Daniel Pipes has argued "from Senegal to Morocco to Egypt to Turkey to Chechnya, Muslims form a membrane around Europe, with vast numbers of potential migrants able with relative ease to enter illegally the continent by land or sea."[265]

The Chicken Coop: A Submissive Europe

If that does not concern you, consider this: Across Europe, explicitly Muslim political parties are cropping up, such as the DENK party in the Netherlands, the Equality and Justice Party (PEJ) in France, and the NBZ Party in Austria.[266] According to one critic, "These purport to help downtrodden Muslim minorities, but are in fact part of a network controlled by Turkey's AKP party that organizes Muslims under an anti-assimilation platform."[267]

For instance, the PEJ, the critic charges, "is an element of a network of political parties built by Turkey's President Erdoğan and AKP to influence each country of Europe, and to influence Europe through its Muslim population."268 "The first party in France established by Turks," the PEJ, has already participated in March 2015 Provincial General Assembly elections, but was eliminated in the first round.269

The French magazine *Marianne*, which counted 68 PEJ candidates in that election, calls the party "Erdoğan's hand in France's polls."270 The piece charges that PEJ is closely connected to Council for Justice, Equality and Peace (COJEP), an international NGO which "represents, everywhere it is based, an anchor for AKP", Erdoğan's political party in Turkey.271 Don't believe it? Well, reports another outlet, "many managers of PEJ are also in charge of COJEP"."272

And what, pray tell, is PEJ's platform? "[A]bolishing the founding secularist law of 1905, which established the separation of church and state; mandatory veils for schoolgirls; and community solidarity (as opposed to individual rights) as a priority. All that is wrapped in the not-so-innocent flag of the necessity to "fight against Islamophobia," a concept invented to shut down the push-back of all people who might criticize Islam before they can even start."273

That's right: Mandatory veils for schoolgirls.

Austria has one of these Erdoğan stalking horses as well. In 2016, "Turkish citizens"—wait, who vote in Austria?—founded the New Movement for the Future (NBZ) party.274 NBZ's goal is "to give Turks a voice in politics across Austria." The NBZ backs Erdoğan and—surprise!—damns the Gülen movement roundly.275

The Netherland's DENK party, "long been accused of being a mouthpiece for" Erdoğan, in March 2017 became the first-ever ethic minority party in the Dutch parliament, winning three seats in the recent election, which was focused on immigration.276

All of this is nothing compared to Bulgaria. The Muslim population there is made up of Turks, Shi'ites, Bulgarians, and Roma.277 Accordingly, Bulgaria sports *three* Muslim political parties. The eldest of these is The Movement for Rights and Freedoms (HÖH), founded in 1990 by Ahmet Doğan.278 In 2014, HÖH held 38 seats in Bulgaria's 240-member parliament—and had four MEPs in the European Parliament (EP) as well. HÖH is in a coalition with the Bulgarian Socialist Party (BSP), and so helps run the country.279 Because Erdoğan is not satisfied with HÖH, however, he has worked to create other pro-Turkish parties in Bulgaria as well.280

Finally, many Germans of Turkish descent have gotten involved in established German parties.281 Notably, a party known as the Allianz

Deutscher Demokraten ("Alliance of German Democrats", or ADD) has arisen there as well, apparently as a reaction to the German Parliament's recognition of the Armenian Genocide.[282] ADD is friendly toward Erdoğan and has been trying to establish an electoral base within immigrant and Muslim communities, but has struggled; for instance, the party had difficulty collecting the 1,000 signatures necessary to participate in a May 2017 state election.[283]

According to Kamel Daoud, an Algerian writer writing in *Le Point*:

> *[An Islamic party's] purpose is to conquer the world, not just have a mandate. Its mechanics were already established....Islamists took power in the name of democracy, then suspended democracy by using their power....Convert the clothes, the body, the social links, the arts, nursing homes, schools, songs and culture, then, they just wait for the fruit to fall in the turban....An Islamist party is an open trap: you cannot let it in. If you refuse it, your country switches to a dictatorship, but if you accept it, you are at risk of submission."[284]*

Submission—not just to Sharia, but in this case to Erdoğan as well.

Extracting the Fox from the Hen House

What is to be done?

First, Europe and its allies must acknowledge that Erdoğan is no longer an ally and, as such, declare his cat's-paw political parties and civil society groups foreign actors as appropriate by country.[285] Second, it must recognize the threat from Sharia-supremacist illegal immigration, changing its policies to deport illegals within the Schengen Region as called for by Hungarian Prime Minister Viktor Orbàn.[286] Third, the EU must harden its outermost borders, including especially in this context by dramatically ramping up maritime security in the waters around Greece and creating defensible barriers on the land bridge from Turkey to both Greece and Bulgaria.

Fourth, thus prepared for Erdoğan's reaction, the EU should go beyond freezing negotiations over Turkey's accession to breaking them off. Along those lines, the European Parliament should eliminate its EU-Turkey Joint Parliamentary Committee. Similarly, Europe should expel Turkey from the Council of Europe, which has through the European Court of Human Rights condemned the country a towering 2,812 times since 1959.[287]

Last, of course, the NATO alliance should expel Turkey. No one can seriously believe NATO currently includes Erdoğan under its nuclear umbrella. If that is true, regardless of whether NATO's governance includes specific provisions to expel a member country, Turkey must be sidelined as quickly as possible, as it acts ever-more like an enemy, not an ally.

A Hen House Full of Foxes

Centuries ago, Muslims invaded and transformed the Christian Byzantine Empire into the Ottoman Empire, an Islamic caliphate.[288] Jan Sobieski defeated that Caliphate army on the battlefield in 1683. Today, a resurgent Turkey seeks to recreate that Empire—and it may not have to attack Europe to do so.

If Europe and its allies fail to act, and illegal immigration explodes again, demographic shifts continue, and Islamic and pro-Turkish political parties flourish, a neo-Ottoman Empire under Erdoğan may defeat the West yet—more like a fox in a henhouse than a barbarian at the gates.

CHRISTOPHER C. HULL, PH.D. is the Executive Vice President at the Center for Security Policy. He is the immediate past chief of staff for a nationally prominent Member of Congress. He has held politics & policy positions including serving as a press secretary in the U.S. House of Representatives, a foreign affairs & trade legislative assistant in the U.S. Senate, a researcher at a major think tank & the majority staff director of a state Senator. Dr. Hull holds a doctorate in government with distinction from Georgetown University & an undergraduate degree magna cum laude, also in government, from Harvard University.

CHAPTER 6

NATO's Turkey Challenge

• BY DANIEL PIPES

I n an inarticulate but important statement, then-National Security
Advisor H.R. McMaster said in a December 2017 closed-door session that
the 'Islamist' threat has been "myopically" treated in the past: "We didn't
pay enough attention how [Islamist ideology] is being advanced through
charities, madrassas and other social organizations." Alluding to prior Saudi
support for such institutions, he noted that it "is now done more by Qatar and
by Turkey."

Dwelling on Turkey, he added that "A lot of Islamist groups have learned
from" its president, Recep Tayyip Erdoğan, and the ruling Justice and
Development Party (*Adalet ve Kalkınma Partisi*, or AKP). The Turks, he went
on, offer a model of "operating through civil society, then the education
sector, then the police and judiciary, and then the military to consolidate
power in the hands of a particular party, which is something we'd prefer not
to see and is sadly contributing to the drift of Turkey away from the West."

McMaster's frank comments raised eyebrows for breaking with the
usual Washington patter that nostalgically recalls the Korean War followed
by decades of near-sacral joint membership in the North Atlantic Treaty
Organization (NATO). His mention of Turkey drifting away from the West
raises several questions: Beyond pious words, how real is the NATO alliance
in 2018? Should Turkey even remain a NATO partner? Does NATO still have
a mission in the post-Soviet era? If so, what is it?

NATO and Islamism

To understand NATO's mission, let's return to the alliance's founding on
April 4, 1949. The Washington Treaty establishing it had enunciated a clear
goal: to "safeguard the freedom, common heritage and civilization of member
states' peoples founded on the principles of democracy, individual liberty,
and the rule of law." In other words, NATO protected Western civilization. At
the time, yes, that meant allying against communism, so NATO focused on the
Soviet threat for 42 long years. Then, one day in 1991 when the Soviet Union

collapsed and the Warsaw Pact vaporized, the alliance faced a crisis of success.

An existential period of self-questioning ensued, asking whether the alliance should continue to exist and whom it might be protecting against. (As it turns out, Russia eventually returned as an opponent, but that is not our topic here.) The most convincing answers offered held that, yes, NATO should continue, and to mobilize defenses against the new great totalitarian threat, Islamism. Fascists, communists, and Islamists differ one from the other in many ways, but they share a common dream of radical utopianism, of molding a superior human who exists to serve his government.

The new Islamist enemy rose to global prominence just as the prior one had been defeated, quickly dispelling airy notions about a liberal consensus or the "end of history." In 1977, Islamists took power in Bangladesh; in 1979, in Iran. Also in 1979, the government of Saudi Arabia turned sharply toward radicalism. In 1989, Islamists took over in the Sudan; in 1996, in most of Afghanistan.

Jihadi attacks on NATO members, and especially the United States, proliferated during this period. Some 800 Americans lost their lives to Islamist violence before 9/11, with the attempted 1993 World Trade Center bombing offering the best insight into the Islamists' supreme ambitions.

By 1995, this threat had become sufficiently apparent that NATO Secretary General Willy Claes compared Islamism to his organization's historic foe: "Fundamentalism is at least as dangerous as communism was." With the Cold War over, he added, "Islamic militancy has emerged as perhaps the single gravest threat to the NATO alliance and to Western security." In 2004, former Spanish prime minister José María Aznar made similar points: "Islamist terrorism is a new shared threat of a global nature that places the very existence of NATO's members at risk." He advocated that the alliance focus on combating "Islamic jihadism and the proliferation of weapons of mass destruction." He called for nothing less than "placing the war against Islamic jihadism at the center of the Allied strategy."

So, right from the beginning of the post-Soviet era, perceptive leaders called for NATO to focus on Western civilization's new main threat, Islamism.

The Islamist Threat

Two countries then symbolized that threat: Afghanistan and Turkey. They represented, respectively, unprecedented external and internal challenges to NATO.

Article 5 of the NATO charter, the critical clause requiring "collective self-defense," was invoked for the first and only time not during the Cuban missile crisis or the Vietnam war but a day after the 9/11 attack. To emphasize: not the Soviet, Chinese, North Korean, Vietnamese, or Cuban Communists but Al-Qaeda and the Taliban hiding in the caves of a peripheral country (Afghanistan) prompted a member state to take this momentous step. That's because Islamists, not Communists, dared to strike the American centers of power in New York City and Washington, D.C.

Further, Al-Qaeda and the Taliban are but a small part of the global jihad movement. The Iranian nuclear buildup, now with a legitimate path to making bombs within the decade, represents the single most deadly problem, especially when one factors in the apocalyptic regime ruling in Tehran and the possibility of an electromagnetic pulse attack.

Small-scale attacks present less danger but occur constantly, from a mosque in Egypt to a bridge in London to a coffee shop in Sydney. Islamist insurgencies have sparked civil wars (in Mali, Libya, Yemen, and Syria) and semi-civil wars (in Nigeria, Somalia, Iraq and Afghanistan). For five months, a branch of ISIS held the city of Marawi in the Philippines. Jihadi attacks occur in non-NATO countries with Muslim majorities and minorities alike: Argentina, Sweden, Russia, Israel, India, Myanmar (Burma), Thailand, and China.

Jihadis have also struck many NATO members, including the United States, Canada, the United Kingdom, Spain, France, the Netherlands, Germany, Denmark, and Bulgaria. Beyond political debilitation and terror, these attacks have seriously impaired military capabilities, by reducing training and distracting up to 40 percent of the active military forces from their core mission and instead doing police work—protecting synagogues, schools, and police stations.

And then there is Turkey.

Dictatorial, Anti-Western, and Anti-NATO Turkey

In the good old days, NATO provided Turkey with security, primarily against the Soviet Union; in turn, Turkey offered it an invaluable southern flank. Even today, Turkey has NATO's second largest military; combined with Americans, they make up, 3.4 million out of 7.4 million troops; together, the two countries contribute 46 percent of the total from 29 allies.

But much changed with the AKP's parliamentary victory in November 2002. Erdoğan famously stated soon after that "Turkey is not a country where moderate Islam prevails," and he lived up to that promise, with his government sponsoring Islamic schools, regulating male-female relations, alcohol, mosque building, and more broadly seeking to rear a "pious generation."

Erdoğan's rule has built on Islamism's despotic nature: he rigged elections, arrested dissident journalists on terrorism charges, created a private army, SADAT, had his police engage in torture, and staged a coup d'état. On the last point: the alleged coup of July 2016 gave the government the opportunity to detain, arrest, or fire over 200,000 Turks, shutter some 130 news outlets, and jail 81 journalists. The Committee to Protect Journalists calls Turkey "the world's biggest prison for journalists."

Without many noticing, a near-civil war now rages in Turkey's southeast, as Erdoğan appeases his new Turkish nationalist allies by trying to eliminate the expression of Kurdish language, culture, and political aspirations. Fear spreads, totalitarianism looms.

NATO's direct problems with Turkey began on March 1, 2003, when the AKP-dominated parliament denied American forces access to Turkish airspace to conduct the war against Saddam Hussein.

The Turkish government threatens to overrun Europe with Syrian refugees. It obstructs NATO relations with close allies such as Austria, Cyprus, and Israel. It has sponsored a turn of Turkish opinion against the West, in particular against the United States and Germany. As an example of this hostility, the mayor of Ankara, Melih Gökçek, tweeted in September 2017 that he prayed for more storm damage after two major hurricanes, Harvey and Irma, ravaged parts of the United States.

Ankara has taken Germans and Americans as hostages for political leverage. Deniz Yücel, a German journalist of Turkish origins, was jailed for a year until the German government agreed to upgrade Turkey's tanks. Peter Steudtner, a German human rights activist, spent several months in jail. Andrew Brunson, Protestant pastor, is the most conspicuous American hostage but there are others, including Ismail Kul, a chemistry professor, his brother Mustafa, and Serkan Gölge, a NASA physicist.

To put this in personal terms, I (and many other analysts of Turkey) cannot even change planes in Istanbul out of fear of being arrested and thrown in jail, serving as a hostage to be traded for some real or imagined Turkish criminal in the United States. Imagine that: Turkey, a supposed ally, is the only country in the world I fear arrest on arrival.

Dissident Turks in Germany have either been assassinated or fear assassinations, such as Yüksel Koç, co-chair of the European Kurdish Democratic Society Congress. Additionally, thugs in Turkish government employ have attacked Americans in the United States, most notably, at the Brookings Institution in 2016 and at Sheridan Circle, outside the Turkish embassy in Washington, in 2017.

The Turkish government sides with Tehran in various ways: it helped the Iranian nuclear program, assisted with the development of Iranian oil fields, helped transfer Iranian arms to Hezbollah, and joined in supporting Hamas. The Iranian chief of staff visited Ankara, perhaps to develop a joint effort against the Kurds. Ankara joined the Astana talks with the Iranian, Russian, and Turkish governments to decide Syria's destiny.

Erdoğan has quasi-joined the Shanghai Cooperative Organization; while a bit of a sham, it is the closest thing to a Russian-Chinese counterpart to NATO. Turkish troops have engaged in joint exercises with Chinese and Russian militaries. Most significantly, the Turkish armed forces are deploying the Russian S-400 anti-aircraft missile system, a step wildly inconsistent with NATO membership.

Then there is the Aegean Army. Yiğit Bulut, a top aide to Erdoğan, stated in February 2018 that Turkey needs a force "fortified with Russian and Chinese-made fighter jets because one day [the U.S. government] ... may very well consider attacking Turkey." Not exactly, you might observe, the sentiments of an ally.

And if that sounds conspiratorially kooky, the possibility does exist, as of this writing, of a U.S.-Turkish confrontation in the Syrian town of Manbij. Tensions have reached such a point that a White House statement informs us that President Trump "urged Turkey to exercise caution and to avoid any actions that might risk conflict between Turkish and American forces."

Turkey Distorts NATO

In addition to its hostility, Turkey's presence in NATO distorts the alliance. NATO should be about fighting Islamism. But if Islamists are already within the tent, how is the alliance going to do so?

This dilemma became public in 2009, with the term of Secretary General Jaap de Hoop Scheffer ending in July. A consensus existed that the new secretary general should be the Danish Prime Minister since 2006, Anders Fogh Rasmussen. In other words, he was the country's prime minster during the Danish cartoon crisis. When Muslim-majority country governments, including the Turkish one, pressed him to take actions against the cartoons, he very correctly stated: "I am the Prime Minister of a modern, free country, I can't tell papers what to print or not to print, it's their responsibility". He even refused to meet with a delegation of ambassadors from Muslim majority countries.

Three years later, however, with Rasmussen a candidate for secretary general of NATO, the Turkish government had its say. Then-Prime Minister Erdoğan recalled the cartoon crisis: "I asked for a meeting of Islamic leaders in [Denmark] to explain what is going on and he refused, so how can he contribute to peace?" A lot of bargaining followed, ending in a compromise: Rasmussen was appointed secretary-general on condition he publicly appease Erdoğan, which he did: "I would make a very clear outreach to the Muslim world. To ensure cooperation and intensify dialogue. I consider Turkey a very important ally and strategic partner, and I will cooperate with it and our endeavors to ensure the best cooperation with the Muslim world". Translated out of bureaucratese, he said: "I wouldn't do anything to upset the prime minister of Turkey."

This signaled, obviously, not a robust NATO leading the fight against Islamism, but an institution hobbled from within and incapable of standing up to one of its two main threats for fear of offending a member government. I personally witnessed this when a NATO Parliamentary Assembly delegation walked out of a meeting my organization had prepared, in deference to its Turkish members.

What to Do

NATO faces a dilemma and choice: Freeze Turkey out, as I advocate, or to keep it in, as is the institutional instinct. My argument holds that Ankara takes steps hostile to NATO, is not an ally, and obstructs the necessary focus on Islamism. In short, Turkey is the first member state go over to the enemy camp, where it will likely remain for a long time.

The argument to keep Turkey in boils down to: Yes, Turkey under Erdoğan is wayward but NATO membership allows a modicum of influence over it until it returns, as it will eventually. Or, in Steven Cook's formulation, "Turkey remains important less because it can be helpful but more because of then trouble that Ankara can cause."

So, which is a higher priority? Free NATO to fulfill its mission? Or maintain influence over Ankara? It comes down to a sense of how long Turkey will remain Islamist, dictatorial, and heading toward rogue status. Seeing the wide anti-Western consensus in Turkey, I want NATO free to be NATO.

Analysts (including myself in 2009) who agree with this conclusion sometimes say, "throw Turkey out"; but NATO lacks a mechanism for expulsion, as no one imagined the current problem back in 1949. That said, many steps are available to diminish relations with Ankara and reduce Turkey's role in NATO.

Abandon Incirlik Air Base: Ankara capriciously restricts access to Incirlik (prompting German troops to depart it) and the base is perilously close to Syria, the world's most active and dangerous war zone. Plenty of alternate sites exist, for example, in Romania and Jordan. According to some accounts, this process has already begun.

Pull American nuclear weapons: Incirlik hosts an estimated 50 nuclear bombs; they should be removed immediately. This vestige of the Cold War makes no military sense and, reportedly, planes based at Incirlik cannot even load these weapons. Worse, it is just conceivable that the host government might seize these arms.

Cancel arms sales: The U.S. Congress overrode an Executive Branch decision in 2017, rejecting a proposed personal arms sale in response to the Turks' DC thuggery. Far more importantly, the sale of F-35 aircraft, the most advanced fighter plane in the American arsenal, must be blocked.

Ignore Article 5 or other requests for help: Turkish aggression must not drag NATO members into war because of the Kurds, and they have made this clear. In reaction, Erdoğan needles NATO for the benefit his domestic audience: "Hey NATO, where are you? We came in response to the calls on Afghanistan, Somalia and the Balkans, and now I am making the call, let's go to Syria. Why don't you come?"

Distance NATO from the Turkish military: Stop sharing intelligence, do not train Turkish personnel, and exclude Turkish participation in weapons development.

Help Turkey's opponents: Stand with the Kurds of Syria. Support the growing Greek-Cyprus-Israel alliance. Cooperate with Austria.

In brief, Communists never provoked an Article 5 and no NATO member ever entered the Warsaw Pact. Islamism, in the shape of Al-Qaeda and Erdoğan, has scrambled the old verities almost beyond recognition, requiring new and creative thinking. NATO needs to wake up to these problems.

DANIEL PIPES is a Senior Fellow at the Center for Security Policy & has led the Middle East Forum as its President since 1994. With an A.B. & Ph.D. from Harvard, he has taught at Chicago, Harvard, Pepperdine & the U.S. Naval War College. He has served in five U.S. administrations, received two presidential appointments & testified before many congressional committees. He is the author of sixteen books on the Middle East, Islam, & other topics. Dr. Pipes writes a column for the Washington Times & his work has been translated into 37 languages. DanielPipes.org contains an archive of his writings and media appearances.

CHAPTER 7

President Erdoğan's Economic and Demographic Crises

• BY DAVID P. GOLDMAN

Turkey cannot persist indefinitely in its present geographic, demographic, and economic configuration. Kurdish fertility is the time bomb under the present Turkish state: By sometime in the 2040's, more than half of all Turkish citizens of military age will come from households where Kurdish is the first language. This portends the eventual secession of Turkey's Kurdish-majority Southeast, something that the neo-Ottoman ideology of the Turkish ruling party opposes just as vehemently as did the Kemalist nationalism of the past.

A great deal of Turkish foreign policy is devoted to postponing if not preventing this eventuality. President Erdoğan's Justice and Development Party had earlier hoped that an Islamic as opposed to a secular nationalist Turkish state would make it possible to assuage Kurdish grievances and better integrate the Kurds as fellow Muslims. Whether such a policy had any possibility of success is now a moot point, because America's 2003 intervention in Iraq made it possible for Iraq's Kurds to establish an autonomous zone in northern Iraq and to build up a formidable military capability. Kurdish self-government in Iraq is far short of a Kurdish state, but it is an important step in the direction of a Kurdish state and an inspiration to Kurdish nationalism.

The 2011 Syrian uprising against the Assad dictatorship, also backed by the United States, provide the occasion for Syria's Kurds to become an important military force and to gain control of Syria's major oil-producing regions and most fertile agricultural land. America's enlistment of the Kurds as an allied force to combat ISIS in Syria and Iraq, and the consequent training and arming of Kurdish militias by American as well as German advisers, add to Turkish concerns. Turkey blames the United States for fomenting a prospective ethnic secessionist movement. From the Turkish vantage point, its NATO ally has sacrificed what Turkey perceives to be existential interests (such as territorial integrity) in favor of ill-considered, ideologically-driven interventions (the Iraq War and the Arab Spring).

As a result, Turkey has pivoted towards the East, and is likely to become a political and economic satellite of China over the next several years. This is an example of natural enemies becoming allies precisely because rivalry would be so damaging to both sides (for example, Britain and Russia before World War I). Turkey for decades has supported the Muslims of what it calls "East Turkestan" (Xinjiang Province), the Uyghurs, who speak a dialect of Turkish. Uyghur separatists have committed several large-scale terror attacks in China and are viewed as a serious threat by the Chinese authorities. Several thousand Uyghurs traveled to Syria, many on passports provided by Turkish embassies in Southeast Asia, to fight alongside Syrian rebels supported by Turkey, and an unknown number have returned to China. During 2017, however, the Erdoğan government cracked down on travel by Uyghurs to Syria, evidently in response to Chinese demands.

More importantly, China's One Belt, One Road Eurasian infrastructure plan offers a solution to Turkey's heretofore incurable cycle of booms and busts. Economically speaking, Turkey has more in common with Latin America than with East Asia or South Asia. Erdoğan's populist government provides easy credit for construction and consumer spending, but the credit expansion finances imports of consumer goods rather than investment in productive plant in Turkey itself. Turkey's trade deficit (now close to 5% of GDP) ballooned in response to credit expansion.

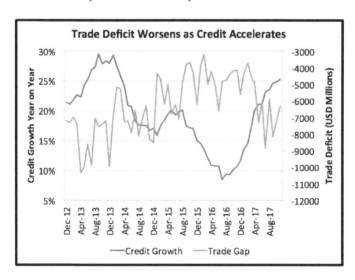

Meanwhile the Turkish lira has depreciated by about 50% during the past five years, resulting in double-digit inflation and interest rates. As a result, the total return of the Turkish stock market during the past five years has been negative 26%, vs an 18% gain for the broad emerging markets index, a 35% gain for India, a 38% gain for China, and an 89% return for the S&P 500 Index. Among all the major economics in the world, Turkey has shown the worst performance during the past five years. Its rising current account deficit threatens to cause another round of devaluation, inflation, higher interest rates, and recession.

A 25% rise in imports pushed Turkey's trade balance to $9.21 billion December 2017, or an annualized 12.5% of GDP. That's a huge number, and clearly unsustainable. Even after seasonal adjustment, that amounts to more than 10% of GDP. By way of comparison, the Greek trade deficit just before the country's 2012 crisis was only 8% of GDP.

The question is why the Turkish lira hasn't collapsed further than it did in 2017. One reason might be that some of the trade deficit isn't really trade at all. About $17 billion of Turkey's $76.7 billion trade deficit during 2017 was due to precious metals imports, a 142% jump over 2016. That might reflect hedging against currency depreciation by Turkish citizens, but it also might reflect money-laundering for Iran, for which a top executive of Turkey's Halkbank with close ties to the Erdoğan government was convicted in Federal court in December. Nonetheless, the numbers are huge by any standard, and the fact that Turkey's currency hasn't nose-dived suggests that Turkey has obtained financing for political reasons, for example, from Qatar.

Qatar is the largest foreign investor in Turkey with more than $20 billion in commitments, with another $19 billion in the pipeline for 2018. Meanwhile Turkey has become the guarantor of the Qatari royal family's security, with a new military base in the tiny country. Turkey backed Qatar during last year's Gulf States boycott, airlifting food after Saudi Arabia closed its border. Qatar meanwhile has started to buy large quantities of Chinese arms, especially missiles that could be directed against Saudi Arabia, and has brought People's Liberation Army personnel to train its armed forces, a relationship put on display at a December military parade in the Qatari capital of Doha. That is noteworthy given the presence of America's largest air force installation in the region, the Al Udeid Air Base, the principal US hub for US operations in Iraq and Afghanistan.

China's One Belt, One Road project acts like a magnetic field on the region: All of the players are lining up towards China, where Turkey and Iran see their economic future. China's direct investment in Turkey remains relatively small, but Turkey will be a key node in China's One Belt, One Road initiative. China is building new railway links to Turkey via Iran, and the Bank of China is financing infrastructure projects inside Turkey. China's second-largest telecom equipment provider ZTE plans to make Turkey its regional technology hub.

One Belt, One Road promises the Sinification of the Turkish economy. What that means concretely can be seen in the telecommunications sector. According to the World Bank, about a third of Turkey's workforce is classified as "informal," which is typical for middle-income developing countries. Everyone has a hustle, but no-one has access to capital, nor rights to property, nor security from the arbitrary intrusion of the authorities. Men work seasonal construction jobs for cash payments and women find things to sell. No one pays taxes; there is no way to collect them, and "informal" workers couldn't afford them in any case. Governments in turn provide paltry services and accumulate debts. An inbred elite milks the state budget and manages monopolies.

China is the first emerging country to fully integrate the informal economy into the formal economy, and it has done so through smartphones and electronic payments. China is on the way to becoming a "cashless society," in which virtually all transactions are electronic and therefore transparent to the tax authorities. Turkey, which has the same rate of smartphone penetration as China, plans to become a cashless society by 2023. It has allowed Chinese telecom providers to buy into the Turkish system and is working with ZTE and Huawei to upgrade its systems. Turkcell, the country's leading mobile broadband provider, has contracted with Huawei to build a 5G telecom network.

As China's labor force peaks and begins to contract during the next decade, Turkish labor will substitute for Chinese labor. With the new fast rail networks in place, Chinese manufacturers will be able to ship parts to Turkey in containers, assemble products there, and sell them to Europe and the rest of the world. Turkey hopes to become a key transshipment hub on the "New Silk Road," a nexus between Europe and Asia, with Chinese funding and Chinese technology.

It remains to be seen to what extent this Eurasian strategy will extricate Turkey from its severe and cyclical economic problems. But there is no extricating Turkey from its demographic dilemma.

Turkey's Kurdish citizens continue to have three or four children while ethnic Turks have fewer than two. By the early 2040s, most of Turkey's young people will come from Kurdish-speaking homes. The Kurdish-majority Southeast inevitably will break away. Erdoğan's hapless battle against the inevitable motivates the sometimes bewildering twists and turns of Turkish policy.

A review of the recently-released 2015 population data shows that the demographic scissors between Kurds and Turks continues to widen. Despite Erdoğan's exhortations on behalf of Turkish fertility, the baby bust in Turkish-majority provinces continues while Kurds sustain one of the world's highest birth rates. Even worse, the marriage rate outside of the Kurdish Southeast of the country has collapsed, portending even lower fertility in the future.

According to Turkstat, the official statistics agencies, the Turkish provinces with the lowest fertility rates all cluster in the north and northwest of the country, where women on average have only 1.5 children. The southeastern provinces show fertility rates ranging between 3.2 and 4.2 children per female.

Turkish Fertility, Highest and Lowest Provinces

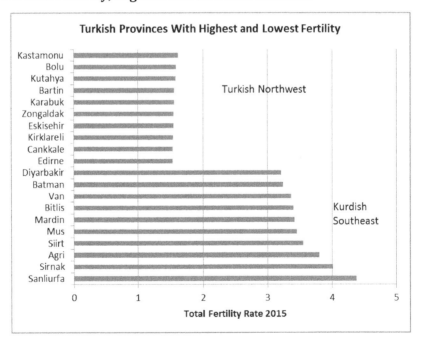

Even more alarming are Turkey's marriage statistics as reported by Turkstat. Between 2001 and 2015, the number of marriages in Istanbul, the country's largest city, fell by more than 30%, and by more than 40% in the capital Ankara. Most of the northern and northwestern provinces report a decline of more than half in the number of marriages. Not only are Turkish women refusing to have children; they are refusing to get married. The plunge in the marriage rate among ethnic Turks makes a further sharp decline in fertility inevitable.

As I reported in my 2011 book *Why Civilizations Die (and Why Islam is Dying, Too)*, Muslim countries that achieve a high rate of adult literacy jump from infancy to senescence without passing through adulthood. Like their Iranian, Algerian, and Tunisian counterparts, Turkish women reject the constraints of Muslim family life as soon as they obtain a high school education. The shock of sudden passage from traditional society into the modern world has produced the fastest-ever fall in fertility rates in the Muslim world.

Erdoğan's attempt to resist the inevitable effects of modernity on Turkish society will fail in the long-term. In the medium term, Erdoğan is likely to add to the political instability of the region.

DAVID GOLDMAN is an American economist, music critic & author, best known for his series of online essays in the Asia Times under the pseudonym Spengler. The pseudonym is an allusion to German historian Oswald Spengler, whose most famous work, Decline of the West (1918), asserted that Western civilization was already dying. Dr. Goldman's writing often focuses on demographic & economic factors. He earned his bachelor's degree at Columbia University in 1973 & acquired a master's degree in music education at the City University of New York. He completed his doctoral studies in economics at London School of Economics in 1976.

CHAPTER 8

Election 2019: Erdoğan's Existential War

• BY BURAK BEKDIL

In his victory speech on the night of April 16, 2017, President Recep
Tayyip Erdoğan said that the referendum that gave him sweeping new
powers was not the end but rather the beginning of a decisive political
struggle that should be crowned in 2019.[289] He was referring to the municipal
elections scheduled for March 2019 and the twin parliamentary and
presidential elections eight months after. Election 2019 will be the first
popular vote to elect the president after the Apr 16 referendum, narrowly
won by Erdoğan, consolidated party leadership, presidency, legislature and,
arguably, the judiciary in the personality of one all-too-strong man.

By November 2019 every Turkish youth younger than 18 will not have
seen in his life a leader –prime minister or president-- other than Erdoğan.
When the former militant Islamist became Turkey's leader the euro had just
become the official currency of 12 European Union (EU) members; Saddam
Hussein's Iraq had rejected UN weapons inspection proposals; President
George W. Bush had created the Department of Homeland Security to fight
terrorism; and Switzerland had just joined the UN.

Since his Justice and Development Party (AKP) came to power in
November 2002 Erdoğan has not lost a single election—municipal,
parliamentary, presidential or a referendum. In theory, Election 2019 will be
a bigger challenge for Erdoğan. Whereas under Turkey's parliamentary
system—in which the prime minister held the executive power- a party could
win parliamentary majority with as low as 30 percent of the national vote
(Erdoğan's AKP won around 60 percent of parliamentary seats with 34
percent of the vote in 2002 elections) the executive presidential system will
require the successful candidate to win at least 50 percent of the vote. But,
effectively, slightly more than a year and half before the presidential election
in November 2019 Erdoğan looks unrivalled despite a rich menu of
internal and external challenges he faces and will likely face in the next
22 months.

Background: Elections 2002-2017

Between 2002 and 2014 AKP's nationwide vote ranged between 34.2 percent (2002) and 49.8 percent (2011). In the country's first presidential election by popular vote in 2014 Erdoğan won 51.8 percent of the vote.

The parliamentary election on June 7, 2015 was tricky for Erdoğan. The AKP lost its parliamentary majority in general elections for the first time since it came to power in 2002. With 41 percent of the national vote (compared with 49.8 percent in the 2011 general elections), the AKP won eighteen fewer seats than necessary to form a single-party government in Turkey's 550-member parliament. More importantly, its parliamentary seats fell widely short of the minimum number needed to rewrite the constitution in the way Erdoğan wanted it so as to introduce an executive presidential system that would give him uncontrolled powers with few checks and balances, if any. [290] Undaunted by what looked like an election defeat, Erdoğan chose to toss the dice again. At his instructions, Prime Minister Ahmet Davutoglu pretended to hold coalition negotiations with opposition parties while secretly laying the groundwork for snap elections. [291] In Erdoğan's thinking, the loss of a few more seats would make no difference to AKP power, but re-winning a parliamentary majority would make the situation totally different. Erdoğan dissolved parliament and called for early elections on Nov 1, calculating that the wave of instability, sparked by countless terror attacks in the country, would push frightened voters toward single-party rule.

Erdoğan's gamble paid off. The November 2015 elections gave the AKP a comfortable victory and a mandate to rule until 2019: 49.5 percent of the national vote, or 317 parliamentary seats, sufficient to form a single-party government but still short of the critical number of 330 necessary to bring a constitutional amendment up for referendum. Once again, political Islam had won in Turkey.[292]

With the surprise support of a right-wing opposition party, the Nationalist Movement Party (MHP), Erdoğan passed the constitutional amendments in parliament and brought them up for referendum on Apr. 16, 2017. In a bitter irony, nearly 55 million Turks went to the ballot box to exercise their basic democratic right to vote; but they voted in favor of giving away their democracy. The system for which they voted looks more like a Middle Eastern sultanate than democracy in the West: 51.4 percent of the Turks voted in favor of constitutional amendments that gave Erdoğan excessive powers to augment his one-man rule in comfort.

The changes made Erdoğan head of government, head of state and head of the ruling party -- all at the same time. He now had the power to appoint cabinet ministers without requiring a confidence vote from parliament, propose budgets and appoint more than half the members of the nation's highest judicial body. In addition, he had the power to dissolve parliament, impose states of emergency and issue decrees. Alarmingly, the proposed system lacked the safety mechanisms of checks and balances that exist in other countries such as the United States. It would transfer powers traditionally held by parliament to the presidency, thereby rendering the parliament merely a ceremonial, advisory body.[293] As Kati Piri, the European Parliament's Turkey rapporteur, said of the referendum: "This is a sad day for all democrats in Turkey."[294]

The 'Sociology' Behind the Average Turk's Love Affair with Erdoğan

Countless theories, academic and otherwise, have tried to explain why Erdoğan has remained unchallenged. Erdoğan's opponents blame him and his one-man rule for the visible, perilous Islamization of the once secular country. In this view, Erdoğan has taken a nation of 80 million souls hostage. That is not true.

There are remarkable parallels between the political sociology of the average Turkish voter and Erdoğan's blend of Islamist/nationalist worldview. These parallels suggest that Erdoğan is, in a way, what the average Turk sees when he looks in the mirror.

But who is the average Turk? What are his ideology, his social habits, education, welfare and values? In the past years there have been a number of useful studies revealing that profile.

By 2014, when Erdoğan won 51.8 percent of the Turkish vote in the presidential election, there were only three Turkish universities in the world's top 500.[295] The infant mortality rate in Turkey was a grim 17 per 1,000 live births[296] while 24 percent of children aged 10 to 14 were in the labor market. [297] Per capita health spending was one-tenth of Italy's. According to the World Economic Forum's Global Gender Gap Report, Turkey ranked 120 in a list of 136 countries.[298] Press freedom in Turkey, according to Freedom House's world map, fell into the red zone of "not free."[299] And the World Press Freedom Index of Reporters Without Borders put Turkey's world ranking at 154.[300]

In 2015, Erdoğan boasted that the number of students studying to be imams [like he once did] rose from a mere 60,000 when his party first came to power in 2002 to 1.2 million in 2015.[301] When those students reach the voting age of eighteen, marry, and have children, their pious families would likely form a new army of five to six million AKP voters.

In the same year a survey by Kadir Has University in Istanbul suggested that a substantial number of Turks were fully aware of the political trajectory of their country but did not really care about the democratic deficit they lived in. The survey found that 56.5 percent of Turks did not think Turkey was a democratic country while 36.1 percent thought it was. Similarly, 59 percent thought that there was no freedom of thought while 33.1 percent said there was. A mere 9 percent of Turks thought there "definitely" was a free press in the country although another 31.3 percent agreed to some extent. These numbers left almost 60 percent who were sure they no longer had these civil liberties.[302]

More alarmingly, when narrowed down to AKP voters—49.5 percent of Turks according to the November 2015 elections—the study found that these Turks did not care all that much about democratic values. Only 58.3 percent of those who voted for the AKP thought Turkey was a democratic country; 56.7 percent thought there was freedom of thought in the country, and 54.8 percent thought there was a free press. In other words, nearly half of AKP voters did not think they lived in a democratic country but were happy to vote for the party anyway, without blaming it for the democratic deficit.

By 2017, fresh data confirmed the socio-political dynamics behind Erdoğan's unshaken popularity. Who was your average Turk in 2017?

Education: In Turkey, the average schooling period is a mere 6.51 years. In the age group 18-24, only 26.6 percent of male Turks and 18.9 percent of female Turks attend a school. The August 2017 OECD Regional Well-Being Index showed that Turkey came dead last out of 362 in the education area, and only 16 percent of Turks over the age of 18 are university graduates.

Sociology: Seventy-four percent of Turks identify themselves as people who perform "all duties" of Islam. Ninety-four percent say they have never had holidays abroad, and 70 percent say they have never participated in any cultural or arts events. Seventy-four percent identify as either conservative or religiously conservative—which, among other reasons, explains Erdoğan's popularity. It makes mathematical sense that Erdoğan, who does not hide his hatred of alcohol consumption for religious reasons, is popular in a country where 79 percent say they never consume alcohol (per capita alcohol consumption in Turkey is as low as 1.5 liters, compared, for example, to 12 liters in Austria).

Welfare: And Turks are poor. Boasting barely $10,000 per capita income, the country has 92% percent of its population living on incomes between $180 and $1,280 per month—with 56 percent earning between $180 and $510 per month. It should be noted that the number of families receiving free coal from Erdoğan's governments rose from 1.1 million in 2003 to 2.15 million in 2014.[303]

Demographics: Erdoğan has persistently prescribed to every Turkish family to have at least three children, ideally five.[304] "Size" has always been at the center of Erdoğan's vision of power: We build the biggest airport, the biggest mosque, the biggest bridge... We are more populous, we are bigger, our country could have been much bigger in size... All the same Erdoğan's call for bigger families has also been a subtle means to expand his voter base: More children in a country like Turkey would mean less education, more poverty and, often, more piety: the groups that tend to vote most for Erdoğan. But things are not moving in the exact direction Erdoğan wishes them to be, with the fertility game in politics tilting in favour of Kurds.

By 2015, the total fertility rate in eastern and southeastern, Kurdish-speaking Turkey was 3.41, compared to an average of 2.09 in the non-eastern, Turkish-speaking areas. The total fertility rate in Turkey dropped from 4.33 in 1978 to 2.26 in 2013. Unsurprisingly, it stood at 3.76 for women with no education and at 1.66 for women with high school or higher degrees.[305] Although Turkey remains the second most populous country in Europe after Germany, with a population of nearly 80 million, and has one of the lowest median ages in Europe at 31.5 - but up from 28.8 in 2009—official figures in 2017 showed the first time that fertility rates had dropped to the replacement rate of 2.1 in 2016.[306]

Terror, Divisions and the Emergence of a Nationalistic Bloc

Turks have traditionally shown tendencies to "unite behind their elected governments" at times they feel threatened by an external force, usually terror, which they often blame on "foreign powers trying to stop their country becoming great again." The governments' inability to successfully counter terror attacks from a multitude of sources do not discredit them; often, on the contrary, such security threats, tackled by the governments in the "Third World rhetoric" generate a national sense of unity behind "the state" which the Turks would often associate with "the government."

In the aftermath of what looked like an election defeat for Erdoğan in June 7, 2015 parliamentary elections [in which Erdoğan's AKP came first but fell short of forming a single-party government] a terrible wave of violence gripped Turkey.

First, the separatist Kurdistan Workers' Party (Partiya Karkerên Kurdistan, PKK), which had been fighting a guerrilla war from mountain hideouts in northern Iraq, declared an end to its unilateral ceasefire begun in 2013.[307] Then on July 20, a Turkish suicide bomber killed more than thirty people at a pro-Kurdish gathering in the small town of Suruc.[308] Claiming that the Turkish state had a secret role in the bombing, the PKK killed two policemen in the town of Ceylanpinar.[309] The three-decades-old violence between the Turkish and Kurdish communities had suddenly roared back with a vengeance. In one of Turkey's bloodiest summers ever, more than a thousand PKK fighters and Turkish security officials were killed.

Then in October, the radical jihadist Islamic State (IS) attacked in the Turkish capital. Two suicide bombers, one Turkish the other Syrian, killed some one hundred people at a pro-peace rally in the heart of Ankara, the worst single terror attack in the country's modern history.[310] In repeat polls less than five months later –and at the peak of terror attacks—the AKP's national vote in Nov. 1, 2015 elections rose by nearly nine percentage points to 49.5 percent.

Erdoğan has a history of emerging as the winner as Turkey becomes more deeply divided along conservative/nationalist vs. secular/liberal lines primarily because he remains the only leader the larger segments of the society [the conservative/nationalist bloc] believe could fight when they feel threatened by "infidel atheists, the enemies within and an army of traitors."

A 2016 research sponsored by the German Marshall Fund revealed that 83 percent of Turks would not agree to their daughter getting married to someone from the opposite ideology. Seventy-eight percent would not do business with the "other" 76 percent would not agree to be neighbors with and 73 percent would not let their children befriend with the children of the "other."[311]

More recently, a research by Bilgi University of Istanbul revealed in December 2017 that a majority of Turkish youth are against the "other." In this study, 90 percent of youth said they would not want their daughters to marry someone "from the 'other' group." While 80 percent of youth said they would not want a neighbor from the "other," 84 percent said they would not want their children to be friends with children from the "other" group. A ratio of youth who have said they would not do business with members of the "other" group also stood at 84 percent. Eighty percent said they would not hire anyone from the "other." Doubtlessly, the results of the study demonstrated the dimensions of high social distance between Turkish youth.[312]

Against that background, starting from the summer of 2015 Erdoğan has gradually changed his party's ideology from strict Islamism to a blend of nationalism and strict Islamism in order to appeal, in addition to conservative votes, to nationalist constituencies which had voted against him in previous elections. The effort paid off. An otherwise fierce critic of Erdoğan, the nationalist opposition MHP supported his bid for executive presidential system. Without MHP's support Erdoğan would not have won the Apr. 16, 2017 referendum which narrowly passed (with 51.4 percent of the national vote). Political observers agree that MHP's critical contribution to that was anywhere between three to four percentage points.[313]

The MHP leadership went further after the referendum and formed an election alliance with Erdoğan's AKP. MHP's chairman, Devlet Bahceli, announced at the end of 2017 that his party would support Erdoğan in Election 2019 in an "indigenous and national alliance."[314] That support is expected to bring an extra five to seven percentage points to Erdoğan in an election where even one percentage point can be a game changer.

The Opposition

The "indigenous and national alliance" between the AKP and MHP leave three main parties in the opposition bloc: The main opposition Republican People's Party (CHP), the center-right IYI Party (Good Party) and the pro-Kurdish Peoples' Democratic Party (HDP). The CHP traditionally appeals to the better-educated Turks with ideological tendencies ranging from social democrat to Kemalist, liberal, left-wing nationalist and others that join forces along their anti-Erdoğanism. The party's popular support has stubbornly stuck at around the 25 percent benchmark and is not expected to make a surprise boom in 2019. Established in 2017, IYI Party is a new comer into the stage, with a woman leader, Meral Aksener, who claims she can win votes from all disenchanted social and political groups in the country. Aksener claims her party's popularity was measured at a promising 20.5 percent[315] in January 2018, but independent observers viewed that claim as total exaggeration. Although it is difficult to predict how IYI Party may evolve from now until Election 2019 a fair guess would be that IYI could garner votes anywhere between five to 10 percentage points.

That picture could make the destination of Kurdish votes critical in 2019. Since 2015, Erdoğan has been enjoying the fruits of his newfound ethnic nationalism. He has ordered the security forces to fight the Kurdish separatist PKK "till they finish it off," and has pursued hawkish politics via the judiciary he controls. Several leading Kurdish MPs are now in jail on terrorism charges. More than 1,400 academics who signed a petition "for peace" have been prosecuted and/or dismissed from their universities. Erdoğan has vowed immediate military action inside neighboring Syria if Syrian and Iraqi Kurds set up a belt of semi-state entity in Turkey's south. He keeps repeating that the emergence of a near-state Kurdish actor in Mesopotamia would be an existential threat to Turkey; hence Turkey's right to militarily retaliate.

Election 2019 will take place at a time when both Erdoğan and the insurgent Kurds will have less appetite for a new peace-based political adventure. Kurds trust him less than they did between 2011 and 2013. At the same time, Erdoğan has discovered that he wins more votes if he plays to nationalist Turkish constituencies rather than to Kurdish ones. He will be more reluctant to shake hands with Kurds than he was in 2013 when his Kurdish peace campaign urged the PKK to declare a unilateral ceasefire—which the group would break in 2015.

The pro-Kurdish HDP's national support is estimated in the 10 percent to 12 percent range. Would the Kurds, traditionally having voted either for Erdoğan or a pro-Kurdish party, tend to vote less for the AKP now that Erdoğan is in a nationalist coalition with the MHP, Kurds' political nemesis? Bekir Agirdir, a veteran political analyst and pollster explains: "In the past, five out of every 10 Kurd would vote for the AKP and four for the HDP. In 2015 only three voted for the AKP and seven voted for the HDP. AKP's alliance with the MHP may lead up only two out of 10 Kurds voting for Erdoğan."[316]

As he campaigns ahead of the 2019 election, Erdoğan will have to find a miracle equilibrium: how to win Kurdish votes without losing nationalist Turkish votes? So far, he has managed this challenge exceptionally well. He has won nationalist votes, and his party has come in first or second in Kurdish regions. In 2019, however, he will face a bigger challenge.

As the opposition bloc stands today its combined vote against Erdoğan's candidacy could be standing at between 40 percent and 45 percent. That is too little to challenge Erdoğan. Moreover, there are no guarantees that the three opposition parties of sometimes clashing ideological preferences should agree on a common candidate against Erdoğan. For instance, it may be too difficult to bring together IYI and HDP voters in support for a common candidate solely on opposition to Erdoğan: IYI's leader, Aksener, a former interior minister, has a past record of hawkish fight against Kurdish uprisings in the 1990s. And her mildly nationalistic/right-wing constituencies often view the HDP as a "terrorist" group disguised as a political party.

A 'Milder Erdoğan' Against Erdoğan?

Some opposition figures have long been toying with the idea of challenging Erdoğan with a "milder Erdoğan:" another conservative who would appeal to conservative Turkey [the majority] but would not run Turkey undemocratically like the "Sultan." The idea looks like the U.S. effort during the Cold War to fight Soviet communism by supporting non-Soviet left in Europe: fight autocratic Islamism by supporting mild Islamism. In theory, it may work. In practice, it probably will not.

There has long been speculation that Erdoğan's former confidante and chief ideological ally, former President Abdullah Gul, might be the right choice. Gul, like Erdoğan, comes from the ranks of militant political Islam. He is one of the co-founders of the AKP. In 2007, with Erdoğan's support, he was elected president of the country—but when the presidency was largely a ceremonial office. After Gul finished his term in 2014, Erdoğan forced him into de facto political exile by not rewarding him with any seat in his government. The two former allies have since publicly disagreed on major issues, with Erdoğan defending his hardline, confrontational polity while Gul has been critical of that polity and advocated, instead, broader civil liberties in line with western democratic practices.

In January 2018, Erdoğan, without naming names, accused any potential former AKP bigwig who may challenge him of high treason. Pro-Erdoğan media preferred to name names: an army of columnists crucified Gul and Ali Babacan, Erdoğan's former economy minister and another likely candidate against Erdoğan, accusing any such traitor of being a pawn in an international conspiracy against Erdoğan.[317] That is a dangerous label to carry in a country like Turkey where millions of potentially violent men have self-tasked themselves of protecting their country and leader from the evil of foreign powers, and where prosecutors wait on alert to indict people on charges of high treason on slightest hint from the president.

Theoretically, there is always the possibility that the opposition can find the right man and agree on a single candidate who would most successfully challenge Erdoğan. Ideally, that man must be a conservative with liberal democratic credentials, a pious Muslim but at the same time a secular Kemalist and a proven Turkish nationalist who could garner Kurdish votes too, but who is not too nationalist so as to push away left-wing liberals and democrats. In practice, however, such a miracle man may not exist.

Major Challenges Beyond the Turkish soil

There has hardly been an important regional or global state actor with which Erdoğan has not openly fought in recent years. Turkey's major diplomatic rows in the past decade has had counterparts including the United States, EU (most notably Germany, the Netherlands and Austria), Switzerland, Russia, Israel, Syria, Iraq, the Iraqi Kurdish Regional Government, Egypt, Libya, the United Arab Emirates, Armenia and Cyprus— in addition to various degrees of open to discreet hostilities with Saudi Arabia, Jordan, Lebanon and Myanmar. Erdoğan's more than confrontational rhetoric aiming at chosen adversaries is both real [reflecting his neo-Ottoman, pan-Turkic Sunni Islamism] and exaggerated language [reflecting his desire to catch votes in a country where the national psyche is deeply isolationist].

At the beginning of 2018, Turkey did not have diplomatic relations with its littoral neighbour and EU member state Cyprus and its eastern neighbour Armenia; Turkey had just ended its six-year-long diplomatic impasse with Israel; had come to the brink of confrontation with Russia (end of 2015); declared President Bashar al-Assad's Syria as a "terrorist state;" did not have full [ambassadorial level] diplomatic relations with Egypt and the Netherlands; was threatening military action against U.S. interests and military assets in Syria; and had a quiet sectarian war with Shiite Iran.

The U.S.: From Strategic Partnership to Strategic Enmity: Turks often demonstrate degrees of confusion when asked about their foreign policy preferences. A public opinion poll in the mid-2000s found that most Turks viewed the US as a threat to world security—but the same poll found that Turks expected the US, before every other ally, to come to Turkey's help if needed.[318] Conspiracy theories have always been abundant in the Turkish psyche. Schoolchildren grow up hearing maxims like "A Turk's only friend is another Turk" and "Our Ottoman ancestors had to fight seven worlds (the big powers)." According to this worldview, the world's major powers construct intricate conspiracies as they tirelessly plot to stop Turkey's rise. In an age of rising populism, Erdoğan has systematically fueled the common thinking that "the entire world is conspiring against us." His Islamist, anti-western, isolationist narrative has found millions of supporters in Turkey.

In August 2017, the Washington-based Pew Research Center's global survey found that 72 percent of Turks saw America as a threat to their country's security. In Turkey, a NATO member state, the U.S. is perceived as a greater threat than Russia or China. "America's influence is a top concern in Turkey," the survey read. "This figure [72 percent] is up 28 percentage points since 2013, when just 44 percent named U.S. power and influence as a major threat." Bizarrely, similar numbers of Turks view the U.S. and IS as a threat to their country. Pew did not ask Turks about their perceptions of IS in 2017, but its 2015 research found that 73 percent of Turks had a negative opinion of IS and 72 percent had a negative opinion of America. (In that poll, 8 percent of Turks had a favorable opinion of IS while 19 percent had no opinion.)

U.S. President Donald Trump's National Security Strategy of December 2017 came amid major policy and ideological divergences between the U.S. and Turkish administrations. Such was the background of the Washington-Ankara axis when Trump unveiled his whitepaper:

1. In May, supporters of Erdoğan, including his security detail and several armed individuals, violently charged a group of peaceful protesters outside the Turkish ambassador's residence in Washington, injuring 11, including a police officer, and prompting the State Department to condemn the attack as an assault on free speech. Washington warned Turkey that the action would not be tolerated. A group of Republican lawmakers called the episode an "affront to the United States."

2. In October, the US and Turkey suspended all non-immigrant visa services for travel between the two countries after the arrest of a US consulate employee in Istanbul.

3. In November, Reza Zarrab, a Turkish-Iranian gold trader who is cooperating with US prosecutors, told jurors in a New York federal court that Erdoğan authorized a transaction in a scheme to help Iran evade US sanctions. Erdoğan called the court a "US plot against Turkey and [his] government."

4. In early December, Turkish and Russian officials announced that they were only weeks away from penning a deal for the acquisition and deployment of Russian S-400 air and anti-missile systems on Turkish soil. This will make Turkey the only NATO member state deploying the S-400 system.

5. Press reports said on December 6 that an arrest warrant had been requested through the Ankara chief prosecutor's office for Brett MacGurk, US Special Presidential Envoy for the Global Coalition to Counter the Islamic State. The petition accuses McGurk of attempting to overthrow the Turkish government and change the constitutional order of the Turkish Republic by "acting in concert with ... armed terrorist organizations."

6. On December 13, US national security adviser HR McMaster condemned Qatar and Turkey for taking on a "new role" as the main sponsors and sources of funding for extremist Islamist ideology that targets western interests.

7. On December 14, Turkish police summoned an FBI official stationed in Turkey in connection with testimony in the Iran sanctions (Zarrab) case.

8. On December 17, Erdoğan slammed a US-backed Syrian Kurdish militant group and said he will clear his country's border with Syria of "terrorists." The "terrorists" he was referring to are the principal land warfare assets of the US military campaign against radical jihadists in Syria and Iraq. Erdoğan slams the US administration almost daily for "giving weapons to a terror organization" and has declared US policy to be in violation of the NATO treaty. Ironically, Erdoğan remains mute about Russian support for the same militant Kurdish group. Russia does not even categorize as terrorist the Kurdistan Workers' Party (PKK), which both Ankara and Washington view as terrorist. (PKK's violent campaign since 1984 has claimed more than 40,000 lives in Turkey.)

9. On December 21, Erdoğan, spearheading an international campaign to condemn Trump's decision to recognize Jerusalem as Israel's capital, said that the US cannot buy the people's will, a reference to Trump's threats to cut funding to countries that vote against Washington on a motion at the UN. "They call the US the cradle of democracy. The cradle of democracy is seeking to buy a nation's will with dollars," Erdoğan said. "Mr. Trump, you cannot buy our will. I am calling on the whole world: Do not sell your struggle for democracy for a few dollars."[319]

Turkey's political goals, ambitions, and planned policy actions in the Middle East are too divergent from Trump's security vision for the region. So is Erdoğan's pro-Islamist, pro-HAMAS, neo-Ottoman policy calculus. In many ways, Trump's "Make America Great Again" campaign is flatly incompatible with Erdoğan's "Make Turkey Great Again" campaign.

A day after the U.S. publicly admitted it is supplying weapons and training to Syrian Kurdish militia—which Turkey views as terrorist-- Erdoğan accused Washington on Jan. 15 of "building an army of terror" on Turkey's border with Syria. Erdoğan said in a public speech: "The U.S. has admitted to building an army of terror along our national borders. It is our responsibility to suffocate this effort before it is born ...

What we have told all our allies and friends is this: do not stand between us and terrorists, between us and murderers, otherwise it may give rise to situations that are unwanted and we will not be responsible."[320] In other words, Erdoğan was threatening military action inside Syria against militia groups equipped and trained by the U.S.

What are the options for the Trump administration to deal with its annoying former ally? Nick Danforth, a senior policy analyst for the Bipartistan Policy Center's national security program, wrote in a January 2018 article:

"American policy makers could soon find themselves facing an acute dilemma: As Mr. Erdoğan becomes more aggressive, the means at Washington's disposal to apply pressure on him increasingly risk destabilizing Turkey even further.

"In an increasingly tense and transactional relationship, targeted steps like these can help curb some of Mr. Erdoğan's more antagonistic behavior. But getting tough on Turkey is unlikely to reverse the negative trajectory of the relationship. And it will ultimately produce diminishing returns.

"As Turkey's political and economic situation deteriorates, the risk grows that further pressure will be counterproductive. Any sanctions with real bite would only increase the already serious possibility of a major economic crisis in Turkey. Rather than leave Turkey more dependent on Washington, such a crisis could well empower those in Ankara who already believe that Turkey has less to lose and more to gain by breaking with the West completely.

"For all of Mr. Erdoğan's anger at America, he now stands to benefit from the very American cynicism he regularly denounces. However infuriating and dangerous American policy makers find him, they will ultimately find the alternative — chaos in Turkey — scarier."[321]

The EU: No Longer the "Anchor:" Although Erdoğan needs the investment climate and foreign cash [portfolio and physical investment] inflows to keep the fragile economy afloat with Turkey's "EU candidate state" status he knows very well that Turkey will not become a member of the European club any time in the foreseeable future. In short: Turkey says it wants to join the EU, but has no intention of complying with membership rules primarily on democratic governance and civil liberties. The EU says it wants Turkey to join, but is fully aware that it does not qualify. Turkey, theoretically, pushes forward in the hope that the EU might someday change its rules; the EU, theoretically, pushes forward in the hope that Turkey might someday miraculously qualify. Neither will happen.

In 2017, three decades after Turkey officially applied to become a full member of the EU, the European Parliament called for Turkey's accession talks to be suspended if Ankara fully implements plans to expand Erdoğan's powers, which he won in the April 16, 2017 referendum. Although the parliament's vote is not binding, it illustrates the gulf that has grown between Ankara and Brussels. The resolution passed by the parliament in Strasbourg "calls on the Commission and the member states ... to formally suspend the accession negotiations with Turkey without delay if the constitutional reform package is implemented unchanged." If the object of the resolution was to rein Erdoğan in, it did not work. Erdoğan remained defiant and said the majority of Turks did not "want the EU anymore," and "the EU is not indispensable for Turkey." [322] Regardless, the tedious round of mutual pretension between Ankara and Brussels is growing less sustainable by the day.

It came as unsurprising, thus, that Germany's Christian Democratic Union (CDU) and the Social Democrats (SPD) reportedly agreed early in January in a coalition draft document that they do not want to close any chapters in Turkey's talks on accession to the EU, nor open any new chapters, "given the state of democracy and human rights in that country."[323]

In another sign of realism, French President Emmanuel Macron told Erdoğan during the Turkish leader's state visit to Paris on January 5, 2018 that there was no chance of progress towards Turkey joining the EU. Macron said it was time to end the hypocrisy of pretending that there was any prospect of an advance in Turkey's membership talks with the EU.[324]

From Russia Not-So-Much With Love: When, in the late 1950s, Kemal Nejat Kavur was serving as the Turkish ambassador to Moscow, Andrei Gromyko, the then Soviet Commissar for Foreign Affairs asked him: "Your Excellency, your country has the most number of men under arms in Europe. If it's against your traditional enemies, the Greeks, it is too big. If, on the other hand, it is against us, it's too small. So, what's the reason for it?" Little seems to have changed on the Ankara-Moscow axis since then.

At the end of 2015, Turkey risked serious tensions with Russia in order to advance its pro-Sunni Islamist agenda in Syria. Russia, together with Iran, provided the lifeline Syrian President Bashar al-Assad needed to stay in power while Turkey stepped up its anti-Assad campaign. In November 2015, Turkey once again zigzagged toward the West when it shot down a Russian military aircraft, citing the violation of its airspace along its border with Syria. Turkey also threatened to shoot down any Russian aircraft that might violate its airspace again. It was the first time in modern history that a NATO ally had shot down a Soviet or Russian military airplane.

An angry Vladimir Putin, Russia's president, imposed punishing economic sanctions, which cost the Turkish economy billions of dollars. Turkey started zigzagging again. In July 2016, Erdoğan apologized for downing the Russian plane, and in August he went to Russia to shake hands for normalization. Once again, Russia was trendy for the Turks, and the West looks passé.

Turkey's newfound love affair with Russia would inevitably have repercussions in Syria, and that pleases Iran. "Not only will Turkey have to 'digest' that [Russian-Iranian-Syrian] line, it will have to join it, entering into a pact with Putin and the ayatollahs. Clearly, this is where Erdoğan has decided is the best place to pledge his allegiance," wrote Meira Svirsky at The Clarion Project.[325] There are already signs.

Turkey and Russia found where they converge [326]: Putin accuses the West of violating agreements by expanding NATO to Russia's borders and fomenting unrest in nearby Georgia and Ukraine, while in Turkey, the pro-Erdoğan media accuses the U.S. of orchestrating the July 2016 coup. There are more alarming signals from Ankara. Mevlut Cavusoglu, the foreign minister, said that Turkey may look outside NATO for defense cooperation.[327]

On December 29, 2017, Turkey and Russia finalized a $2.2 billion deal for the Turkish acquisition of Russian-made S-400 air and anti-missile defense system.[328] This will be the first time that the S-400 system will be deployed on NATO soil.

Nevertheless, Turkey's forceful tactical cooperation with Russia will not evolve into a strategic alliance. Turkey's newfound peace with Russia is too fragile and a one-way direction rather than mutually-beneficial productivity: Erdoğan learned by experience that Russia is too big for him to bite; that Russia will not "punish" Turkey as long as Turkey aligned its policy, especially at the Syrian theatre, with Russia [and Iran in the Syrian case], a tough condition ostensibly acceptable for Erdoğan today but not so easily digestive in the future. The historic mutual mistrust between Ankara and Moscow remains too alive.

Turkish Belly-Dancing to Persian Santouri: Iran, for Turkey, is another Russia story. After having fought several inconclusive wars, Ottoman Turks and Safavid Persians decided, in 1639, to embrace a new code of conduct that would last in the next centuries: cold peace. After Iran's Islamic Revolution in 1979, the Turkish-Iranian cold peace turned less cold as the then-staunchly secular Turkish establishment feared that the mullahs in Iran could wish to undermine Turkey by exporting its Islamic revolution to Turkish soil.

The cold peace in the 21st century took a different turn after Turkey metamorphosed from staunch state secularism into elected Islamism. Theoretically the cold peace should have moved from cold to just peace. It did not. Simply because Turkish Islamism was too Sunni, and Iran's too Shiite. The cold war was to stay with its golden rule respected by both Ankara and Tehran: pretend to respect your rival; do not openly confront; and cooperate along the lines of common enemies—there are plenty of them.

For years and years Ankara thought it could win hearts and minds in Tehran by emphasizing convergences rather than divergences. The Turks opposed sanctions on Iran, and later helped Iranians evade them. Then there was the common enemy: Israel. But none has sufficed: Like in most acts of the passionate Turkish-Persian screenplay the moments of emotional, Muslim-to-Muslim fraternity are misleading. For the mullahs of various conservative flavors Turkey remains too western, too treacherous and too Sunni. And for the neo-Ottomans in Ankara Iran remains too discreetly hostile, too ambitious, too untrustworthy and too Shiite.

Why Muslim Fraternity With Arabs Is A Myth: Turkish textbooks have taught children how treacherous Arab tribes stabbed their Ottoman ancestors in the back during the First World War, and even how Arabs collaborated with non-Muslim Western powers against Muslim Ottoman Turks.[329] A pro-Western, secular rule in the modern Turkish state in the 20th century coupled with various flavors of Islamism in the Arab world added to an already ingrained anti-Arabism in the Turkish psyche.

Erdoğan's indoctrination, on the other hand, had to break that anti-Arabism if he wanted to revive the Ottoman Turkish rule over a future united *ummah*. The Turks had to rediscover their "Arab brothers" if Erdoğan's pan-Islamism had to advance into the former Ottoman realms in the Middle East. For that purpose, the Turkish Education Ministry added Arabic courses to its curriculum[330] and the state broadcaster, TRT, launched an Arabic television channel.[331] Erdoğan claimed that "Arabs stabbed us in the back was a lie"[332] while even the Arabs do not claim they did not revolt against the Ottomans in alliance with Western powers.

But facts are different. The Turkish-Arab fraternity along Muslims lines remains a myth. For instance, the Saudi-led Gulf blockade of Qatar imposed in June 2017 came as a complete shock.[333] One of Erdoğan's Sunni brothers had taken out the sword against another: Turkey's Sunni brothers in Arabia had once been sympathetic to his ideas but no longer are.

Only two years ago, Turkey and Saudi Arabia were mulling the idea of a joint military strike in Syria.[334] For the Sunni Saudis, the Turks were allies only if they could be of use in any fight against Shiite Iran or its proxies, such as the Baghdad government or the Syrian regime. For the Saudis, Turkey was only useful if it could serve a sectarian purpose. Meanwhile, as Turkey, together with Qatar, kept on championing Hamas, Saudi Arabia and Egypt distanced themselves from the Palestinian cause and consequently from Turkey. Both the Saudi kingdom and Egypt's al-Sisi regime have viewed Hamas, a tactical Iranian satellite, with hostility, whereas Turkey gave it logistical and ideological support. Another reason for the change in Saudi Arabia's position toward Turkey—from "friendly" to "semi-medium-hostile"—is Saudi Arabia's newfound alliance with Egypt's President Abdelfattah el-Sisi. El-Sisi replaced the Muslim Brotherhood president, Mohamed Morsi, in Egypt, while Turkey and Qatar, have effectively been the embodiments of the Muslim Brotherhood in the region. As a result, Erdoğan offered to build a Turkish military base in the Kingdom, for example, but in June 2017, Saudi officials turned him down.[335]

More recently, a tiny sheikdom had to remind Erdoğan that his expansionist, "*ummah*-ist" policy design for the Middle East was no more than a fairy tale he persistently wanted to believe. In December 2017, United Arab Emirates (UAE) Foreign Minister Sheikh Abdullah bin Zayed Al Nahayan shared a tweet[336] that accused Turkish troops of looting the holy city of Medina a century ago. In response, Erdoğan himself lashed out:

"Some impertinent man sinks low and goes as far as accusing our ancestors of thievery … What spoiled this man? He was spoiled by oil, by the money he has."

But that was not the end of what looks like a minor historical debate. The row symbolized the impossibility of what Erdoğan has been trying to build: An eternal Arab-Turkish fraternity.

Anwar Gargash, UAE's Minister of State for Foreign Affairs, said there was a need for Arab countries to rally around the "Arab axis" of Saudi Arabia and Egypt. Gargash also said that "the Arab world would not be led by Turkey."[337]

The realist idea that "the Arab world would not be led by Turkey" was in fact a simple confirmation of the findings of a 2016 poll. The pollster Zogby found in its research that 67 percent of Egyptians, 65 percent of Saudis, 59 percent of UAE citizens, and 70 percent of Iraqis had an unfavorable opinion of Turkey.[338]

Directionless Turkey: Geographically speaking, Turkey is a peninsula. Politically speaking, it is a landlocked country. Its political/military bonds with its traditional allies, the U.S. and NATO, have never been weaker. It is an EU candidate state with no prospect of membership. It has no diplomatic relations with its southern littoral neighbour Cyprus and eastern neighbour Armenia. It is in a cold sectarian war with its eastern neighbour Iran and the Iraqi government it controls in its southeast. Its trade-centric ties with the Iraqi Kurds look like a loose cannon. It is involved in military confrontation with the Syrian Kurds. The Syrian regime across the southern border is Turkey's worst regional nemesis. It has deeply problematic ties with Egypt, the most populous Arab nation. It has worse than shaky relations with Saudi Arabia and its Gulf allies, except Qatar. It is too hostile to Israel and champions the "Palestinian cause" in ways "more Palestinian than Palestinian." Turkey thinks it is in a safe alliance with Russia, but this is only a tactical, probably temporary, period of calm based on safeguarding Russian interests rather than common interests. Once again, the country is directionless and the Turks keep thinking they are friendless.

Conclusions

Election 2019, for the Turks, will be a difficult choice between the bad and the potentially worse. Twenty-two months before what most analysts view as the most critical Turkish vote in the 21st century all credible indications point to another Erdoğan victory.

If that happens, Turkey will be further dragged into the elected darkness of Islamist polity, with Erdoğan further consolidating power and advancing his agenda of "raising devout generations" at home and "making Turkey great again" abroad. That will be bad news for secular and liberal Turks, Turkey's one-time Western allies and the Middle East. Erdoğan's election also will formalize the now emerging coalition of Islamist and nationalist ideologies in Turkey, most probably merging them, gradually, inside the AKP, ending the rivalry between Turkey's Islamists and nationalists. That in the longer term will be Turkey's new, powerful "right-wing" bloc.

The opposition looks too weak. Even if the anti-Erdoğan bloc could produce a plausible candidate to run against him it will not be easy to challenge the strongman. Erdoğan controls the army, police and judiciary. An opposition candidate believed to be posing a serious challenge to Erdoğan could end up in jail on fabricated charges ranging from terrorism to high treason.

Moreover, the Turkish ballot box is not a credible source to judge contenders in a democratic race. For instance, an EU parliamentary organization warned before the April 2017 referendum that the democratic legitimacy of the vote was in question. It mentioned that the lawmakers' ability to campaign for the 'No' vote [against Erdoğan] had been undermined by the government. "The conditions for a free and fair plebiscite on proposed constitutional reforms simply do not hold," said a report released by the EU Turkey Civic Commission.[339] Observers from the Organization for Security and Cooperation in Europe (OSCE) confirmed cases of intimidation against the 'No' campaign across the country.[340] Also, after the vote, the opposition claimed election rigging. Only an hour into the vote count, the Supreme Board of Elections declared as valid voting papers without official seals. That practice was clearly in violation of the election laws. The opposition also claimed that in some cities the election observers from the 'No' groups were removed from their polling stations.[341]

Although Erdoğan's re-election as president and the potentially unpleasant options emerging after that do not promise a bright future for Turkey or any of the countries that must deal with Turkey, Erdoğan's defeat could be even more chaotic.

Some of Erdoğan's 20 million to 25 million voters are not just party loyalists but potentially violent groups committed to protect their leader against what they believe will be an international conspiracy in case Erdoğan gets defeated at the ballot box. They will find it hard to believe that the "Sultan" has lost but will instead tend to believe that this must be a plot which they must physically fight. Such an Islamist/nationalist reaction to Erdoğan's election defeat would be a prelude to civil war between pro- and anti-Erdoğan forces, possibly in scenes reminiscent of the left-right street fighting that saw thousands of victims in the 1970s.

There have been worrying signals that the pro-Erdoğan camp may be getting organized for paramilitary warfare. In October 2016, Turkey's religious affairs general directorate, or "Diyanet," issued a circular for the formation of "youth branches" to be associated with the country's tens of thousands of mosques. Initially, the youth branches would be formed in 1,500 mosques. But under the plan, 20,000 mosques would have youth branches by 2021, and finally 45,000 mosques would have them. Observers feared the youth branches could turn into Erdoğan's "mosque militia."[342]

Then there is the curious case of SADAT, an international defense consultancy company, owned by a retired Islamist general who is now one of Erdoğan's chief advisors. [343] SADAT defines its mission as "providing consultancy and military training services at the international defense and interior security sector." Opposition lawmakers have been inquiring about SADAT's activities, suspecting its real mission may be to train official or unofficial paramilitary forces to fight Erdoğan's multitude of wars inside and outside Turkey: "Inside" will mean fighting future dissidents and opposition and "outside" most probably means training jihadists fighting Erdoğan's sectarian wars in countries such as Syria.[344,345]

Most recently, a new organization under the curious banner "the People's Special Forces (HOH)" has emerged. The group defines itself as a "patriotic" gathering of volunteers and does not hide its pro-Erdoğan ideology. Within a year after its formation, its members reached over 22,000 people, some of whom love to pose for cameras with heavy guns.[346]

Ironically, HOH burst onto the political scene when Erdoğan passed a controversial state of emergency decree that grants immunity to civilians deemed to have helped thwart an attempted coup. The new law says people who acted to "suppress" [*i.e.*, killed, for instance, others to thwart a putsch] the July 2016 coup attempt would not face prosecution. Critics, including former President Gul, say that the language of the law is so vague that it could provoke [pro-Erdoğan] groups to attack and kill opposition protesters, link it to the failed coup and escape prosecution.[347]

No matter how the vote count officially ends, Election 2019 will unlikely bring any good fortune to Turkey.

CHAPTER 9

Turkey's War on Minority Schools

• By Uzay Bulut

In recent years, Turkey is mostly in the news for its unending crisis situations that include but are not limited to Islamic State (IS) jihadist activities and an increasingly Islamizing education system with courses about "jihad"[348] introduced to curricula.

The media is also filled with reports about the Turkish government's targeting, arresting, repressing, dismissing and, in some cases, torturing of Turkish citizens.[349] Turkey's Human Rights Joint Platform (IHOP) reported on 18 September 2017 that since the failed coup attempt of 2016, at least 140,000 people had lost their jobs. At least 60,000 people had been arrested. Trustees were appointed by the government to at least 980 companies, 94 municipalities, and 145 media outlets.[350]

According to a by Committee to Protect Journalists, Turkey remains the world's worst jailer of journalists for the second consecutive year when it comes to jailing reporters for their work, with 73 journalists behind bars.

Also, the Turkish Minister of Justice announced that, as of this writing, 69,301 students currently were behind bars in Turkey.[351] "Under statutory decrees, 5,717 academics from 117 universities in 81 cities have been discharged", the Turkish news outlet Bianet reported on September 19.[352]

Much of the world media seems to be shocked particularly by the recent purging of academics: What has happened to Turkey, which is commonly assumed by the West to be a "democratic" and "secular" country? The government's targeting of educators and schools, however, in fact has been a norm in Turkey for decades. And the main victims have been minority citizens.

A closer look at what has for decades been done by Turkish governments to minority schools and how this has possibly affected Turkey culturally and intellectually will provide us with a clearer understanding of why the country is in a deep cultural and political chaos today.

Majority-Christian Before Islam

Discrimination against non-Muslim communities in Turkey did not start with the ruling Islamic government of the Justice and Development Party (AKP). Christians, Jews, Yazidis and Alevis in what is today termed "Turkey" have for centuries been exposed to persecution and slaughters.

Originally from Central Asia, Turkic nomadic tribes were Islamized in the tenth century, replacing their shamanistic religions. They then targeted Armenia, and Asia Minor, and started conquering them following the defeat of the Byzantines at the Battle of Manzikert (Malazgirt) in 1071. The scholar Brian Todd Carey writes that "The enduring legacy of Manzikert comes from its convenient use by historians, from the medieval period to now, as a turning point in Byzantine history, a military defeat often portrayed as the beginning of the decline of Byzantium and a martial event that ushered in the cultural transformation of Asia Minor from a bastion of Christian Orthodoxy to the eventual Islamic heartland of modern Turkey."[353]

Asia Minor and Armenia were ruled by the Byzantine (Eastern Roman) Empire when Muslim Turks arrived in the eleventh century and started occupying large territories in the region which were then majority-Christian and had sizable Jewish communities. According to professor Franklin Hugh Adler, Jews have been living continuously in Asia Minor from Biblical times, mentioned by Aristotle and several Roman sources, including Josephus.

Adler writes: "Jews, in fact, had inhabited this land long before the birth of Mohammed and the Islamic conquests of the seventh and eighth centuries, or for that matter, the arrival and conquests of the Turks, beginning in the eleventh century. On the eve of the birth of Islam, most of world Jewry lived under Byzantine or Persian rule in the lands of the Mediterranean basin."[354]

The Greeks, Armenians, and Assyrians were among the original inhabitants and builders of the cities in the region. Even the names of the region originate from Greek: "Anatolia" (literally, "place of the rising sun" in Greek) and "Asia Minor" (from the Greek "Mikra Asia" - Little Asia). Ancient Asia Minor was the site of the kingdoms and cities such as Thrace, Pontus, Armenia, Assyria, and Troy. The accomplishments of the peoples of Asia Minor both in the ancient world and during the Byzantine Empire were enormous in many fields, including but not limited to historiography, philosophy, literature, art, architecture, trade, as well as advancements in scientific inquiry and method.

In 1299, however, Asia Minor fell to the Ottoman Empire and, after its collapse, became Turkey. And this history is largely the history of persecution and discrimination against non-Muslims—Christians, Jews,

Yazidis, Alevis, and others as well as of the decline of the cultural growth of the region.

The Ottoman Empire, which in 1515 imposed the death penalty on anyone using a printing press to print books in Turkish or Arabic, also greatly thwarted the cultural development of the peoples under its rule. That prohibition is widely cited by historians as one of the major reasons for the intellectual and scientific collapse of Islam at the dawn of the industrial revolution. Ironically, because of that ban, the first books to be published in the Ottoman Empire were in Hebrew in the city of Safad (now located in northern Israel). [355]

Scholar Theo Pavlidis writes[356]:

> "The printing press had been invented by Gutenberg around the time of the fall of Constantinople. It did not go unnoticed in Ottoman lands, but this invention of the devil (as religious leaders claimed) was banned by a decree issued by Bayazid II in 1485. However, a Jewish press was approved about 20 years later on the condition it prints only texts in the Hebrew alphabet. An Armenian press was approved in 1567 and a Greek one in 1627, each limited to the respective alphabets. Printing of Arabic characters was considered sacrilegious and it was not permitted. It was only in 1727, almost 300 years after the invention of the printing press, that printing in Turkish with Arabic characters was allowed."

Christian Persecution and Genocide

Many Western news outlets refer only to the persecution of the Christians in Ottoman Turkey in the 20th century as the historical background in their coverage of the discrimination that Christians in Turkey are currently subjected to.

The scholar Raymond Ibrahim rightfully challenged a 2009 news report of *Reuters*, which merely mentioned the 20th century, rather than how the territory which is now termed 'Turkey" was first invaded by Turkish Islamic armies. [357]

"Christians," wrote Ibrahim, "are merely the remnant descendants of the original, and conquered, inhabitants of 'Turkey,' or 'Anatolia'... Why does this account begin with the 20th century? Why not begin with, say, the battle of Manzikert (1071), when the invading Seljuk Turks first gained major ground in Anatolia, annexing a major chunk from the Byzantines, and slaughtering Christians by the thousands?"

The Islamic conquest of the region was completed with the Ottoman invasion of Constantinople (now Istanbul) in 1453, bringing an end to Byzantine Empire. [358] Under the Ottoman rule, the Christians and Jews became "dhimmis", third-class, barely "tolerated" people in their dispossessed land, and having to pay a tax—the jizya—in exchange for so-called "protection."[359]

What completely changed the demographics and culture of the region was the 1914-1923 Christian genocide. Before the genocide, the population of the territory that is now Turkey was about 15 million, about 4.5 million of which was Christian (nearly a third)[360]. Today, one can hardly even talk of a Christian minority in Turkey, whose entire population is almost 80 million. Only 0.2 % of Turkey's population today is Christian or Jewish. What has happened?

As dhimmis, Christians across Ottoman Turkey were exposed to widespread discrimination, pressures, and massacres such as the mass killings in the mid-1890s.[361] The 1914-1923 genocide, however, dwarfed the previous massacres. The greatest reason for the shrinking of Christian population is that Christians were largely exterminated during and after the World War One by the Turkish Committee of Union and Progress (CUP), otherwise known as the Young Turks, and the Turkish nationalist movement that later founded the Turkish Republic in 1923.

The scholars Colin Tatz and Winton Higgins write in their 2016 book *The Magnitude of Genocide* that the Young Turks "adopted an authoritarian ethnic nation-state based on Türklük ('Turkishness'), which included linguistic uniformity and Islamic adherence... Thereupon the non-Turkish-speaking Christian minorities in Anatolia became a 'problem' to be solved as part of the ethnic nation-building enterprise." The Armenian genocide "was certainly racially based in the ethnic, religious, and linguistic senses.[362]

"Turkish paramilitaries dealt with the three Christian minorities (Armenians, Assyrians, and Greeks) through pogroms, deportations, and other atrocities laced with spectacular and gratuitous sadism. The Turks deployed concentration camps and special killing units; they engaged in massacres, public butchering, drownings, and poisonings; they employed elementary gas chambers, medical experiments, starvation, and death marches. (A quarter of a century later, the German Nazi regime would assiduously replicate all of these genocidal methods.) French-Armenian historian Raymond Kevorkian estimates the death toll included 1.5 million

Armenians, between 750,000 and 900,000 Greeks, and between 275,000 and 400,000 Christian Assyrians."

The genocide was also religiously based—Islamic jihad was a major determinant of the atrocities committed against Christians. The historian, Tigran Matosyan, writes in his article "Comparative Cases of Armenian and Jewish Cases of Genocide"[363] that:

"In the case of the Armenian Genocide, the Young Turks harkened back to the concept of Holy War. By declaring jihad in November 1914, the Turkish government intended to channel Muslim religious sentiments not only against the Christian powers but also against the 'disloyal infidels' within the Ottoman state. To understand how successful this propaganda technique was in 1915-1916, one should turn to survivor accounts and memoirs that describe the Turkish and Kurdish mobs attacking Armenian caravans with shouts and cries of 'Allah' and 'Jihad'."

In 2007, the International Association of Genocide Scholars (IAGS) announced that "the Ottoman campaign against Christian minorities of the Empire between 1914 and 1923 constituted a genocide against Armenians, Assyrians, and Pontian and Anatolian Greeks."[364]

Turkey: Ethnicization of Islam

In an attempt to make a clear distinction between his government and previous Turkish governments, Turkish President Recep Tayyip Erdoğan often uses the terms "Old Turkey" and "New Turkey". To him, his government represents the "New Turkey", a new regime that has unchained the shackles of the "Old Turkey", an anti-democratic state. To that effect, he says, he has introduced widespread democratic reforms in the country. To his critics, however, the "Old Turkey", founded by Mustafa Kemal Ataturk in 1923, was a democracy with equal rights for all and the "New Turkey", ruled by Erdoğan, is an authoritarian regime that violates rights and freedoms of Turkey's citizens. But is there really that much difference between the so-called "old" and "new" Turkey?

First of all, secularism in the sense of equality among religions or at least respect for all religions has never existed in Turkey.

A year after the Turkish republic was established in 1923, the Presidency of Religious Affairs, referred to in Turkish simply as the Diyanet, was established in 1924 after the abolition of the Ottoman Caliphate, by the then-ruling Kemalist government as a successor to Sheikh ul-Islam (the authority that governed religious affairs of the Muslims in the Ottoman Empire).[365] Although the Diyanet has many branches, the first duty of the

High Board of Religious Affairs, according to its official website, is "To make decisions, share views and answer questions on religious matters by taking into consideration the fundamental source texts and methodology, and historical experience of the Islamic religion as well as current demands and needs."[366]

Contrary to Turkey's claims of being a secular republic, the objective of the Diyanet, appears to keep religion (Islam) under the control of the state, and to keep the public under the control of the state by means of religion.[367]

The newly founded Turkish republic not only regarded Islam as the dominant religion and institutionalized it with the establishment of the Diyanet, but also turned Islam into an "ethnic identity." Professor Yeşim Bayar explains in her book "Formation of the Turkish Nation-State, 1920–1938"[368]:

> "During the early 1920s the debate about the constituent elements of Turkishness brought forth the issue of the specific positioning of religion and ethnicity within the matrix of belonging.

> "Throughout this period, the place of Islam as a determinant of the rules of belonging was revealed in various speeches and statements by the political elite. As Rasih Bey conveyed: [When we say] Turk, it means Islam. All the Muslim world and also Europe accept that the world of Islam is referred to as [that of the Turks].

> "During the 1920s the addresses of the deputies equally express how they perceived the Muslim character of the nation as part of definition of Turkishness. Mehmet Seref (Aykut) Bey's statement is an instance of this ethnicization of religion: The Turks took the Koran in their hands, and they shed all their blood for its glorification. Here is the history of Islam. This is a nation which... has executed the sacred and sublime duty that had been handed over to it without batting an eye. During his address to the TBMM [Turkish parliament] in 1922, Mustafa Kemal asserted: Turk and Islam- the Turkish state is going to be the most fortunate state in the world owing to the fact that it is the source for the manifestation of these two [elements]."

Muslim Turks: 'The True Owners of Turkey'

In the founding phase of the new republic, the Turkish MPs in the parliament also dealt with questions such as "who are the true owners of Turkey?" and "what to do to the minorities?"

"The MPs in Ankara conceptualized the term minorities as those who were not the true owners of the nation," writes Bayar. "The Greek-Orthodox and Armenian communities were especially singled out as having been the ungrateful children of the Ottoman Empire, as having abused Ottoman tolerance. Mustafa Kemal's speech at the Adana Turkish hearth (March 1923) was strong in its denunciation of the Armenians[369]:

> "The Armenians have no right whatsoever in this beautiful country. Your country is yours, it belongs to Turks. This country was Turkish in history; therefore, it is Turkish and it shall live on as Turkish to eternity... Armenians and so forth have no rights whatsoever here. These bountiful lands are deeply and genuinely the homeland of the Turk."[370]

Turkey's current President Recep Tayyip Erdoğan and many officials of his Justice and Development Party (AKP) have made several anti-Western statements. For example, Erdoğan said on November 27, 2014: "I speak openly; foreigners love oil, gold, diamonds, and the cheap labor force of the Islamic world. They like the conflicts, fights and quarrels of the Middle East. Believe me, they don't like us."[371] Engaging in anti-Western rhetoric is not a new phenomenon for Turkey, however. According to Bayar:

> "During this period [1920-1938], the nationalist elite very often and zealously articulated anti-Western and anti-Christian sentiments... The Western world represented a body which was working toward the annihilation of Islam. Within this framework, the issue of minorities was further conceptualized as a struggle between Muslims and Christians... All internal tensions were attributed to external sources (i.e., Western powers)."[372]

1924 Treaty of Lausanne: Creation of Turkey

Turkey was one of the last states that sat down to the negotiation table with the Allied Powers. The 1924 Treaty of Lausanne, which set the boundaries of republican Turkey, also became the defining document for the rights and freedoms to be provided for the non-Muslim minorities.[373]

"Under the Lausanne treaty the Armenian, Jewish and Greek Orthodox communities were recognized as minorities," Bayar writes. "Accordingly, they were accorded certain rights and freedoms as Turkish nationals. These included freedom of movement; the right to establish, manage and control their own charitable, religious and social institutions; the free use of any language in private intercourse, in commerce, in the press and before the courts; and the protection of their religious establishments."[374]

These rights were officially given to Armenian, Greek, and Jewish minorities, however, not of the Turkish free will, but due to Western insistence and pressures.

"During the Lausanne process, many deputies in Ankara expressed that the disagreements over the definition of minority rights in Lausanne were due to Western powers', and specifically Britain's, insistence in protecting their own interests. It was thought that under the guise of equality for all the West was trying to push Christian groups into a more privileged position. According to the deputies, the desired outcome for the Allied Powers was the ultimate weakening of Turkey—a Muslim country—through the destroying of its national unity."[375]

This treaty has never been fully implemented, however. Christians and Jews have been exposed to systematic discrimination, pressures and even pogroms since the founding of the Turkish republic in 1923. Moreover, there is not a single minority in Turkey that has enjoyed the right to own and freely manage their schools, which are actually the inheritance of their ancestors.

According to a 2013 report by Turkey's History Foundation entitled *the Minority Schools from Past to Present*, in the Ottoman Empire, there were 6,437 schools that belonged to religious minorities in 1894 and in Istanbul alone, there were 302. There are only 22 minority schools in Istanbul today. All of the minority schools across Anatolia have been closed down.[376]

The report emphasized that since the early years of the republic, the schools of minority citizens were seen "sources of mischief that promote divisive ideas" and quoted the correspondence of the officials of the Turkish ministry of national education as evidence.

According to the report, there are no departments at universities that train Armenian or Hebrew teachers and the "principle of equality" guaranteed by the 1923 Lausanne Treaty is not practiced by Turkey.

Let's now have a look at how the schools of Armenians, Greeks, and Jews across Turkey have "melted away" since the founding of the Turkish republic and how the government has not even allowed Kurds, Yazidis, and Alevis to run private- or state-funded schools.

Armenian schools

After the 1915 Armenian genocide, many properties belonging to Armenians, including schools, became "lost" or were stolen. That is, they were either destroyed or seized by Turkish government authorities or private persons.

The researcher Raffi Bedrosyan writes that Armenian church and school buildings "disappeared or were converted to other uses. If not burnt and destroyed outright in 1915 or left to deteriorate by neglect, they became converted buildings for banks, radio stations, mosques, state schools, or state monopoly warehouses for tobacco, tea, sugar, etc., or simply private houses and stables for the Turks and Kurds."[377]

The confiscation of Armenian schools continued for decades—even after the founding of the Turkish republic in 1923.

In 1936, the Turkish government requested that minority foundations provide a list of their owned assets and properties. In 1974, new legislation was passed that stated that non-Muslim trusts could not own more property than that which had been registered under their name in 1936.

"The Turkish government continued the seizure of Armenian assets and the legalization of it up until the 2000s," writes Bedrosyan. "With legislation brought in 1974, more than 1,400 legally obtained assets of the Istanbul Armenian charitable foundations since 1936, were declared illegal and seized by the state."[378]

Dr. Tessa Hofmann, a scholar of Armenian studies, wrote a comprehensive report entitled *"Armenians in Turkey Today"* in 2002.[379]

"Schools are subjected to abusive interference concerning the education of teachers, the number of weekly hours teaching is allowed in the Armenian language, who is and is not allowed to attend an Armenian school or how schools are run. For instance, the authorities can and do paralyze the operations of schools at will. Violent attacks on schools also occur on occasions, though they are more often targeted at churches or cemeteries."

For example, during the anti-Greek pogroms of 6-7 September in 1955, eight Armenian schools were destroyed by Muslim mobs. From 1992 to 1994, a new wave of violence against Armenian schools in Istanbul broke out when the post-Soviet Republic of Azerbaijan once again failed to recapture Karabakh, or Artsakh, an historically Armenian land. In January 1994, Turkish professor Baskin Oran stated that Armenian schools and churches were stoned and shot at.[380]

Even today it is still difficult for the Armenian community, which numbers around 60,000, to maintain their schools as the Armenian population keeps declining and pressures on the community are still widespread. For example, racist and hate-filled graffiti were written on the walls of several Armenian schools in Istanbul last year (2016).[381]

Greek Schools

The Turkish government has also confiscated much of the real estate including schools belonging to Greek Orthodox Christians. The current Greek population in the country is estimated at fewer than two thousand. As the Greek community has become nearly extinct due to many state-sponsored attacks and much pressure, many Greek schools are now used by Turks.[382]

Helsinki Watch carried out a fact-finding mission to Turkey in October 1991 and published a comprehensive report.[383]

"Helsinki Watch found that education is a matter of great concern to the Greek minority. Greek children are not allowed to study Greek history; teachers from Greece who are supposed to teach the children Greek, English, music, gym and art are not permitted to arrive in Turkey until the school year is well under way; Greek-language textbooks are old and out of date; students are discouraged from speaking Greek; and the Greek community cannot control the hiring or assignment of teachers or access to schoolbooks.

"A man reported: 'Greek clerics are not allowed to enter the Greek schools; if they do, they are called in by police and interrogated. Also, there's a small chapel in the Greek consulate; sometimes we go there for holidays. If the police see you, they call you in and interrogate you'.

"Helsinki Watch concludes that the Greek minority has been denied equal treatment in education and the right to control its schools, in violation of international human rights agreements, the Lausanne Treaty and the Turkish Constitution."

But finding these facts was no easy task for Helsinki Watch as Greeks were not willing to speak out about their problems due to fear of violence: "Greeks in Istanbul who met with Helsinki Watch looked over their shoulders apprehensively, afraid their conversations were being observed. A principal of a Greek school continually asked a teacher to lower her voice as she described problems of the Greek children. A well-dressed, middle-class businessman shook with fright as he related his difficulties and fears. Some Greeks who were asked by intermediaries to meet with us refused. Interviews with Greeks willing to talk were arranged in a secretive, cloak-and-dagger fashion."[384]

The Greek community is literally on the verge of extinction today - all the governmental and public pressures against the Greek-speaking Orthodox citizens bore fruit: In 2016, only nineteen Greek students graduated from three Greek schools in Turkey, reported the weekly newspaper Agos.[385] In the 1926-27 school year, however, there were 58 schools belonging to Greek community in Turkey with 7213 students. Only five have survived, according to Yannis Demircioglu, the principle of the Greek Zografyan High School.

Greek schools have also been subject to violent attacks. During the anti-Greek pogroms on 6–7 September 1955, for example, Turkish mobs devastated the Greek districts of Istanbul, destroying and looting their places of worship, homes, offices, and businesses, among others. The Greek Patriarchate in Istanbul reported that thirty-six Greek schools had been devastated during the attacks.[386]

Turkey's Greek-speaking Orthodox citizens still cannot freely obtain education in their institutions. The Halki seminary in Istanbul, or the Theological School of Halki, the main theological school of the Ecumenical Patriarchate of Constantinople, was closed down by the Turkish state in 1971[387] and has not been reopened.

Jewish Schools

Dr. Andrew Bostom, the author of several books and articles about Turkey and Islamic antisemitism, examines in his book *The Legacy of Islamic Antisemitism: From Sacred Texts to Solemn History* what he calls "the tragic living legacy of Turkish antisemitism: from the archetypal Islamic Jew hatred and general anti-dhimmi attitudes of the Ottoman Empire, to their persistence and transmogrification into racially-based antisemitism by the bizarre and bigoted Turco-centric racial theories promoted under Ataturk and his successors."[388]

"Ignorance about the plight of Jews under Turkish rule—past, including Ottoman Palestine, and present—is profound," writes Bostom, who—unlike many Western analysts or historians—does not shy away from discussing the persecution of Jews under Kemalist governments: "Ataturk's regime and the CHP-lead Republican governments of his successors manifested their own discriminatory attitudes towards non-Muslims, generally, including specific outbursts of antisemitic persecution—most notably the Thracian pogroms of July, 1934."

It was during this period that Jewish "Alliance" Schools were exposed to pressures and were eventually closed down.[389]

In Turkey, in 1912, the Alliance Israélite Universelle, the first modern international Jewish organization, possessed 71 boys' schools and 44 girls' schools, of which 52 were in European Turkey (including the Balkans) and 63 in Asian Turkey (including Iraq, etc.).[390]

The Alliance was founded in 1860 to "help their fellow Jews, wherever they were suffering for or discriminated against because of their religion". The network of schools established by the Alliance aimed "to improve the position of the Jews in the Turkish Empire by instruction and education."[391]

Sadly, the Turkish regime has largely destroyed the Jewish cultural heritage and the important network of Alliance schools, which could have greatly contributed to Turkey.

The researcher Ahmet Hilmi Guven wrote in his PHD thesis:[392]

"In early 1924, Alliance directors in the provinces began to report that the Turkish educational authorities were creating problems, refusing to recognize the schools as Alliance institutions, insisting that they be called communal schools. In March 1924, the Alliance schools were ordered by the Ministry of Education to cease all contact with the organization in Paris. Juridically, this spelled the end of the Alliance in Turkey.

"Characterization of these schools changed with the 1924 law of Unification of Education, into communal schools, and with the introduction of Turkish as the language of instruction, these schools ceased to be Alliance schools."

The last of the Alliance Israélite Schools in Turkey was closed down in 1937.

Riza Nur, the Turkish envoy at the Conference of Lausanne and the Minister of National Education of Turkey, had addressed the Turkish parliament in 1923 to brief the deputies about the negotiations in Lausanne. He said:

> *"[Referring to the population exchange with Greece] Minorities will not remain here. With the exception of Istanbul.... [Voices from the floor: Armenians?] But my dear friends, how many Armenians are there? [Voices from the*

floor: the Jews?] There are about 30.000 Jews in Istanbul.
They have not caused any trouble so far [noises from the
floor]. You know the Jews: they would go in whichever way
they are pulled. Of course, it would be better if they were not
here."[393]

The closure of Alliance schools was a strong blow to the Jewish existence in Turkey, thus helping Nur come one step closer to realizing his "dreams."

Assyrian schools

The people of the world's oldest Christian communities - variously referred to as Syriacs and Chaldeans, but best known as Assyrians - have inhabited the Middle East since the beginning of recorded history. The scholar Hannibal Travis wrote in his comprehensive article *Native Christians Massacred – The Ottoman Genocide of the Assyrians during World War I*, that:

> *"The Assyrians and other Ottoman Christians, like the Jews,*
> *had suffered from centuries of discrimination and official*
> *segregation; were charged with being agents of foreign*
> *powers and scapegoated for military defeats and looming*
> *threats in a rhetoric of ethnic elimination; and were*
> *physically and culturally exterminated in large numbers by*
> *means of massacres, rapes, expulsions, and attacks on homes*
> *and religious institutions carried out by genocidal state*
> *apparatuses and local irregular forces."[394]*

Once the rulers of the greatest empire in history, Assyrians have been turned into a persecuted minority in their native lands. [395] After being exposed to the 1915 genocide at the hands of Ottoman Empire, Assyrian Christians were left out of the 1924 Treaty of Lausanne, which set the boundaries of republican Turkey. The legal rights of Assyrians were not even mentioned in the Lausanne Treaty. Because of that, Assyrians are still not officially recognized as a distinct community and they do not have a primary school or other government-funded institutions in Turkey.[396]

Sait Susin, the chairman of the Beyoglu Assyrian Church of the Virgin Mary Foundation in Istanbul, said in an interview with the Turkish newspaper Radikal in 2012:[397]

> *"When we applied to open a kindergarten that would teach*
> *Assyrian, our demand was denied on the grounds that the*

Turkish citizens belonging to the Assyrian community are not considered a minority, but are merely part of the Turkish nation.

"Our origins go back 3,500 years. The Assyrian language is one of the oldest languages in the world, with a history of 5,500 years. However, it is about to be forgotten, since we are not allowed to establish schools in which we can use our language as the language of education. ... I am the head of the only Assyrian foundation, but I don't know the Assyrian language."

The Istanbul-based newspaper Agos reported in September 2017 that when the application of Assyrians was rejected, they took on a legal struggle and were finally able to open the Mor Efrem kindergarten without any economic support from the government in 2013. But there is still not a Syriac elementary school in Istanbul where the graduates of the kindergarten would be able to enroll.[398]

The Virgin Mary Ancient Syriac Church Foundation in the Beyoğlu district of Istanbul is still struggling to open a Syriac elementary school in the city. The officials of the foundation stated that it is impossible for them to open an elementary school without governmental financial support.

In the Ottoman Empire in 1913-1914, however, there were 2,580 schools belonging to non-Muslims, and 29 of those were Assyrian schools. The last Assyrian school in Turkey, which was located in the city of Mardin, was closed down in 1928 and afterwards, Assyrians were not allowed by Turkish governments to open a primary school where they would be educated in their native language for the next 90 years.

Non-Existent Kurdish Schools

"Soon after the establishment of the Republic of Turkey," reported[399] the Human Rights Watch (HRW), "its government embarked upon a radical program of nation-building. Ethnic diversity was perceived as a danger to the integrity of the state, and the Kurds, as the largest non-Turkish ethnic group, obviously constituted the most serious threat. They were decreed to be Turks, and their language and culture were to be Turkish. All external symbols of their ethnic identity were suppressed.... There was no official discrimination against those Kurds who agreed to be assimilated: they could reach the highest positions in the state apparatus. Those who refused, however, often met with severe repression.

"The use of Kurdish—along with other languages—was prohibited in teaching as was its public use. By 1930, publishing in languages other than Turkish was prohibited by an act of parliament that was heralded under the slogan of "Citizen, Speak Turkish!" (Vatandas, Türkçe Konus!). The Kurdish names of towns and villages in southeastern Turkey were also changed to Turkish."

Kurdish activists in Turkey have been trying to keep their language alive with their own resources and efforts. Even these very limited endeavors, however, are systematically repressed and even criminalized by the Turkish government.

For example, the first Kurdish private primary school in Turkey—named after Ferzad Kemanger, an Iranian-Kurdish teacher hanged by Iran in 2010—was closed down in October of 2016 by the decision of the governor's office in Diyarbakir, in a note that read in part: "The school was closed because it was against the regulations of the Ministry of National Education." The door of the school was sealed by police officers. The school had opened in Diyarbakir in 2014 and had 238 students between the ages of 5 and 11. [400]

A 2015 survey called *Public Dynamics Before the June 2015 Elections*, which was carried out with 2,201 participants from forty-nine Turkish cities, revealed that the views of the vast majority of the Turkish public on the use of Kurdish as a language of instruction were in line with the official ideology of the Turkish government.

In the survey, the voters of the ruling AKP (Justice and Development Party - 78 %) and of the opposition parties - CHP (Republican People's Party - 85 %), and MHP (Nationalist Movement Party - 91 %) - agreed that "All children in Turkey should receive their primary education in Turkish no matter what ethnic group they come from."[401]

Non-existent Yazidi and Alevi schools

The religion of the Yazidis, a persecuted and indigenous ethno-religious minority in the Middle East, has not been recognized by the Turkish state. Even the section of "religion" in Yazidi identity cards has been left empty or has been registered as "x" or left blank.[402] The estimated number of Yazidis in the country is currently around 350, excluding recent asylum seekers from Iraq and Syria.

As for Alevis, the largest religious minority in Turkey, they are not even recognized as a religious community by the Turkish regime either. A law enacted in 1925 during the rule of the CHP, which is still in effect in Turkey, bans Alevi religious centers and denies their faith. Hence, neither Alevis nor

Yazidis have schools in which their children can be educated in accordance with their cultures and values.

The current political crises in Turkey are not only the products of the authoritarian policies of the ruling AKP (Justice and Development Party) government. The Turkish state has allowed only two ideologies to grow and take root in Turkey: Turkish nationalism and Islam. Turkey's domestic politics as well as foreign policy have largely been shaped by these two ideologies. All other ideas, cultures, philosophies and religions have been systematically repressed. Even Turkish ex-Muslims and critics of Islam were subject to much pressure and even murdered. For example, Turan Dursun, a former mufti and imam and an open critic of Islam, was brutally assassinated in front of his house in Istanbul on September 4, 1990[403].

By having destroyed the Armenian, Greek, Jewish, Assyrian, Yazidi, and other non-Muslim or non-Turkish communities and their heritage for over a century, Turkey has also largely destroyed free thought, intellectual diversity, and learning, as well as the opportunity to live in meaningful and peaceful coexistence. What now remains is governmental authoritarianism and cold-blooded murder accompanied by a brutal war environment and continued pressures against minorities and dissidents.

UZAY BULUT is a Turkish journalist formerly based in Ankara, but currently working in Washington, D.C. She graduated from Istanbul's Bogazici University in 2007 with a BA in Translation & Interpreting Studies. She holds a master's degree in Media & Cultural studies from Ankara's Middle East Technical University. Ms. Bulut's journalistic work focuses mainly on the Kurdish issue, antisemitism & Turkey's ethnic & religious minorities.

CHAPTER 10

Censorship in Turkey: The Obliteration of Turkey's Independent Media

• By Deborah Weiss

Information is power. A free and independent press is critical to an informed citizenry. It is therefore not by happenstance that as Turkey descends into authoritarianism, Turkey's President, Recep Tayyip Erdoğan, and his ruling party (the AKP), are using a wide panoply of censorship tactics as a way to cement their power. Turkey and the region in which it resided prior to its existence as a nation state, have a long history of censorship, as complicated as the history of Turkey itself.

Background

Previously an Islamic State under the Ottoman Empire, the new State of Turkey, established in 1923, was, according to its constitution, intended to be a secular state.[404] Turkey's history is intimately intertwined with Islam, however. Since 2014, when then-Prime Minister Recep Tayyip Erdoğan became the first "elected" President of Turkey, working with the Justice and Development Party (AKP), Turkey is once again becoming Islamized,[405] at the same time it is sliding toward authoritarian rule.[406]

While Islamic blasphemy has always been outlawed in Turkey, as it has been in several other Islamic countries, freedom of expression more broadly, and press and media freedom in particular, have been steadily eroding since 2010. Things have only gotten worse since Erdoğan took his seat as President in 2014.[407] Indeed, Erdoğan has used his win in the election as a means to undermine Turkey's democracy. Interestingly, he once famously asserted that "Democracy is like a train. You get off once you have reached your destination."[408]

2013 was a turning point in Turkish history. Peaceful protests to save Istanbul's Gezi Park from a government-supported plan to build a shopping center were met with an overly harsh response from the government. [409] Protestors were beaten, one was killed, and the use of live munition was reported as was the sexual assault of female protestors. The authorities' disproportionate reaction helped the demonstration morph into country-wide anti-government protests that lasted for weeks. Hundreds of thousands of protestors participated.

In turn, the government's abuse only got worse. According to Amnesty International's special report on the Gezi Park protests, authorities violated the human rights of protestors "on a massive scale". The report states that tear gas was aimed directly onto protestors, passersby, and sprayed into residential and medical facilities; that chemicals were added to the water cannons that were also aimed at protestors; that plastic bullets were shot onto protestors' heads and upper bodies; that women were sexually abused; and that many protestors were unlawfully detained. The level of violence employed by the government was inappropriate, excessive and illegal. Alarmingly, the government even sent out one of its military units to control the crowds.

As protestors labelled then-Prime Minister Erdoğan a "dictator", he in turn labelled the protestors "extremists" and warned that those "supporting terrorists" would be held accountable, implying that retribution would follow. [410] Note that Erdoğan does not use the plain meaning of the word "terrorist" as it is understood in the West, but instead labels as a "terrorist" anybody who opposes his government.

Turkey's handling of the situation was indicative of a government unwilling to tolerate dissent. [411] The demonstrations were some of the most significant in recent Turkish history and the unrest shook up Turkey to its core. The events that transpired around the Gezi Park protests are considered to be a marker in Turkey's slide toward authoritarian rule.

A few years later, in July of 2016, there was an attempted coup to oust Erdoğan's Administration, for which Erdoğan blamed Turkish Sunni cleric Fethullah Gülen, who resides in the United States, and was the founder of the Gülen Movement.[412]

The coup attempt failed due to pro-government citizen protests, but the government's response was harsh and has had long-lasting consequences. Erdoğan declared a state of emergency, which was originally intended to last three months, but had been extended every three months. In the end, it lasted for over a year, from July 15, 2016 through the end of October 2017.[413]

During this time, decrees were issued, [414] which had the effect of changing pre-existing laws. Among the most important were those that increased censorship and decreased human rights, political rights, civil rights and rights for minorities, especially the Kurds. Government corruption also drastically increased.

Since 2005, the European Union (EU) had been engaging in discussions with Turkey, contemplating the possibility of Turkey becoming an EU member. Because Turkey is no longer functioning as a democracy under Erdoğan-AKP rule, however, these long-standing negotiations have come to a halt.

The actions of Turkey's government appear to have thwarted all hope for those who aspired to see Turkey become a true democracy. The problems in Turkey are many, but this paper will be confined to specifically address the state of censorship in Turkey during recent and current times.

Jailing Journalists

A free and independent press is a mainstay of a healthy democracy and critical for the freedom of a nation's citizens. It is therefore no coincidence, that the Turkish government under Erdoğan-AKP rule has targeted journalists and the media for intimidation, abuse and jail, using various means of repression and censorship as a tool of tyrannical power.

Over the past five years, Turkey's freedom of expression and press freedom in particular, have drastically declined. Indeed, Freedom House now ranks Turkey's press as "Not Free" as opposed to Free or Partly Free.[415]

Turkey's criminal code includes over three hundred provisions that restrict freedom of expression, religious freedom and freedom of association,[416] all of which are considered fundamental freedoms under the UN Declaration of Human Rights. Under President Erdoğan's rule, hundreds of journalists have been arrested, many of whom do not receive due process or fair trials when prosecuted.[417] Oftentimes, the crimes for which journalists are prosecuted are used as pretext for shutting down factual reporting about the Turkish government or its officials. This includes reporting that criticizes Erdoğan's Administration or that simply supports policies that are in disagreement with those of the Erdoğan government.[418] Additionally, journalists and their families are often precluded from travelling. Indeed, those "under investigation" including politically motivated investigations subsequent to the coup attempt, often have their passports taken away, as do their relatives.

During its twelve-year reign, the AKP has gradually increased its censorship efforts, even prior to the failed coup attempt of 2016. It has always been the case that under the AKP, reporting on "sensitive subjects" was dangerous. Sensitive topics include Kurdish rights, terrorism, the Gülen Movement, criticism of the Turkish government, criticism of the government's policies or government officials (especially the President) and criticism of Islam. [419]

Additionally, numerous broadcast stations were precluded from timely reporting of the results of the June 2015 election, [420] despite the fact that the European Court of Human Rights has criticized Turkey for violating the right to free expression. Much of the reporting that did take place regarding the 2015 election results was extremely partisan and biased. [421]

Media Cover-Up of the Gezi Park Protests

The Gezi Park protests and the government's response constituted one of the most significant periods in recent Turkish history. The government's escalated use of force to break up the protests and the media's steadfast refusal to report on it revealed Turkey's dwindling right to peaceable assembly, freedom of expression, political dissent, and a free and independent media. For example, while CNN International and foreign media broadcast the massive protests, CNN Türk was broadcasting a program about penguins.[422] Turkish media were loathe to report the protests for fear of reprisal, especially if they were critical of the government.

According to the Turkish Journalists Union, at least 72 journalists who persisted in covering the protests lost their jobs. Scores wound up in jail [423] and some were beaten by police. Several channels that aired coverage were issued fines. The pro-AKP media which was permitted to report on the demonstrations largely disseminated disinformation about the events and false reports about the protestors' conduct.

Demonstrators had to rely heavily on social media for updates, causing a boom in its use and importance. Erdoğan blamed Twitter and Facebook for contributing to the protests and temporarily detained scores of people for their tweets and Facebook posts. Though the government denied blocking social media and other relevant websites, when 3G networks and VPNs became temporarily inaccessible, many believed the government was behind it.

Whether the Turkish government overtly pressured the media into censorship and the dissemination of disinformation or whether the media self-censored due to fear makes little difference. The government's authoritarian response to the Gezi Park protests and the media's accompanying cover-up marked a significant backsliding of Turkish democracy.

After the Coup Attempt

Even before the unsuccessful coup attempt in July 2016, Turkey had more journalists in jail than any other country in the Council of Europe. According the Committee to Protect Journalists (CPJ), as of 2016, 81 members of the press sat imprisoned in Turkish jails. [424] This constitutes one third of the entire number of jailed journalists world-over. Indeed, Turkey has more jailed journalists than any other country in the world, including Iran and China. After the attempted coup, the crackdown on the media heightened to a crisis level. During the state of emergency, several decrees were issued that allowed the government to fire journalists, close media outlets and seize their property. And that's exactly what it did. 125,000 judges, teachers, policemen and civil servants were fired by the government. 45,000 people were arrested. Many journalists lost their jobs. 170 media outlets were closed, [425] including 16 television stations, approximately 8 radio stations, and 45 newspapers. Media outlets that survived were largely transferred to supporters of the AKP.

During the state of emergency, 700 journalists had their credentials revoked. [426] Many journalists were placed under investigation, primarily as a means of intimidation. Anti-AKP media organizations were fined; journalists were prosecuted and sometimes harassed. Erdoğan and his cronies would criticize journalists publicly, and often these criticisms led to subsequent death threats against the journalists via social media. Those in the press who were unsympathetic to the AKP also had their non-media livelihoods threatened, for example, if they were business owners. The message was clear: if you don't support with the Turkish government or its policies, censor yourself or lose your job, income stream, and perhaps even your liberty or your life.

Frequently, journalists are not prosecuted outright for their journalism. Instead, they are charged with serious crimes, defamation, or support for terrorism and terror ties pursuant to the overly broad anti-terrorism laws. [427] Clearly these bodies of law are used as cover to jail or intimidate journalists who express unfavorable views. The emergency decrees exacerbated the situation exponentially.

For example, the Gülen Movement was classified as a terrorist organization shortly before the failed coup. Subsequently, any newspapers or broadcasting stations that were connected to or owned by the Gülen movement were closed and their property seized. Journalists who wrote positively about the Gülen movement were prosecuted as being members of a terrorist organization. Most notably, the newspaper *Zaman* and its English language version, *Today's Zaman*, were folded just days after the coup attempt for their ties to the Gülen Movement. [428] These newspapers were the largest opposition newspapers in Turkey.

Some of the other laws under which journalists were aggressively pursued by the Turkish government include[429]:

- Penal Code Article 301 which criminalizes insults to "Turkishness" or official Turkish institutions (often used to punish journalists who criticized Turkey's security troops, for example in the Armenian genocide;

- Penal Code Article 312 which criminalizes incitement to religious and racial hatred (and has somehow been used against those calling for peace with the Kurds);

- Penal Code Article 314 which makes membership in a terrorist organization a crime, (but is used often against journalists who support the Kurds, all of whom the government of Turkey considers terrorists);

- Penal Code Article 220 which penalizes anyone who praises a criminal organization or its objective. Penalties are increased if the message is conveyed through the press or broadcasting. Clearly this section is designed to impinge on free speech rights and interfere with a free and independent press.

- Penal Code Article 125 criminalizes those who defame or libel a person or the religious views of another (also used to punish journalists);

- Penal Code Article 216 bans incitement of hatred or violence based on ethnicity, class, or religion and is often used against journalists;

- Anti-Terrorism laws, i.e., The Law on the Fight Against Terrorism of Turkey and several provisions of the Penal Code are also written in an overbroad manner and used against journalists. They include accusations of "propaganda" for opposing viewpoints or unfavorable reporting. [430]

Turkey's so-called "blasphemy laws" extend beyond the protection of the Islamic religion or Allah and include prohibitions against badmouthing Islam's practitioners or believers in Islam. (See, *e.g.*, Penal Code Articles 125 and 216).

Even after the interim government of the AKP and the cessation of the emergency period, Turkey continues to crack down on, pursue, and intimidate media outlets and journalists. A free and independent media in Turkey no longer exists. The media sector in Turkey has been totally eviscerated and honest reporting is now criminalized. Factual reports that show the government in a bad light or opinion editorials that support oppositional views are banned from the public square. Even cartoons and satire against the government are no laughing matter.

Internet Censorship

The right to receive and impart information is part and parcel of the human right of free expression and media freedom. In today's world of information technology, the internet is a major source of news. It is undoubtedly for that reason that the Turkish government has been on the forefront of internet censorship, shutting down more and more sites with each passing year under AKP and Erdoğan reign.

Internet censorship and the blocking of websites in Turkey has been par for the course, but in time, it is only getting worse. In 2014, the Turkish parliament passed a law giving the Telecommunications Authority (TIB) the power to block websites without a court ruling. [431] Over the years, Turkey has periodically blocked YouTube, Twitter, blogger services and multitudes of other websites based on content or subject matter. Indeed, some of these sites have been subject to total blackouts throughout the country. In the second half of 2014, Twitter's Transparency report revealed that Turkey made 477 requests for Twitter to remove tweets based on their content. This is more than five times as many removal requests than any other country in the world, and an increase of 150 percent from the first half of the year.[432]

As of March 2015, Turkey blocked approximately 68,000 websites, claiming 49 of them violated Turkey's blasphemy laws. Included in this list were Charlie Hebdo and all websites that republished Hebdo's satirical cover of the Muslim Prophet Mohammad. It also blocked the website of Turkey's first atheist organization claiming it was blasphemous, though the government didn't explain how.[433] With the threat of blanket bans on Twitter and Facebook looming large, many social media sites were pressured to self-censor for content even in the absence of a court order.[434]

In addition to sites that were deemed "blasphemous" or "insulting" to Islam, websites that contained information (read "reporting") on controversial political subjects or that expressed anti-AKP opinions were also blocked. As with other media, website blocking and various forms of online internet restrictions showed a sharp rise after the attempted coup of 2016. For example, Twitter, Facebook and YouTube experienced temporary blocks on many occasions as did WhatsApp. Sometimes specific posts or accounts were blocked even when social media was generally accessible. Additionally, specific hashtags were blocked such as #Istanbul and #Ankara, especially after terrorist attacks. These blocks effected millions of Turkish citizens.[435] Posts with satire on these subjects were additionally subject to removal.

As of April 2017, approximately 127,000 websites have been blocked[436] based on religious, social or political content. This includes, but is not limited to, content on Islamic blasphemy, criticism of the nation of Turkey or Turkish government officials, reporting in support of the Kurds, reporting in support of the Gülen Movement, or criticism of the government's anti-Terrorism policies or their implementation.

Four Case Studies In Censorship

There exists almost an innumerable number of censorship cases in Turkey that make it impossible to comprehend the full scope and impact of oppressive tactics surrounding the issue of free expression. Following, however, is a small sampling of cases.

CASE #1: *The Afterlife is No Joke: Fazil Say, 2013*[437]

Fazil Say was a 44-year-old renowned classical and jazz pianist who was charged under the Turkish Penal Code Article 216 for so-called "blasphemous tweets."

He was known to regularly send tweets that denigrated Muslims. In this particular case, he was accused of retweeting a comment stating that all the thieves, low-lifes and buffoons are "Allahists". He was also accused of sending a tweet making fun of the afterlife, using the words of a famous poet. Say was convicted and given a suspended sentence of 10 months.

CASE #2: *Free Speech Advocacy is Blasphemous: Sevan Nişanyan, 2013*[438]

On the heels of Say's conviction, came the conviction of Armenian writer and human rights activist Sevan Nişanyan. Nişanyan was advocate for the Armenian people and wrote frequently on national identity, religion, and Turkey's genocide against the Armenians. He was well-known to be an atheist and frequently received death threats. Nişanyan wrote a blog entry criticizing the government's response to the *Innocence of Muslims* YouTube video. (This video received notoriety after then-Secretary of State Hillary

Clinton falsely blamed the video for the attack on the U.S. consulate in Benghazi.)

The Turkish government had condemned those who insult the Islamic Prophet Mohammad in response to the video and called for the prohibition of criticism of the Muslim Prophet. Nişanyan disagreed with Turkey's handling of the situation and posted his opinion on a blog. He argued that disrespectful speech is part of free speech and should be protected as such. He thinks that people should have the right to believe and speak as they wish, so long as it is done peaceably.

Subsequently, a government Minister publicly verbally attacked Nişanyan for his statements. As a result, Nişanyan received hundreds of death threats. He was prosecuted in twelve Turkish courts and was convicted to 15.5 months in jail for blasphemous speech under Article 216 of the Turkish Penal Code. Not insignificantly, Nişanyan was already serving a two-year jail sentence for alleged building code violations. Selective prosecution is commonplace in Turkey, however, and many thought Nişanyan was specifically targeted for expressing his views on the Armenian genocide and religion. It is likely that the building code violation prosecution was pretextual. After the conviction for his blog post, Nişanyan was interviewed. He correctly noted that his case was indicative that free speech in Turkey, especially regarding Islam, was in grave danger.

CASE #3: *The Red Stiletto Tweet,* 2014[439]
In 2014, an unnamed woman tweeted a photo of a woman's foot in a red stiletto high-heeled shoe stepping on pages of the Quran. Then-Mayor of Ankara, Melih Gökçek of the AKP filed a complaint and the woman was arrested. Gökçek is reported to have filed approximately 3,000 lawsuits against those who have insulted him personally, an act which is illegal under Turkish law as he's a government official.

Gökçek retweeted the blasphemous red stiletto tweet with the caption, "No one has a right to insult our religion". Ironically, his shared tweet is the most notable place that this forbidden photo can be found.

CASE #4: *Wikipedia: Reports on Turkish Government Verboten,* 2017
The blocking of Wikipedia in 2017 constitutes one of Turkey's largest and most significant censorship scandals. The Turkish government had requested that Wikipedia remove entries that reported on Turkey's support for various terrorist groups[440] as well as its involvement with the Syrian conflict. When Wikipedia denied the request, Turkey's response was to

permanently block Wikipedia on a country-wide scale, restricting access to it in all languages.[441] Many people were able to circumvent the blocks using a virtual private network (VPN). The government has since blocked many of the VPNs as well.[442]

Propaganda

Though Turkey's constitution guarantees freedom of expression, its promise rings hollow as it is gutted by the overbroad anti-terrorism laws, the referendums passed during the extended "state of emergency" and the pro-government judicial interpretations issued by biased courts. (Over 2500 judges and prosecutors have been fired, jailed or "gone missing". Evidence-free accusations of ties to the Gülen Movement were used to justify the mass firings).[443]

As discussed previously, the media are pressured to self-censor under threat of prosecution, job loss, and other types of harassment and intimidation. Additional government control of the media takes the form of propaganda and influence over reporting. Part of this has been achieved merely by ensuring that those now running media outlets are government sympathizers. After cleaning house of virtually all journalists that reported independently from the government, the government seized the assets of much of the remaining media and transferred control to pro-AKP supporters. Moreover, those who report favorably on the government are enticed by preferential treatment.

The government, in effect, now has control over much of the media and can determine or heavily influence what topics are reported and how. All objectivity has been lost. The media no longer has any balance. Turkish citizens have nowhere to go for unbiased information or alternative viewpoints.[444]

It's critical to note that the role of a free and independent press is to provide accurate information to the public and to hold the government accountable. This check on government power in Turkey has ceased to exist. For example, the obliteration of objective reporting played a substantial role in the outcome of the vote on the referendum to make amendments to the Turkish Constitution, held in May 2017. The referendum proposed was effectively tailor-made to fit President Erdoğan, and even though citizens "voted" on the referendum, the media informing them was biased and one-sided. Information on key elements of the referendum was not provided.[445] For this and numerous other problems pertaining to the referendum vote (that are not the subject of this paper), the anti-referendum position had little chance of winning.

The government's relationship to the media has moved from censorship to co-opting to state control of the media. It is the consensus of many human rights and free press advocates that the free and independent press in Turkey has been obliterated with no signs of resuscitation on the horizon.

Turkey and the Organization of Islamic Cooperation

The Organization of Islamic Cooperation (OIC) is a body comprised of 56 UN Member States plus the Palestinian Authority. It was formed after the demise of the Ottoman Empire with the purpose of galvanizing the Islamic *ummah* and serving as its unified voice. Many experts believe that the OIC constitutes a proto-Caliphate.[446]

One of the main objectives of the OIC is to criminalize so-called "Islamophobia",[447] which, while ill-defined, in application includes anything that sheds a negative light on Islam, even, and perhaps especially, if true. Notably, Turkey was a founding member of the OIC. [448] Furthermore, from 2004-2014, the OIC was headed by Secretary General Ekmeleddin İhsanoğlu from Turkey.[449]

The OIC constitutes the largest voting bloc in the UN. Under İhsanoğlu's leadership, the OIC spearheaded numerous UN resolutions to condemn "defamation of religions", by which it meant "defamation of Islam". Indeed, the first proposed resolution on this topic was titled "Defamation of Islam" but it failed to get sufficient support. Subsequent resolutions embodied similar text, calling only the religion of Islam out by name, but the titles of the resolutions were changed to "Defamation of Religions."

Additionally, in 2005, the OIC launched its *Ten Year Programme of Action*, a major component of which was to combat "Islamophobia". It promulgated, along with then-Secretary Hillary Clinton, an international process to implement the now-infamous Resolution 16/18, which in practice serves largely to whitewash the religious motivations of Islamic terrorist groups. It operates through engagement and dialogue with the relevant communities and "training" national security professionals not to see religious ideology as a root cause of terrorism, despite the admission of such by the terrorist groups themselves.[450]

Essentially, the OIC is attempting to impose Islamic blasphemy laws on Western countries by using language that masks the true nature of the speech censorship sought. Rather than couching religiously offensive language as "blasphemy", the OIC has deftly referred to such speech as "defamation", "slander" or "Islamophobia", all words that naïve Westerners associate with bigotry, prejudice or false statements.

In 2012, then-Prime Minister Erdoğan, prior to becoming President, similarly called on the West to declare that "Islamophobia is a crime against humanity". He pushed for "international legal regulations against attacks on what people deem sacred, on religion."[451] Erdoğan echoes the OIC's assertion that freedom of speech has limits, can be abused and precludes the expression of speech deemed blasphemous. "Freedom of thought and belief ends where the freedom of thought and belief of others start. You can say anything about your own thoughts and beliefs, but you will have to stop when you are at the border of others [sic] freedoms."[452]

It is, of course, impossible to determine where one person's thoughts stop and another's start. Additionally, blasphemy laws are often used to persecute religious minorities. If a Christian asserts that Jesus is the Son of God, that could be viewed as blasphemous to Islam and therefore outlawed. Moreover, these laws often are coupled with corruption and mere accusations wind up jailing people simply to settle personal or familial scores. Erdoğan, like İhsanoğlu, called for domestic and international laws to outlaw speech blasphemous speech. Though it was worded in religiously neutral language, in its application and intent, it was clear that his outrage applied only to Islamic blasphemy.

Erdoğan announced that Turkey would immediately work to ban blasphemous, sacrilegious and offensive speech. Boasting, he proclaimed his belief that Turkey could lead the world by example in outlawing such speech.[453] The "respect" demanded by Erdoğan, the OIC and other Islamic supremacists is really a demand for compliance with Islamic blasphemy laws. Reciprocity for such respect to other religions is neither expected nor given. Turkey is inching toward world leadership as an Islamic nation, as the OIC encourages other Muslim countries to move in this direction as well.

Conclusion

Speech censorship and the complete evisceration of the independent media sector in Turkey should be seen within the context of Turkey's creeping authoritarian government and its slide toward tyranny and oppression.

Free speech censorship and government-controlled media is taking place in the midst of a climate of fear. Religious freedom and freedom of association have drastically declined. Many non-governmental organizations (NGOs), and think tanks have been folded by the Turkish government. There is no more academic freedom and no more freedom of thought on political matters in any forum. In effect, the criminalization of the media has gone hand in hand with the criminalization of political opposition.

While Turkey has always had some degree of censorship, especially regarding Islamic blasphemy, in years prior to Erdoğan's rule, some degree of economic and political reforms had been made,[454] giving hope that Turkey might one day be a true democracy. Erdoğan has since reversed many of those reforms, however. With the rise of the Presidential state, Turkey is no longer a nation of laws but a nation of men.

With the ascendency of the Erdoğan Presidency comes the gradual realization of Erdoğan's vision of Turkey as an Islamic state. At the same time, we have witnessed a drastic backsliding of human rights, political rights, and civil rights in Turkey, including but not limited to the freedom of expression and a free and independent press.

These rights are now dead in Turkey and with it the hope of her citizens. The dream of Turkish democracy is fast becoming a nightmare of corruption and Islamic authoritarianism. The United States and other Western countries should admit this unfortunate fact and stop pretending that Turkey is the democratic republic that it feigns to be.

DEBORAH WEISS, ESQ., is a Senior Fellow at the Center for Security Policy. She is an attorney, author & public speaker specializing in free speech & terrorism-related issues & is considered an expert on the Organization of Islamic Cooperation (OIC) & the Council on American Islamic Relations (CAIR), the U.S. branch of HAMAS. Formerly, Ms. Weiss was the Manhattan Director for the Forbes for President Campaign; Assistant Corporation Counsel in the Giuliani Administration & a Counsel for the Committee on House Oversight in Congress. She is the author of dozens of published articles as well as author/contributing author of several books.

References

[1] https://www.youtube.com/watch?v=GdBAUNQ5b2w

[2] http://ahmetsaltik.net/tag/rt-Erdoğan-demokrasi-bizim-icin-bir-tramvaydir-istedigimiz-duraga-gelince-ineriz/

[3] We know this because when one of Erdoğan's advisors was confronted by an American Turkish-speaker who complained that the translation was NOT what the then Turkish Prime Minister said, the aid's face turned visibly red. He was totally caught off guard and demanded that the American Turkish-speaker shut up.

[4] https://web.archive.org/web//http://www.thememriblog.org/turkey/blog_personal/en/2595.htm

[5] For more on the role of truces in Islam, see , see Modern Islamic Warfare—An Ancient Doctrine Marches On, pages 27-29.

[6] https://www.salon.com/2016/06/30/turkeys_double_game_on_isis_and_support_for_extremist_groups_highlighted_after_horrific_istanbul_attack/

[7] https://www.alarabiya.net/articles/2011/09/14/166814.html

[8] *Ibid.*

[9] https://en.wikipedia.org/wiki/Yusuf_al-Qaradawi

[10] https://www.youtube.com/watch?v=_ob1bkqBHCE

[11] Alevis are a separate group in Turkey that are more closely religiously aligned with the Shiism of Iran and Iraq. Turkish Sunnis see these Alevis as lowlifes, brigands, and sexually "permissive." Erdoğan's government is doing its best to make them into Sunnis, by building mosques in Alevi towns and villages. Alevis do not pray and congregate in mosques. For more on the Alevis, see https://en.wikipedia.org/wiki/Alevism.

[12] https://www.dailysabah.com/diplomacy/2017/12/06/jerusalem-red-line-for-all-muslims-president-Erdoğan-says

[13] Quran: Chapter 5:20-21

[14] http://www.hurriyetdailynews.com/obama-names-turkish-pm-Erdoğan-among-trusted-friends-11897

[15] https://www.yenisafak.com/en/news/money-intimidation-cannot-buy-will-Erdoğan-tells-us-2911257

[16] For more on this concept, see Modern Islamic Warfare…, p.33.

[17] Known in Islamic law (Shari'a) as "Dar al-Harb"

[18] Frank Gaffney, Center for Security Policy, "The Muslim Brotherhood in America," https://www.centerforsecuritypolicy.org/the-muslim-brotherhood-in-america/

[19] Sayed Qutb Shaheed, "Milestones," http://www.izharudeen.com/uploads/4/1/2/2/4122615/milestones_www.izharudeen.com.pdf

[20] For a comprehensive explanation of the USCMO's origin and its impact to American pillars of society, please reference the Center for Security Policy's book publication "Star Spangled Shariah: The Rise of America's First Muslim Brotherhood Party" released on 1 September 2015, https://www.centerforsecuritypolicy.org/2015/09/15/bookrelease-star-spangled-shariah-the-rise-of-americas-first-muslim-brotherhood-party/

21 University of Minnesota, Human Rights Library, "The Cairo Declaration on Human Rights in Islam," http://hrlibrary.umn.edu/instree/cairodeclaration.html

22 Center for Security Policy, "Book Release: Star Spangled Shariah: The Rise of America's First Muslim Brotherhood Party," 15 September 2015 https://www.centerforsecuritypolicy.org/2015/09/15/book-release-star-spangled-shariah-the-rise-of-americas-first-muslim-brotherhood-party/

23 Gregg Carlstrom, "Egypt Declares Brotherhood Terrorist Group," *Al Jazeera*, 25 December 2013 http://www.aljazeera.com/news/middleeast/2013/12/egypt-declares-brotherhood-terrorist-group-201312251544398545.html

24 "Egypt court upholds Muslim Brotherhood ban," *Al Jazeera*, 6 November 2013 http://www.aljazeera.com/news/middleeast/2013/11/egypt-court-upholds-muslim-brotherhood-ban-2013116101936365849.html?xif=]

25 "Egyptian court sentences 529 Brotherhood members to death," *Reuters*, 24 March 2014 https://www.reuters.com/article/us-egypt-brotherhood-courts/egyptian-court-sentences-529-brotherhood-members-to-death-idUSBREA2N0BT20140324

26 Amena Bakr and William Maclean, "Egypt's Brotherhood struggles to regroup in exile," *Reuters*, 23 May 2014 https://www.reuters.com/article/us-egypt-brotherhood-exile/egypts-brotherhood-struggles-to-regroup-in-exile-idUSBREA4M0BJ20140523

27 US Council of Muslim Organization, Press Releases, "Witnessing Turkish Democracy in Action," August 27, 2014, http://www.uscmo.org/council-news/

28 See for full details From the Archives of the Muslim Brotherhood in America: An Explanatory Memorandum on the General Strategic Goal for the Group in North America at http://www.centerforsecuritypolicy.org/wpcontent/uploads/2014/05/Explanatory_Memoradum.pdf

29 "An Explanatory Memorandum on the General Strategic Goals for the Group in North America," as published by the Center for Security Policy. PDF available online at http://www.centerforsecuritypolicy.org/wpcontent/uploads/2014/05/Explanatory_Memoradum.pdf

30 *Ibid.*

31 Robert Spencer, Jihad Watch, "Asked to condemn Hamas, Hussam Ayloush of Hamas-linked CAIR gives dishonest, bullying answer," 20 November 2013 http://www.jihadwatch.org/2013/11/asked-to-condemn-hamas-hussam-ayloush-of-hamas-linked-cair-gives-dishonest-bullying-answer

32 Robert Spencer, Jihad Watch, "Nihad Awad of Hamas-linked CAIR refuses to condemn Hamas," 26 January 2011 http://www.jihadwatch.org/2011/01/nihad-awad-of-hamas-linked-cair-refuses-to-condemn-hamas

33 U.S. Department of State, "Foreign Terrorist Organizations," https://www.state.gov/j/ct/rls/other/des/123085.htm

34 Christopher Holton, Center for Security Policy, Free Fire, "HAMAS, the Muslim Brotherhood and the Islamic State," 31 May 2017 https://www.centerforsecuritypolicy.org/2017/05/31/hamas-the-muslim-brotherhood-and-the-islamic-state/

35 Yaakov Lappin, Special to Investigative Project on Terrorism, "Shin Bet Investigation Exposes Depth of Turkey's Hamas Support," 15 February 2018 https://www.investigativeproject.org/7349/shin-bet-investigation-exposes-depth-of-turkey

36 *Ibid.*

37 *Ibid.*

38 Burak Bekdil, Gatestone Institute International Policy Council, "Hamas: Turkey's Longtime Love," 22 February 2018 https://www.gatestoneinstitute.org/11933/turkey-hamas-Erdoğan

39 Burak Bekdil, "Turkey's Islamic government fully backs Hamas," *Ahval News*, 22 February 2018 https://ahvalnews.com/israel-turkey/turkeys-islamic-government-fully-backs-hamas-analyst

40 Jonathan Schanzer, "Hamas Still Finds Harbor in Turkey," The Weekly Standard, 8 June 2016 http://www.weeklystandard.com/hamas-still-finds-harbor-in-turkey/article/2002746

41 U.S. Council of Muslim Organizations, "Witnessing Turkish Democracy in Action," 27 August 2014 http://www.uscmo.org/council-news/

42 The Muslim Link, "'A Symbol of Friendship' : Turkish PM Lays Stone for $100M Masjid Complex In Maryland" http://www.muslimlinkpaper.com/community-news/3358-a-symbol-of-friendship

43 *Ibid.*

44 Republic of Turkey, The Presidency of Religious Affairs, "Prof. Dr. Mehmet Görmez," https://web.archive.org/web/20170404050258/http://diyanet.gov.tr/en/kategori/prof-dr-mehmet-gormez/120

45 Islamic Circle of North America, World Bulletin, News Desk, "Muslims unite at 13th MAS-ICNA in Chicago," 1 January 2015 http://www.icna.org/muslims-unite-at-13th-mas-icna-in-chicago/

46 The Muslim Link, "Thousands gather as Erdoğan officially opens Diyanet Complex," 15 April 2016 https://issuu.com/muslimlink/docs/04_15_2016_web

47 Dick Uliano, "Maryland Mosque opens its doors to the faithful," *WTOP*, 2 April 2016 http://wtop.com/local/2016/04/dicks-turkish-mosque-story-photos/slide/1/

48 Diyanet Center of America, https://diyanetamerica.org/

49 Republic of Turkey, The Presidency of Religious Affairs https://www.facebook.com/diyanetenglish/

50 Ahmet Cetin Guzel, "MUSIAD USA Strongly Condemns Atrocious Terrorist Attack in Ankara, Turkey," *Turkish American News*, 11 October 2015 http://www.turkishamericannews.com/turkish-american-news/item/3964-musiad-usa-strongly-condemns-atrocious-terrorist-attack-in-ankara-turkey

51 U.S. Council of Muslim Organizations, Board Members https://web.archive.org/web/20160317103557/http://www.uscmo.org/board-members/

52 Clifford May, "Recalling the lessons of Armenia," *Washington Times*, 28 April 2015 https://www.washingtontimes.com/news/2015/apr/28/clifford-may-recalling-the-lessons-of-armenia/

53 US Council of Muslim Organizations, "USCMO Statement on 1915 Turkish-Armenian Events," 19 April 2015 http://www.uscmo.org/pressreleases/

54 Islamic Circle of North America, "USCMO Statement on 1915 Turkish-Armenian Events," 19 April 2015 https://www.icna.org/uscmo-statement-on-1915-turkish-armenian-events/

55 Turkish American Cultural Society of New England, "Letter to Connecticut State Senator Steve Cassano," 11 March 2016 https://www.cga.ct.gov/2016/gaedata/tmy/2016SB-00438-R000314-Turkish%20American%20Cultural%20Society%20of%20New%20England-TMY.PDF

56 Yasin Aktay, "Greetings and a message from Western Muslims," *Yeni Şafak*, 6 February 2016 https://web.archive.org/web/20160211043643/http://www.yenisafak.com/en/columns/yasinaktay/greetings-and-a-message-from-western-muslims-2026629

57 Aktay

58 *Ibid.*

[59] *Ibid.*

[60] John Guandolo, Understanding the Threat, "CAIR Is HAMAS," https://www.understandingthethreat.com/cair-is-hamas-2/

[61] Editor, "Erdoğan meets with representatives of Muslim Community in the US," *Yeni Şafak*, 23 September 2016 https://www.yenisafak.com/en/news/Erdoğan-meets-with-representatives-of-muslim-community-in-the-us-2535813

[62] Editor, "Erdoğan meets with representatives of Muslim Community in the US," *Yeni Şafak,* 23 September 2016 https://www.yenisafak.com/en/news/Erdoğan-meets-with-representatives-of-muslim-community-in-the-us-2535813

[63] *Ibid.*

[64] Jeff Mason, Ece Toksabay, "Biden seeks to ease Turkey tensions over coup suspect Gülen," Reuters, 24 August 2016 https://www.reuters.com/article/us-turkey-security-usa/biden-seeks-to-ease-turkey-tensions-over-coup-suspect-Gülen-idUSKCN10Z0WF

[65] Associated Press, "US, Turkey at an impasse over extraditing Muslim cleric," *Fox News*, 25 August 2016 http://www.foxnews.com/us/2016/08/25/us-turkey-at-impasse-over-extraditing-muslim-cleric.html

[66] http://www.iiit.org/news/iiit-and-dca-sign-an-mou & https://diyanetamerica.org/news/dca-signed-mou-with-iiit/

[67] https://www.thefairfaxinstitute.org/news/diyanet-center-imams-visit-iiit & http://www.iiit.org/news/turkish-imams-and-diyanet-center-visit-iiit March 2017

[68] Diyanet Center of America, "Ibn Haldun University Opens US Office at the DCA Complex," 16 July 2017 https://diyanetamerica.org/news/ibn-haldun-university-opens-us-office-at-the-dca-complex/

[69] Diyanet Center of America, "DCA Organizes Panel, Opens Booth at ICNA-MAS Convention in Baltimore," 20 April 2017 https://diyanetamerica.org/news/dca-organizes-panel-opens-booth-at-icna-mas-convention-in-baltimore/

[70] Diyanet Center of America, "Coordination Meeting with Turkish Religious Leaders (Imams)," 21 March 2017 https://diyanetamerica.org/news/coordination-meeting-with-turkish-religious-leaders-imams/

[71] Muslim Legal Fund of America, Muslim "Non-profit Leadership Conference-Maryland," https://www.mlfa.org/event/muslim-nonprofit-leadership-conference-maryland/#.WOFlZBvysb4

[72] The Salem Award Foundation for Human Rights and Social Justice, "2006 Charles Swift and Neal Katyal," http://salemaward.org/salem-award/award-winners/2006-charles-swift-and-neal-katyal/

[73] Constitutional Law Center for Muslims in America, "Staff," https://www.clcma.org/our-people/staff

[74] Robert Spencer, Jihad Watch, "Scalia: Supreme Court decision on Gitmo "will make the war harder on us. It will almost certainly cause more Americans to be killed," 12 June 2008 https://www.jihadwatch.org/2008/06/scalia-supreme-court-decision-on-gitmo-will-make-the-war-harder-on-us-it-will-almost-certainly-cause

[75] OYEZ, "Hamdan v. Rumsfeld," https://www.oyez.org/cases/2005/05-184

[76] Muslim Legal Fund of America, "Project," https://www.mlfa.org/projects/#.WN1Df6K1tPY

[77] The Counter Jihad Report "A Last, Desperate Plea to Excuse Hamas Support," *IPT News*,12 January 2017 https://counterjihadreport.com/2017/02/13/a-last-desperate-plea-to-excuse-hamas-support-2/

[78] Center for Security Policy, "Genesis of the US Council of Muslim Organizations Muslim Brotherhood Political Party," 19 May 2014

https://www.centerforsecuritypolicy.org/2014/05/19/genesis-of-the-us-council-of-muslim-organizations-muslim-brotherhood-political-party/

[79] Muslim Legal Fund of America, "Projects: Constitutional Law Center for Muslims in America," https://www.mlfa.org/projects/#.WqgdsUxFx9A

[80] Samidoun: Palestinian Prisoner Solidarity Network, "Take action: Call the US Congress to request commutations for the Holy Land Five," 20 December 2016 http://samidoun.net/2016/12/take-action-call-the-us-congress-to-request-commutations-for-the-holy-land-five/

[81] Drew Zahn, "Will 'legal jihad' silence online critics of Islam?" *WND*, 4 July 2009 http://www.wnd.com/2009/07/102989/#3cxb7lpyccF9K3zw.99

[82] Muslim Legal Fund of America, "Constitutional Law Center for Muslims in America Issues Advisory on Muslim Ban 2.0," 8 March 2017 https://www.mlfa.org/clcma-issues-advisory-muslim-ban-2-0/#.WN3OSaK1tPY

[83] Resident Fatwa Committee, Assembly of Muslim Jurists of America, "AMJA Post-Election Statement: Principles and Roadmap," 28 November 2016 http://www.amjaonline.org/en/articles/entry/amja-post-election-statement-principles-and-roadmap

[84] 104th US Congress, Jerusalem Embassy Act of 1995, PUBLIC LAW 104–45—NOV. 8, 1995, https://www.congress.gov/104/plaws/publ45/PLAW-104publ45.pdf

[85] Center for Security Policy, "NATO Ally Turkey Working with U.S. Muslim Brotherhood," 3 April 2017 https://www.centerforsecuritypolicy.org/2017/04/03/nato-ally-turkey-working-with-u-s-muslim-brotherhood/

[86] *Ibid.*

[87] American Muslims for Palestine Live Video, https://www.facebook.com/ampalestine

[88] Center for Security Policy, "Turkey's Erdoğan Declared Ummah Leader at DC Muslim Brotherhood Rally Condemning Trump Recognition of Jerusalem," 20 December 2017 https://www.centerforsecuritypolicy.org- /2017/12/20/turkish-president-Erdoğan-declared-ummah-leader-at-washington-dc-muslim-brotherhood-rally-condemning-trump-recognition-of-jerusalem/

[89] *Ibid.*

[90] Safvan Allahverdi, "Thousands in Washington protest US Jerusalem decision," *Anadolu Agency*, 17 December 2017 http://aa.com.tr/en/americas/thousands-in-washington-protest-us-jerusalem-decision/1007136

[91] Center for Security Policy, "Turkey's Erdoğan Declared Ummah Leader at DC Muslim Brotherhood Rally Condemning Trump Recognition of Jerusalem," 20 December 2017 https://www.centerforsecuritypolicy.org/2017/12/20/turkish-president-Erdoğan-declared-ummah-leader-at-washington-dc-muslim-brotherhood-rally-condemning-trump-recognition-of-jerusalem/

[92] Samuel Osborne, "Turkey president Erdoğan tells Trump declaring Jerusalem Israel's capital is a 'red line' for Muslims," 5 December 2017 http://www.independent.co.uk/news/world/asia/donald-trump-jerusalem-israel-capital-turkey-Erdoğan-muslims-diplomatic-ties-palestinians-recep-a8092411.html

[93] Safvan Allahverdi, "Trump's Jerusalem plans 'reckless and dangerous'," *Anadolu Agency*, 6 December 2017 http://aa.com.tr/en/americas/trumps-jerusalem-plans-reckless-and-dangerous-/991780

[94] *Ibid.*

[95] US Council of Muslim Organizations, "A Statement of the US Council of Muslim Organizations on President Trump's Recognition of Jerusalem as the Capital of Israel," 7 December 2017 http://www.uscmo.org/

96 Sara Malm, "Islamic leaders declare Trump's Jerusalem decision 'null and void' and call for the city to be recognised as Palestine's capital," *Daily Mail*, 13 December 2017 http://www.dailymail.co.uk/news/article-5174769/Erdoğan-against-Trumps-recognition-Jerusalem.html

97 Syed Shafiq, "Organisation of Islamic Cooperation Declare East Jerusalem as the Capital of Palestine," *TheEurasia Times*, 14 December 2017 https://eurasiantimes.com/organisation-of-islamic-cooperation-istanbul/

98 "OIC declares East Jerusalem as Palestinian capital," *Al Jazeera*, 14 December 2017 http://www.aljazeera.com/news/2017/12/oic-leaders-reject-trump-decision-jerusalem-171213095417995.html

99 "Ankara to open diplomatic mission in East al-Quds: Erdoğan," *PressTV*, 17 December 2017 http://www.presstv.com/Detail/2017/12/17/545924/Ankara-to-open-diplomatic-mission-in-East-alQuds-Erdoğan

100 Sendika, "AKP opens the way for civil war with state of emergency decree absolving civilians in 'suppressing' terrorism," 24 December 2017 http://sendika62.org/2017/12/akp-opens-the-way-for-civil-war-with-state-of-emergency-decree-absolving-civilians-in-suppressing-terrorism-463893/

101 *Ibid.*

102 Lukas Mikelionis, "Erdoğan: Recognizing Jerusalem as Israel's capital is 'red line' for Muslims," *Fox News*, 5 December 2017 http://www.foxnews.com/politics/2017/12/05/Erdoğan-recognizing-jerusalem-as-israel-s-capital-is-red-line-for-muslims.html

103 Nicole Gaouette, "Despite Haley threat, UN votes to condemn Trump's Jerusalem decision," *CNN*, http://www.cnn.com/2017/12/21/politics/haley-un-jerusalem/index.html

104 Bilgin Sasmaz, "16th annual MAS-ICNA Convention kicks off in Chicago," *Anadolu Agency*, 29 December 2017 https://aa.com.tr/en/americas/16th-annual-mas-icna-convention-kicks-off-in-chicago/1017712

105 "Erdoğan'dan MAS-ICNA Kongresi'nde ABD ve İsrail'e Kudüs uyarısı," *Anadolu Ajansı*, 30 December 2017 https://aa.com.tr/tr/dunya/Erdoğandan-mas-icna-kongresinde-abd-ve-israile-kudus-uyarisi/1018469?amp=1 AND https://translate.google.com/translate?hl=en&sl=tr&u=http://aa.com.tr/tr/dunya/Erdoğandan-mas-icna-kongresinde-abd-ve-israile-kudus-uyarisi/1018469%3Famp%3D1&prev=search AND https://www.haberler.com/cumhurbaskani-Erdoğan-dan-mas-icna-kongresi-nde-10402247-haberi/

106 "Multilingual website devoted to R4BIA sign now running," *Anadolu Agency*, 27 August 2013 https://aa.com.tr/en/world/multilingual-website-devoted-to-r4bia-sign-now-running/222902

107 Diyanet Center of America, "President of Diyanet Visit USA," 18 January 2018 https://diyanetamerica.org/news/president-of-diyanet-visit-usa/

108 *Associated Press*, "Erdoğan criticized for speaking of martyrdom for small," *Washington Post*, 27 February 2018 girlhttps://www.washingtonpost.com/world/europe/Erdoğan-criticized-for-speaking-of-martyrdom-for-small-girl/2018/02/27/a53e6630-1ba8-11e8-98f5-ceecfa8741b6_story.html?utm_term=.9798d969d9e8

109 The White House, President Donald J. Trump, National Security Strategy of the United States of America, December 2017 http://nssarchive.us/wp-content/uploads/2017/12/2017.pdf

110 Sharon-Krespin, Rachel, "Fethullah Gülen's Grand Ambition: Turkey's Islamist Danger," *Middle East Quarterly*, Winter 2009, pp. 55-66. http://www.meforum.org/2045/fethullah-Gülens-grand-ambition

[111] "Bediuzzaman and Risale-i Nur Service," 19 November 2009. A Google translation accessed 19 February 2018 at http://www.risalesohbet.net/genel/bediuzzaman-ve-risale-i-nur-hizmeti.html. See also "Said Nursi," *Harvard Divinity School, Religious Literacy Project*, at https://rlp.hds.harvard.edu/faq/said-nursi

[112] Findley, Carter Vaughn, " Hizmet among the Most Influential Religious Renewals of Late Ottoman and Modern Turkish History". https://content.ucpress.edu/chapters/12909.ch01.pdf

[113] Fethullah Gülen's Official Website, https://fGülen.com/en/fethullah-Gülens-life/1304-biography/24648-introduction. See also Sharon-Krespin, Rachel in the *Middle East Quarterly*.

[114] Aras, Bulent, "Turkish Imam's Moderate Face," *The Middle East Quarterly*, September 1998, pp. 23-29. http://www.meforum.org/404/turkish-islams-moderate-face

[115] Fethullah Gülen, https://fGülen.com/en/

[116] Holton, Christopher and Clare Lopez, "Gülen and the Gülenist Movement: Turkey's Islamic Supremacist Cult and its Contributions to the Civilization Jihad," *Center for Security Policy*, 2015. https://www.centerforsecuritypolicy.org/2015/12/18/book-release-the-Gülen-movement-turkeys-islamic-supremacist-cult-and-its-contributions-to-the-civilization-jihad/

[117] Gülen's essay, "Prophet Muhammad as Commander," is published in full at his website: https://fGülen.com/en/fethullah-Gülens-works/faith/prophet-muhammad-as-commander

[118] *Ibid.*

[119] Holton and Lopez, Gülen and the Gülenist Movement, p. 41.

[120] Singer, Paul and Paulina Firozi, "Turkish faith movement secretly funded 200 trips for lawmakers and staff," *USA Today*, October 29, 2015. https://www.usatoday.com/story/news/politics/2015/10/29/turkish-faith-movement-secretly-funded-200-trips-lawmakers-and-staff/74535104/ . see also Holton and Lopez.

[121] The American Islamic College website is at http://www.aicusa.edu/

[122] The Virginia International University website is at https://www.viu.edu/

[123] The Respect Graduate School website is at https://www.respectgs.us/respect-graduate-school/

[124] The Gülen Institute website is at http://www.Güleninstitute.org/

[125] SERKAN DEMİRTAŞ, "Gülen earns $500 million annually from US activities: Turkish intel report," *Hurriet Daily News*, May 27, 2017. http://www.hurriyetdailynews.com/opinion/serkan-demirtas/Gülen-earns-500-million-annually-from-us-activities-turkish-intel-report--113608

[126] Amsterdam & Partners, LLP, "Empire of Deceit: An Investigation of the Gülen Charter School Network, Book 1". http://empireofdeceit.com/pdf/Empire_of_Deceit_final.pdf

[127] Atlas Foundation sponsors "Dialogue Trips," including to Turkey. Its website is at http://atlaslouisiana.org/

[128] Raindrop Foundation is an umbrella group with a Raindrop Turkish House presence in Arkansas, Kansas, Louisiana, Mississippi, New Mexico, Oklahoma, Tennessee and Texas. Its website is at http://www.raindropturkishhouse.org/

[129] Fethullah Gülen is the Honorary President of the Niagara Foundation. Its website is at https://www.niagarafoundation.org/

[130] The California-based Pacifica Institute website at http://pacificainstitute.org/ declares openly that Gülen's *Hizmet* movement provides its inspiration

[131] The Citizens Against Special Interest Lobbying in Public Schools (CA.S.I.L.I.P.S.) is a group of volunteer citizens and concerned parents who have carefully documented many of the Gülen charter schools and also post information about Gülenist corporations and non-profit organizations. http://turkishinvitations.weebly.com/

[132] Singer, Paul and Paulina Firozi, "Turkish faith movement secretly funded 200 trips for lawmakers and staff," *USA Today*, October 29, 2015. https://www.usatoday.com/story/news/politics/2015/10/29/turkish-faith-movement-secretly-funded-200-trips-lawmakers-and-staff/74535104/

[133] Whyte, Liz Essley, *The Center for Public Integrity* in *USA Today*, February 9, 2017. https://www.usatoday.com/story/news/politics/2017/02/09/state-legislators-trips-to-turkey/97602934/

[134] Holton and Lopez, "Gülen and the Gülenist Movement," pg. 49.

[135] Cagaptay, Soner, "The New Sultan: Erdoğan and the Crisis of Modern Turkey," 2017.

[136] *Ibid.*, pg. 135

[137] *Ibid.*

[138] Cagaptay, pp. 136-137

[139] Yüksel A. Aslandoğan, PhD, "What Really Happened in Turkey on July 15, 2016?" https://fGülen.com/en/what-went-wrong-with-turkey/51552-what-really-happened-in-turkey-on-july-15-2016

[140] Nelson, Steven, "D.C. Police: 12 Turkish Guards Charged for Beating Protesters, No Probable Cause Yet to Charge Erdoğan," *U.S. News*, June 15, 2017. https://www.usnews.com/news/articles/2017-06-15/dc-police-12-turkish-guards-charged-for-beating-protesters-no-probable-cause-yet-for-Erdoğan-arrest

[141] Weiser, Benjamin and Carlotta Gall, "Banker From Turkey Is Convicted in U.S. Over Plot to Evade Iran Sanctions," *New York Times*, January 3, 2018. https://www.nytimes.com/2018/01/03/world/europe/turkey-iran-sanctions-trial.html

[142] Rubin, Michael, "Why the Reza Zarrab guilty plea matters to Turkey and the world," *The Washington Examiner*, November 28, 2017. http://www.washingtonexaminer.com/why-the-reza-zarrab-guilty-plea-matters-to-turkey-and-the-world/article/2641919

[143] Hayward, John, "Speaker of Turkish National Assembly Declares 'Jihad' Against Kurds," *Breitbart*, 29 January 2018. http://www.breitbart.com/national-security/2018/01/29/speaker-turkish-national-assembly-declares-jihad-kurds/

[144] Reuters Staff, "Erdoğan tells Cyprus not to test Turkey over gas standoff," *Reuters*, February 13, 2018. https://www.reuters.com/article/us-cyprus-natgas-turkey/Erdoğan-tells-cyprus-not-to-test-turkey-over-gas-standoff-idUSKBN1FX0XZ

[145] Uzay Bulut Twitter page, https://twitter.com/UzayB

[146] The Explanatory Memorandum is a key 1991 document written by the U.S. Muslim Brotherhood that lays out its motivation, intent, and scope of its subversive activity in the U.S. It was presented as a key piece of evidence by the Department of Justice in the 2008 Holy Land Foundation HAMAS terror funding trial. See for full details *From the Archives of the Muslim Brotherhood in America: An Explanatory Memorandum on the General Strategic Goal for the Group in North America* at http://www.centerforsecuritypolicy.org/wpcontent/uploads/2014/05/Explanatory_Memoradum.pdf

[147] "An Explanatory Memorandum On the General Strategic Goal for the Group In North America", 5/22/1991. *The Investigative Project on Terrorism*, https://www.investigativeproject.org/documents/misc/20.pdf

[148] The Official Website of the Diyanet Center of America is at https://diyanetamerica.org/about-us/divine-ground-between-us/

[149] "NATO Ally Turkey Working with U.S. Muslim Brotherhood," *Center for Security Policy*, April 3, 2017. https://www.centerforsecuritypolicy.org/2017/04/03/nato-ally-turkey-working-with-u-s-muslim-brotherhood/

[150] For example, in March 2017, a nationwide delegation of Muslim imams and chaplains gathered at the Diyanet Center for the bi-annual Religious Services Coordination Meeting—after which, they visited the as Center and met with Imam Mohamed Magid. https://diyanetamerica.org/news/coordination-meeting-with-turkish-religious-leaders-imams/

[151] Dr. Yasar Colak, the President of the DCA, signed the MOU on 24 January 2017 with Dr. Abubaker Al-Shingieti, the Executive Director of the International Institute of Islamic Thought (IIIT), to establish training programs for religious clergy, academic exchange programs, and other educational initiatives. https://diyanetamerica.org/news/dca-signed-mou-with-iiit/

[152] "NATO Ally Turkey Working with U.S. Muslim Brotherhood," *Center for Security Policy*, April 3, 2017. https://www.centerforsecuritypolicy.org/2017/04/03/nato-ally-turkey-working-with-u-s-muslim-brotherhood/

[153] Group photo taken September 8, 2017 is featured prominently at the DCA website: https://diyanetamerica.org/news/prince-georges-county-police-chief-meeting/

[154] Funeral Prayer for Cpl. Mujahid Ramzziddin, February 23, 2018. https://diyanetamerica.org/news/funeral-prayer-for-cpl-mujahid-ramzziddin/

[155] "CAIR Offers Condolences on Death of 'Fallen Hero' Slain Maryland Muslim Police Officer," February 23, 2018. https://www.cair.com/

[156] Rossomando, John, "Muslim Leaders Insist Islamic State Not Islamic," *Investigative Project on Terrorism (IPT)*, , September 10, 2014. https://www.investigativeproject.org/4562/muslim-leaders-insist-islamic-state-not-islamic

[157] "President of Religious Affairs Erbas accepted Awad, President of the Council of American Islamic Relations," January 11, 2018. http://www.diyanet.gov.tr/tr-TR/Kurumsal/Detay/11190/diyanet-isleri-baskani-erbas-amerikan-islam-iliskileri-konseyi-baskani-awadi-kabul-etti See also: https://diyanetamerica.org/news/president-of-diyanet-visit-usa/

[158] CAIR Board Elects New Chairman, *CAIR*, March 11, 2015. https://www.cair.com/press-center/press-releases/1306-cair-board-elects-new-chairman.html

[159] "Video Gallery: Presentation on terrorism by Dr. Parvez Ahmed," http://www.atlanticinstitutesc.org/index.php/about-us/multimedia/184-presentation-on-terrorism-by-dr-parvez-ahmed

[160] "Terror In The Name Islam - Unholy War Not Jihad," *Atlantic Institute of Central Florida*, https://theatlanticinstitute.org/orlando/terror-name-islam-unholy-war-not-jihad

[161] "Turkey's Unethical Interference in American (Muslim) Civic Society is Dangerous," *Patheos*, April 6, 2017. http://www.patheos.com/blogs/altmuslim/2017/04/turkeys-unethical-interference-in-american-civic-society-is-dangerous/

[162] Ross, Chuck, "EXCLUSIVE: DNC Official Shared Political Intel With Turkish Government Officials, Paid For Pro-Turkey Op-Ed," *Daily Caller*, 12/07/16. http://dailycaller.com/2016/12/07/exclusive-dnc-official-shared-political-intel-with-turkish-government-officials-paid-for-pro-turkey-op-ed/

[163] Murat Guzel**Error! Bookmark not defined.**, MUSIAD-USA Board Member, http://www.musiad.us/about-us/

[164] From the TASC Facebook page, 22 September 2016: https://www.facebook.com/tasc.steeringcomittee/posts/1593146700987865:0

[165] Ross

[166] "Murat Guzel Political Campaign Contributions 2014 Election Cycle," *CampaignMoney.com*, https://www.campaignmoney.com/political/contributions/murat-guzel.asp?cycle=14

[167] Congressional Record, November 19, 2014.
https://www.congress.gov/crec/2014/11/19/CREC-2014-11-19-pt1-PgE1633-5.pdf

[168] Soylu, Ragip, "US congressman refunds Gülenist donations in fear of violating federal rules," *Daily Sabah*, December 7, 2014. https://www.dailysabah.com/world/2014/12/07/us-congressman-refunds-Gülenist-donations-in-fear-of-violating-federal-rules

[169] The Sakina Collective claims to be a registered non-profit organization dedicated to teaching about Islam. Although its website claims that it offers "Weekly Classes, Day Trips & Outings, Family Majalis, Youth Activities, Weekend Retreats, and Annual Conferences," at the moment it seems to comprise a couple of staff members, a Facebook page, and a bare bones website. http://246761799267694862.weebly.com/

[170] The 22 April 2017 Faith Climate event at the Respect Graduate School, one of several for the week, was featured prominently on the CAIR Philadelphia website: https://pa.cair.com/news/faith-climate-action-week/

[171] Sixdouse, Eksi B., *Gülen Scans* comprises scanned pages of Fethullah Gülen books in the Turkish language. https://www.flickr.com/photos/eksib612/sets/72157631747801352/

[172] These include, but are not limited to: The Acacia Foundation; the Foundation for Inter-Cultural Dialogue, the Arizona Institute of Interfaith Dialog; the Interfaith Dialog Center; the Istanbul Center; the Raindrop Turkish House; the Mid-Atlantic Federation of Turkic American Associations; the Niagara Foundation; the Pacifica Institute; the Pioneer Academy of Science, the Rumi Forum; the Turkish-American Association of Kentucky; the Turkish-American Federation of the Midwest; the Turkish-American Society of Nebraska; the Turkish Cultural Center New Jersey; the Turkish Cultural Center of Pennsylvania; the Turquoise Council of Americans and Eurasians, and the Texas West America Turkic Council.

[173] Amsterdam & Partners, LLC, "Empire of Deceit: An Investigation of the Gülen Charter School Network, Book 1." http://empireofdeceit.com/pdf/Empire_of_Deceit_final.pdf

[174] State of Arizona Senate Fiftieth Legislature, First Regular Session, 2011: SR 1010 "A RESOLUTION RECOGNIZING AND SUPPORTING THE FRIENDSHIP BETWEEN THE REPUBLIC OF TURKEY AND THE STATE OF ARIZONA." https://www.azleg.gov/legtext/50leg/1r/bills/sr1010s.htm

[175] The Turkish government has taken down the entire *Zaman* archive, but evidence of this may be found in the Wikileaks cables. https://wikileaks.org/plusd/cables/09ANKARA82_a.html

[176] Amsterdam & Partners, *Empire of Deceit*

[177] Caroline Finkel, *Osman's Dream: The Story of the Ottoman Empire, 1300–1923*, Basic Books, pp. 286–87; cited in "Battle of Vienna," *Wikipedia*, available at https://en.wikipedia.org/wiki/Battle_of_Vienna, accessed January 19, 2018.

[178] Baron Bodissey, "The Other September 11th," Gates of Vienna, September 11, 2006, available at http://gatesofvienna.blogspot.com/2006/09/other-september-11th.html, accessed January 19, 2018.

[179] Norman Davies, *God's Playground, a History of Poland: The Origins to 1795* (New York, N.Y.: Columbia University Press, 1982), p. 487; cited in "Battle of Vienna," *Wikipedia*, available at https://en.wikipedia.org/wiki/Battle_of_Vienna, accessed January 19, 2018.

[180] Stephen R. A'Barrow, *Death of a Nation: A New History of Germany* (Book Guild Publishing, 2016), p. 73; Richard Overy, *A History of War in 100 Battles* (Cambridge, U.K.: Oxford University Press, 2014), p. 58; cited in "Battle of Vienna," *Wikipedia*, available at https://en.wikipedia.org/wiki/Battle_of_Vienna, accessed January 19, 2018.

[181] S.C. Tucker, *A Global Chronology of Conflict*, Vol. Two (ABC-CLIO, LLC: Santa Barbara, Calif., 2010), p. 661; cited in "Battle of Vienna," *Wikipedia*, available at https://en.wikipedia.org/wiki/Battle_of_Vienna, accessed January 19, 2018.

[182] Walter Leitsch, "1683: The Siege of Vienna," *History Today*. July 1983: 33 (7), available at http://www.historytoday.com/walter-leitsch/1683-siege-vienna, accessed January 16, 2018, which reads in part, "The defeat of the Ottoman Army outside the gates of Vienna 300 years ago is usually regarded as the beginning of the decline of the Ottoman Empire. ...[I]t marks a turning point: not only was further Ottoman advance on Christian territories stopped, but in the following war that lasted up to 1698 almost all of Hungary was reconquered by the army of Emperor Leopold I. From 1683 the Ottoman Turks ceased to be a menace to the Christian world. ...The battle of Vienna was a turning point in one further respect: the success was due to the co-operation between the troops of the Emperor, some Imperial princes and the Poles. ...However the co-operation between the two non-maritime neighbours of the Ottoman Empire in Europe, the Emperor and Poland, was something new."

[183] Philip Carl Salzman, "Multiculturalists Working to Undermine Western Civilization," The Gatestone Institute, December 16, 2017, available at http://www.meforum.org/7105/multiculturalists-work-to-undermine-western-civilization?utm_source=Middle+East+Forum&utm_campaign=d12ae6f5c4-salzman_mef_2017_12_19&utm_medium=email&utm_term=0_086cfd423c-d12ae6f5c4-33884745&goal=0_086cfd423c-d12ae6f5c4-33884745, accessed January 15, 2018.

[184] Salzman, http://www.meforum.org/7140/mass-migration-uninvited-guests.

[185] Cairo Declaration on Human Rights, http://www.fmreview.org/sites/fmr/files/FMRdownloads/en/FMRpdfs/Human-Rights/cairo.pdf, accessed January 19, 2018.

[186] Salzman, http://www.meforum.org/7140/mass-migration-uninvited-guests.

[187] "Getting off the train: Mr Erdoğan's commitment to democracy seems to be fading," *The Economist*, February 4, 2016, available at https://www.economist.com/news/special-report/21689877-mr-Erdoğans-commitment-democracy-seems-be-fading-getting-train, accessed February 2, 2018.

[188] Daniel Pipes, "Erdoğan: 'Turkey Is Not a Country Where Moderate Islam Prevails,'" *Lion's Den*, June 14, 2004, updated September 14, 2004, available at http://www.danielpipes.org/blog/2004/06/erdo287an-turkey-is-not-a-country-where?utm_source=Middle+East+Forum&utm_campaign=b779b4f2b8-bekdil_mef_2017_12_09&utm_medium=email&utm_term=0_086cfd423c-b779b4f2b8-33884745&goal=0_086cfd423c-b779b4f2b8-33884745, accessed January 19, 2018.

[189] Burak Bekdil, "Erdoğan: No Moderate Islam," *The Gatestone Institute*, December 4, 2017, available at http://www.meforum.org/7078/Erdoğan-no-moderate-islam, accessed January 15, 2018.

[190] Bekdil, http://www.meforum.org/7078/Erdoğan-no-moderate-islam.

[191] *Hurriet Daily News*, "Erdoğan criticizes Saudi Crown Prince's 'moderate Islam' pledge," November 10, 2017, available at http://www.hurriyetdailynews.com/Erdoğan-criticizes-saudi-crown-princes-moderate-islam-pledge-122262?utm_source=Middle+East+Forum&utm_campaign=b779b4f2b8-bekdil_mef_2017_12_09&utm_medium=email&utm_term=0_086cfd423c-b779b4f2b8-33884745&goal=0_086cfd423c-b779b4f2b8-33884745, accessed January 19, 2018; cited in Bekdil, http://www.meforum.org/7078/Erdoğan-no-moderate-islam.

[192] Eliott C. McLaughlin, "Saudi crown prince promises 'a more moderate Islam'," *CNN*, October 25, 2017, available at http://www.cnn.com/2017/10/24/middleeast/saudi-arabia-prince-more-moderate-islam/index.html?utm_source=Middle+East+Forum&utm_campaign=b779b4f2b8-bekdil_mef_2017_12_09&utm_medium=email&utm_term=0_086cfd423c-b779b4f2b8-33884745&goal=0_086cfd423c-b779b4f2b8-33884745, accessed January 19, 2018; cited in Bekdil, http://www.meforum.org/7078/Erdoğan-no-moderate-islam.

[193] Pew Research Center on Religion and Pubic Life, "Europe's Growing Muslim Population: Muslims are projected to increase as a share of Europe's population—even with no future migration," November 29, 2017, http://www.pewforum.org/2017/11/29/europes-growing-muslim-population/, accessed January 16, 2018. By contrast, compare A. Paul and R. Schweinfurth, "Dramatischer Appell," *Bayerische Staatszeitung*, October 16, 2015, available at https://www.bayerische-staatszeitung.de/staatszeitung/kommunales/detailansicht-kommunales/artikel/dramatischer-appell.html, accessed February 2, 2018: "By the year 2020, [Christian Social Union member Uwe Brandl] forecasts around 20 million people of Muslim background in the Federal Republic of Germany: 'This will ensure a profound change in our society.'" Pew has a dramatically lower estimate, even at its extreme upper bound and projected forward to 2050: "in a "high" migration scenario in which both regular migration and the heavy flows of refugees from the Middle East were to continue indefinitely into the future, Germany's Muslim population would be expected to more than triple by 2050, growing from 4.9 million (6.0%) to 17.5 million (19.7%)." Moreover, the earlier Pew-Templeton estimate for 2020 was 5,530,000, according to projections available at the Pew-Templeton Global Religious Futures Project, "Explore the Data," available at http://www.globalreligiousfutures.org/explorer/custom#/?subtopic=15&chartType=bar&data_type=percentage&year=2020&religious_affiliation=all&countries=Germany&age_group=all&pdfMode=false&gender=all, accessed February 2, 2018.

[194] Pew, http://www.pewforum.org/2017/11/29/europes-growing-muslim-population/.

[195] *Ibid.;* Clare Lopez of the Center for Security Policy reports that she has seen the French figure challenged credibly, and believes that it is well in excess of 10%. For instance, as early as 2007, the conservative National Front party estimated that six to eight million Muslims resided in France, according to Jonathan Laurence and Justin Vaïsse, *Intégrer l'Islam*, Odile Jacob, 2007, p. 35; were that true, the percentage would have been as high as 12.9%, given a total population of 61,966,193 that year, according to PopulationPyramid.net, "France: 2007," available at https://www.populationpyramid.net/france/2007/, accessed February 2, 2018. The U.S. government put the figure at approximately 10% in 2009; see "Background Note: France," U.S. Department of State, December 10, 2009. State also assessed that "There are an estimated 5 million to 6 million Muslims (8 to 10 percent of the population), although estimates of how many of these are practicing vary widely," according to the 2008 Report on International Religious Freedom, U.S. Department of State, September 2008. See also Thomas F. X. Noble, *et al.*, *Western Civilization: Beyond Boundaries* (6th ed.), Boston: Wadsworth Cengage Learning, 2009. Likewise, Interior Minister Claude Guéant said that as of June, 2010, before the illegal immigration crisis of 2015, "We estimate that there are about 5 to 6 million Muslims in France today." However, note that those figures were based on geographic origin. Other studies found that only about a third of the five to six million identified as Muslims based on geographic origin—so approximately two million—actually said they were practicing believers. See Michael Cosgrove, "How does France count its Muslim population?" *Le Figaro*, April 7, 2011, available at http://plus.lefigaro.fr/note/how-does-france-count-its-muslim-population-20110407-435643, accessed February 2, 2018. One critic estimated that France's population was 11% in 2011; see Jean-Paul Gourévitch, *La croisade islamiste*, Pascal Galodé, 2011, p.136.; Jean-Paul Gourévitch, *Les migrations en Europe*, Acropole, 2007, p. 362. In 2016, a French polling company known as IFOP estimated that three and four million Muslims lived in France, making up 5.6% of those older than 15, and 10% of those younger than 25, and criticized those calling their growth a "great replacement" of French of Gaullic extraction; see "Religion, famille, société : qui sont vraiment les musulmans de France," *Le JDD*, available at http://www.lejdd.fr/Societe/Religion/Religion-famille-societe-qui-sont-vraiment-les-musulmans-de-France-810217, accessed February 2, 2018.

[196] Pew, http://www.pewforum.org/2017/11/29/europes-growing-muslim-population/.

[197] *Ibid.*

162

[198] "File:Turksineurope.png," WikiMedia Commons, accessible at https://commons.wikimedia.org/wiki/File:Turksineurope.png, accessed January 16, 2018.

[199] Nick Squires, "A year on from EU-Turkey deal, refugees and migrants in limbo commit suicide and suffer from trauma," *The Telegraph (UK)*, March 14, 2017, available at http://www.telegraph.co.uk/news/2017/03/14/year-eu-turkey-deal-refugees-migrants-limbo-commit-suicide-suffer/, accessed January 16, 2018; another source puts the figure at $6 billion (Ceylan Yeginsu, "Refugees Pour Out of Turkey Once More as Deal With Europe Falters," *The New York Times*, September 14, 2016, available at https://www.nytimes.com/2016/09/15/world/europe/turkey-syria-refugees-eu.html, accessed January 16, 2018.).

[200] United Nations High Commissioner for Refugees (UNHCR), "UNHCR Projected Global Resettlement Needs 2018," 23rd Annual Tripartite Consultations on Resettlement, Geneva, 12-14 June, 2017, p. 37, available at http://www.unhcr.org/en-us/protection/resettlement/593a88f27/unhcr-projected-global-resettlement-needs-2018.html, accessed January 19, 2018.

[201] Squires, http://www.telegraph.co.uk/news/2017/03/14/year-eu-turkey-deal-refugees-migrants-limbo-commit-suicide-suffer/.

[202] *Ibid.*

[203] UNHCR Refugees Operational Portal, available at http://data2.unhcr.org/en/situations/mediterranean?page=1&view=grid&Type%255B%255D=3&Search=%2523monthly%2523, accessed January 16, 2018.

[204] Drew H. Kinney, "Civilian Actors in the Turkish Military Drama of July 2016," *Eastern Mediterranean Policy Note* No. 10, Cyprus Center for European and International Affairs, September 19, 2016, pp. 1–10, available at http://www.emgr.unic.ac.cy/wp-content/uploads/EMPN_10.pdf, accessed January 16, 2018.

[205] Nick Schifrin, "Erdoğan's crackdown targets every aspect of Turkish society," *PBS News Hour*, August 30, 2017, available at https://www.pbs.org/newshour/show/Erdoğans-crackdown-targets-every-aspect-turkish-society, accessed January 16, 2018; another report suggested instead that more than 290 were killed and only 1400 wounded. See Duncan Robinson and Mehul Srivastava, "US and EU leaders warn Turkey's Erdoğan over post-coup crackdown: Brussels official suggests Ankara is using pre-prepared lists for purge," *Financial Times (UK)*, July 18, 2016, available at https://www.ft.com/content/b82ef35a-4cc3-11e6-88c5-db83e98a590a, accessed January 16, 2018.

[206] Robinson and Srivastava, https://www.ft.com/content/b82ef35a-4cc3-11e6-88c5-db83e98a590a.

[207] *Ibid.*

[208] *Ibid.*

[209] *Ibid.*

[210] *Ibid.*

[211] *Ibid.*

[212] *Ibid.*

[213] Alix Culbertson, "Europe on 'BRINK OF WAR' as Turkey gathers boats to ship migrants to Greece over EU anger," *The Express (UK)*, November 30, 2016, available at https://www.express.co.uk/news/world/737480/Europe-war-Turkey-migrants-Greece-EU-Erdoğan, accessed January 19, 2018.

[214] Yeginsu, https://www.nytimes.com/2016/09/15/world/europe/turkey-syria-refugees-eu.html.

[215] Daniel Pipes, "Italy's Apocalypse," *The Washington Times*, November 2, 2017, available at http://www.danielpipes.org/18001/italy-apocalypse, accessed January 15, 2018.

[216] Robert Fisk, "Fethullah Gülen is facing extradition to Turkey by Donald Trump—so he should read up about his country," *The Independent (UK)*, July 13, 2017, available at http://www.independent.co.uk/voices/robert-fisk-gulan-turkey-Erdoğan-isis-extradition-middle-east-terrorist-raqqa-kurdish-america-a7838861.html, accessed January 16, 2018.

[217] See Quran 4:34, "Men are in charge of women by [right of] what Allah has given one over the other and what they spend [for maintenance] from their wealth. So righteous women are devoutly obedient, guarding in [the husband's] absence what Allah would have them guard. But those [wives] from whom you fear arrogance - [first] advise them; [then if they persist], forsake them in bed; and [finally], strike them. But if they obey you [once more], seek no means against them. Indeed, Allah is ever Exalted and Grand." Quran.com, 4:34, SAHIH INTERNATIONAL, available at https://quran.com/4/34, accessed February 2, 2018.

[218] Fisk, http://www.independent.co.uk/voices/robert-fisk-gulan-turkey-Erdoğan-isis-extradition-middle-east-terrorist-raqqa-kurdish-america-a7838861.html.

[219] Rachel Sharon-Krespin, "Fethullah Gülen's Grand Ambition: Turkey's Islamist Danger," *Middle East Quarterly*, Winter 2009, pp. 55-66, available at http://www.meforum.org/2045/fethullah-Gülens-grandambition, accessed February 2, 2018; cited in Christopher Holton and Clare Lopez, *THE GÜLEN MOVEMENT Turkey's Islamic Supremacist Cult and its Contributions to the Civilization Jihad*, Civilization Jihad Reader Series Volume 8, Washington, D.C.: Center for Security Policy Press, December 10, 2015, pp. 11-12, available at https://www.centerforsecuritypolicy.org/wp-content/uploads/2015/12/Gülen_Final.pdf, accessed February 2, 2018.

[220] Christopher Holton, "HOLTON: Islamic Radicals Mount Influence Operation On Louisiana Leges," Counter Jihad Report, April 11, 2014, available at https://counterjihadreport.com/tag/prophet-muhammad-as-commander/, accessed February 2, 2018.

[221] M. Fethullah Gülen, *An Analysis of the Prophet's Life, The Messenger of God MUHAMMAD*, The Light, Inc.: Somerset, New Jersey, 2005, p. 212, available at http://www.fethullahGülenconference.org/resources/books/messengerofgod.pdf, accessed February 2, 2018; cited in Holton and Lopez, p. 6, https://www.centerforsecuritypolicy.org/wp-content/uploads/2015/12/Gülen_Final.pdf.

[222] "Trials in Times of Misfortune," *Fethullah Gülen*, available at https://fGülen.com/en/home/1247-fGülen-com-english/uncategorised/27136-fethullah-Gülens-legal-cases-in-turkey-and-us-immigration-case, accessed February 2, 2018; drawn from James C. Harrington, *Wrestling with free speech, religious freedom, and democracy in Turkey*, University Press of America, May 2011.

[223] See *e.g.* "Turkey Wants U.S. To Extradite Exiled Cleric Blamed For Attempted Coup," *NPR*, September 12, 2016, available at https://www.npr.org/2016/09/12/493573629/turkey-wants-u-s-to-extradite-exile-cleric-blamed-for-attempted-coup, accessed February 2, 2018.

[224] Gulsen Solaker, "Turkey targets foster families in post-coup crackdown: government official," *Reuters*, November 28, 2016, available at https://www.reuters.com/article/us-turkey-security-children/turkey-targets-foster-families-in-post-coup-crackdown-government-official-idUSKBN13N10X?feedType=RSS&feedName=worldNews, accessed January 16, 2018; for more specific statistics on the crackdown, including a lower total from a later date, see also Judith Vonberg, Lauren Said-Moorhouse and Kara Fox, "47,155 arrests: Turkey's post-coup crackdown by the numbers," *CNN*, April 15, 2017, available at http://www.cnn.com/2017/04/14/europe/turkey-failed-coup-arrests-detained/index.html, accessed January 16, 2018.

[225] Solaker, https://www.reuters.com/article/us-turkey-security-children/turkey-targets-foster-families-in-post-coup-crackdown-government-official-idUSKBN13N10X?feedType=RSS&feedName=worldNews.

[226] Ceylan Yeginsu and Safak Timur, "Turkey's Post-Coup Crackdown Targets Kurdish Politicians," *The New York Times*, November 4, 2016, available at

164

https://www.nytimes.com/2016/11/05/world/europe/turkey-coup-crackdown-kurdish-politicians.html, accessed January 16, 2018.

[227] Solaker, https://www.reuters.com/article/us-turkey-security-children/turkey-targets-foster-families-in-post-coup-crackdown-government-official-idUSKBN13N10X?feedType=RSS&feedName=worldNews.

[228] *Ibid.*

[229] *The Chicago Tribune,* "Editorial: The purges in Turkey — and Washington's milquetoast response," August 2, 2016, available at http://www.chicagotribune.com/news/opinion/editorials/ct-turkey-Erdoğan-coup-crackdown-purge-edit-0804-jm-20160802-story.html, accessed January 16, 2018.

[230] Solaker, https://www.reuters.com/article/us-turkey-security-children/turkey-targets-foster-families-in-post-coup-crackdown-government-official-idUSKBN13N10X?feedType=RSS&feedName=worldNews.

[231] Alix Culbertson, "Europe on 'BRINK OF WAR' as Turkey gathers boats to ship migrants to Greece over EU anger," *The Express (UK),* November 30, 2016, available at https://www.express.co.uk/news/world/737480/Europe-war-Turkey-migrants-Greece-EU-Erdoğan, accessed January 19, 2018.

[232] Elana Beiser, "Turkey's crackdown propels number of journalists in jail worldwide to record high," Committee to Protect Journalists, December 13, 2016, available at https://cpj.org/reports/2016/12/journalists-jailed-record-high-turkey-crackdown.php, accessed January 19, 2018; cited in Zia Weise, "Turkey jails more journalists than any other nation. Those in detention are all terrorists, Erdoğan says." *PRI,* June 28, 2017, available at https://www.pri.org/stories/2017-06-28/turkey-jails-more-journalists-any-other-nation-those-detention-are-all-terrorists?utm_source=Middle+East+Forum&utm_campaign=9ecde3e15f-totten_michael_2017_10_19&utm_medium=email&utm_term=0_086cfd423c-9ecde3e15f-33884745&goal=0_086cfd423c-9ecde3e15f-33884745, accessed January 19, 2018.

[233] Tuvan Gumrukcu and Michael Nienaber, "Turkey jails reporter from Germany's Die Welt paper: court witness," *Reuters,* February 27, 2017, available at https://www.reuters.com/article/us-turkey-security-germany-journalist/turkey-jails-reporter-from-germanys-die-welt-paper-court-witness-idUSKBN1662FQ, accessed January 19, 2018.

[234] The letter from 166 lawmakers in the Bundestag, the lower house of the German parliament, read in part, ""Intellectual debate is the best instrument against terrorism, which paradoxically is what he is being accused of." AFP, "German lawmakers urge Turkey to free Die Welt journalist," *The Local,* February 25, 2017, available at https://www.thelocal.de/20170225/german-lawmakers-urge-turkey-to-free-die-welt-journalist, accessed January 19, 2018.

[235] Ned Levin, Ruth Bender and Andrea Thomas, "Merkel Denounces Arrest in Turkey of German Journalist," *The Wall Street Journal,* available at https://www.wsj.com/articles/merkel-denounces-arrest-in-turkey-of-german-journalist-1488315732, accessed January 19, 2018.

[236] Gumrukcu and Nienaber, https://www.reuters.com/article/us-turkey-security-germany-journalist/turkey-jails-reporter-from-germanys-die-welt-paper-court-witness-idUSKBN1662FQ.

[237] AFP, https://www.thelocal.de/20170225/german-lawmakers-urge-turkey-to-free-die-welt-journalist.

[238] *Ibid.*

[239] Squires, http://www.telegraph.co.uk/news/2017/03/14/year-eu-turkey-deal-refugees-migrants-limbo-commit-suicide-suffer/.

[240] Emily Tamkin, "Did Turkey Just Kill the Refugee Deal With Europe?" *Foreign Policy,* March 14, 2017, available at http://foreignpolicy.com/2017/03/14/did-turkey-just-kill-the-refugee-deal-with-europe/, accessed January 16, 2018.

[241] "Human Rights Council hears from 23 dignitaries and concludes its high-level segment," United Nations Human Rights Office of the High Commissioner, available at http://www.ohchr.org/EN/NewsEvents/Pages/DisplayNews.aspx?NewsID=21259&LangID=E, accessed January 15, 2018; Esener also spoke at a May 2017 OSCE meeting during the "[e]xchange of views on national experiences and international co-operation in countering terrorism," and may well have raised the issue at that time; see "ANNOTATED AGENDA," 2017 OSCE-wide Counter-Terrorism Conference Preventing and Countering Violent Extremism and Radicalization that Lead to Terrorism Vienna, 23-24 May 2017, available at http://www.osce.org/secretariat/315886?download=true, accessed January 15, 2018.

[242] Shadia Nasralla and Andrea Shalal, "Turkish referendum: Up to 2.5 million votes could have been manipulated, says foreign observer," *The Independent (UK),* April 19, 2017, available at http://www.independent.co.uk/news/world/europe/turkish-referendum-million-votes-manipulated-recep-tayyip-Erdoğan-council-of-europe-observer-a7690181.html, accessed January 19, 2018.

[243] Andrea Thomas, Anton Troianovski and Ned Levin, "Tensions Escalate Between Germany and Turkey," *The Wall Street Journal,* July 27, 2017, available at https://www.wsj.com/articles/tensions-escalate-between-germany-and-turkey-1501148072, accessed January 19, 2018.

[244] Kareem Shaheen, "Erdoğan to continue crackdown as Turkey marks failed coup," *The Guardian (UK),* July 16, 2017, available at https://www.theguardian.com/world/2017/jul/15/Erdoğan-repeats-support-death-penalty-on-anniversary-of-turkey-coup-attempt, accessed January 16, 2018.

[245] *Ibid.*

[246] Bodissey, http://gatesofvienna.blogspot.com/2006/09/other-september-11th.html, accessed January 19, 2018.

[247] The Commission on Security and Cooperation in Europe (CSCE), "TURKISH PRESSURE ON NGO PARTICIPATION IN THE OSCE," November 27, 2017, available at https://www.csce.gov/international-impact/turkish-pressure-ngo-participation-osce, accessed January 19, 2018; Henrik Clausen, "OSCE: Turkey refuses to even discuss Human Rights!," Gates of Vienna, September 11, 2017, available at https://gatesofvienna.net/2017/09/turkish-non-delight-at-osce-warsaw/, accessed January 19, 2018; see also "STATEMENT BY AMBASSADOR RAUF ENGİN SOYSAL PERMANENT REPRESENTATIVE OF TURKEY 2017," Human Dimension Implementation Meeting Opening Plenary Session, Warsaw, September 11, 2017, available at http://www.osce.org/odihr/339031, accessed January 19, 2018.

[248] "Turkish temper tantrum at OSCE," available at https://youtu.be/DQ7bjJ2JpxY?t=160, accessed January 19, 2018; see also Soysal, http://www.osce.org/odihr/339031.

[249] Soysal, http://www.osce.org/odihr/339031.

[250] For an overview of that evidence, see Mustafa Akyol, "Who Was Behind the Coup Attempt in Turkey?" *The New York Times,* July 22, 2016, available at https://www.nytimes.com/2016/07/22/opinion/who-was-behind-the-coup-attempt-in-turkey.html, accessed January 19, 2018; for a counter-argument, see Dylan Matthews, "Turkey's coup: the Gülen Movement, explained," *Vox,* September 13, 2016, available at https://www.vox.com/2016/7/16/12204456/Gülen-movement-explained, accessed January 19, 2018.

[251] Dexter Filkins, "Turkey's Thirty-Year Coup: Did an exiled cleric try to overthrow Erdoğan's government?" October 17, 2016, available at https://www.newyorker.com/magazine/2016/10/17/turkeys-thirty-year-coup, accessed January 19, 2018.

252 Dylan Matthews, "Turkey's coup: the Gülen Movement, explained," *Vox*, September 13, 2016, available at https://www.vox.com/2016/7/16/12204456/Gülen-movement-explained, accessed January 19, 2018.

253 CSCE, https://www.csce.gov/international-impact/turkish-pressure-ngo-participation-osce.

254 Mehmet Guzel, "German journalist stands trial in Turkey on terror charges," *AP*, October 11, 2017, available at https://apnews.com/51b13920cc5743099a27351905d1aca9, accessed January 19, 2018.

255 *Ibid.*

256 Julian E. Barnes and David Gauthier-Villars, "NATO Apologizes To Irate Turkey," *The Wall Street Journal*, November 18-19, 2017, available at https://www.wsj.com/articles/nato-apologizes-for-offending-turkey-1510941321, accessed February 8, 2018.

257 *Ibid.*

258 Helena Smith, "Confrontational Erdoğan stuns Greek hosts on Athens visit," *The Guardian (UK)*, December 7, 2017, available at https://www.theguardian.com/world/2017/dec/07/turkish-president-Erdoğan-to-make-landmark-visit-to-greece, accessed January 16, 2018.

259 See Reuters, "Turkey begins assault on Kurdish-held enclave in Syria," *The Guardian (UK)*, January 19, 2018, available at https://www.theguardian.com/world/2018/jan/19/turkey-begins-assault-kurdish-enclave-in-syria; Bernard-Henri Lévy, "Stand Up to Erdoğan's Brutality," *The Wall Street Journal*, February 7, 2018, https://www.wsj.com/articles/stand-up-to-Erdoğans-brutality-1518046582, both accessed February 8, 2018.

260 UNHCR, pp. 7 and 37, http://www.unhcr.org/en-us/protection/resettlement/593a88f27/unhcr-projected-global-resettlement-needs-2018.html.

261 UNHCR, p. 10, http://www.unhcr.org/en-us/protection/resettlement/593a88f27/unhcr-projected-global-resettlement-needs-2018.html.

262 Pew, http://www.pewforum.org/2017/11/29/europes-growing-muslim-population/.

263 *Ibid.*

264 *Ibid.*

265 Daniel Pipes, "Accepting Europe's Anti-Immigration Parties," *The Washington Times*, November 30, 2017, available at http://www.danielpipes.org/18063/accepting-europe-anti-immigration-parties, accessed January 15, 2018.

266 Alexander H. Joffe, "Europe's 'Red-Green Alliance': A Dystopian Scenario," *Middle East Forum*, November 26, 2017, available at http://www.meforum.org/7037/europes-red-green-alliance, accessed January 15, 2018; drawn from Alexander H. Joffe, "The British Political Crisis and European Politics: A Dystopian Scenario," The Begin-Sadat Center for Strategic Studies, November 13, 2017, available at https://besacenter.org/perspectives-papers/britain-political-crisis/?utm_source=Middle+East+Forum&utm_campaign=ce6e8fbf90-joffe_mef_2017_11_25&utm_medium=email&utm_term=0_086cfd423c-ce6e8fbf90-33884745&goal=0_086cfd423c-ce6e8fbf90-33884745, accessed January 15, 2018.

267 Yves Mamou, "Islamization of Europe: Erdoğan's New Muslim Political Network," *Gatestone Institute*, June 11, 2017, available at https://www.gatestoneinstitute.org/10509/france-islamic-party, accessed January 15, 2018, cited in Alexander H. Joffe, "Europe's 'Red-Green Alliance': A Dystopian Scenario," *Middle East Forum*, November 26, 2017, available at http://www.meforum.org/7037/europes-red-green-alliance, accessed January 15, 2018; drawn from Alexander H. Joffe, "The British Political Crisis and European Politics: A Dystopian Scenario," The Begin-Sadat Center for Strategic Studies, November 13, 2017, available at https://besacenter.org/perspectives-papers/britain-political-

crisis/?utm_source=Middle+East+Forum&utm_campaign=ce6e8fbf90-joffe_mef_2017_11_25&utm_medium=email&utm_term=0_086cfd423c-ce6e8fbf90-33884745&goal=0_086cfd423c-ce6e8fbf90-33884745, accessed January 15, 2018.

[268] Mamou, https://www.gatestoneinstitute.org/10509/france-islamic-party.

[269] *Ibid.*

[270] Martine Gozlan, "La main d'Erdoğan dans les urnes de France : 68 candidats du PEJ aux législatives," *Marianne*, May 19, 2017, available at https://www.marianne.net/politique/la-main-d-Erdoğan-dans-les-urnes-de-france-68-candidats-du-pej-aux-legislatives, accessed January 19, 2018.

[271] *Ibid.*

[272] Alexandre Sulzer, "Egalité et Justice, le parti islamo-turc qui se lance aux départementales," *l'Express (France)*, June 3, 2015, available at https://www.lexpress.fr/actualite/politique/egalite-et-justice-le-parti-communautariste-islamo-turc-qui-se-lance-aux-departementales_1658413.html, accessed January 19, 2018, cited in Mamou, https://www.gatestoneinstitute.org/10509/france-islamic-party.

[273] Mamou, https://www.gatestoneinstitute.org/10509/france-islamic-party.

[274] *Ibid.*

[275] Chris Tomlinson, "Turkish Migrants Form New Political Party in Austria," *Breitbart London*, January 17, 2017, available at http://www.breitbart.com/london/2017/01/17/migrants-form-political-party-austria/, accessed on January 19, 2017, cited in Mamou, https://www.gatestoneinstitute.org/10509/france-islamic-party.

[276] Kate Mansfield, "Trouble brewing in Netherlands as Erdoğan supporters win first seats in Dutch election," *Express (UK)*, March 16, 2017, available at https://www.express.co.uk/news/world/779891/dutch-election-turkish-dutch-party-denk-win-first-seats-netherlands-parliament, accessed January 19, 2018, cited in Mamou, https://www.gatestoneinstitute.org/10509/france-islamic-party.

[277] Mamou, https://www.gatestoneinstitute.org/10509/france-islamic-party. Note that *contra* Pew's estimate, *supra*, of Muslims comprising 11.1% of the Bulgarian population, M. Mamou claims that Muslim "Turks, Shi'ites, Bulgarians, and Roma...together represent 7-8% of the total population" of Bulgaria. As a source, M. Mamou links to https://en.wikipedia.org/wiki/Muslim, accessed February 2, 2018, which appears to have no direct reference to Bulgaria.

[278] Mamou, https://www.gatestoneinstitute.org/10509/france-islamic-party. Note also that according to Clare Lopez, Center for Security Policy, the long-time communist Bulgarian dictator Todor Zhivkov had been ousted only in November 1989, and communists were still in control of Bulgaria in 1990, albeit beginning to call themselves 'socialists.' Thus Dogan's party was *allowed* to form that year—allowed by the KGB and Bulgarian security forces.

[279] Mamou, https://www.gatestoneinstitute.org/10509/france-islamic-party.

[280] *Ibid.*

[281] *Ibid.*

[282] *Ibid.*

[283] *Ibid.*

[284] *Ibid.*

[285] My CSP colleague Clare Lopez has long made this fundamental point. See e.g. Clare Lopez, "A Counterjihad Security Architecture for America," *Pundicity*, February 25, 2016, available at http://lopez.pundicity.com/18654/counterjihad-security-architecture, accessed of February 8, 2018, which includes the section "Whither Turkey?" that reads, "The Turkish regime under President Recep Tayyip Erdoğan harbors neo-Ottoman jihadist aspirations and under current leadership cannot be considered a viable NATO or Western ally unless its behavior significantly turns toward supporting U.S. and NATO objectives. Rather, Turkey is a

destabilizing force in the Middle East, especially because of its apparently fixed resolve to oust the Syrian regime of Bashar al-Assad. Further, this jihadist Turkish leadership views Israel as a Jewish enemy and Iran and Saudi Arabia both as Islamic rivals for regional domination. Turkey has supported IS since its inception because it views the group as a capable proxy force against Bashar al-Assad. Turkey also supports other jihadist militias including Ahrar al-Sham. Ankara's permission for IS and other jihadis to use Turkey as a gateway to Syrian battlefields, establish terror training camps on its territory, and find safehaven there, eventually will threaten Turkey itself. Turkey's enduring enmity towards the Kurds, both within Turkey and elsewhere, ensures ongoing, destabilizing efforts by Ankara to attack, counter, and degrade the Kurds' equally determined nationalist aspirations. Pro-West, anti-jihadist Kurds are a natural ally for the U.S. and should be recognized and aided as such."

[286] See Marton Dunai, "Hungary PM says EU should deport all illegal migrants: website," *Reuters,* September 22, 2016, available at https://www.reuters.com/article/us-europe-migrants-hungary-orban/hungary-pm-says-eu-should-deport-all-illegal-migrants-website-idUSKCN11S0TU?il=0, accessed February 8, 2018.

[287] These specific ideas are drawn from Lévy, https://www.wsj.com/articles/stand-up-to-Erdoğans-brutality-1518046582.

[288] Salzman, http://www.meforum.org/7140/mass-migration-uninvited-guests.

[289] http://www.sozcu.com.tr/2017/gundem/cumhurbaskani-Erdoğan-referandum-ardindan-aciklama-yapiyor-1798747/

[290] http://www.hurriyetdailynews.com/turkish-style-presidential-system-needed-Erdoğan-repeats-78988

[291] https://www.reuters.com/article/us-turkey-politics/turkeys-main-opposition-accuses-Erdoğan-of-blocking-coalition-efforts-idUSKCN0Q80TJ20150803

[292] https://www.theguardian.com/world/2015/nov/01/turkish-election-akp-set-for-majority-with-90-of-vote-counted

[293] http://edition.cnn.com/2017/01/18/europe/turkey-Erdoğan-power-bill/

[294] https://www.zerohedge.com/news/2017-04-16/eu-rapporteur-turkey-warns-turkish-talks-will-be-suspended-if-Erdoğan-gets-unchecked

[295] https://www.timeshighereducation.com/world-university-rankings/2014/world-ranking#!/page/0/length/25/sort_by/rank/sort_order/asc/cols/stats

[296] "Mortality rate, infant," World Bank, Washington, D.C., accessed Oct. 8, 2014.

[297] "Child Labour Persists around the World: More than 13 Percent of Children 10-14 Are Employed," International Labour Organization, Geneva, June 10, 1996.

[298] *Gender Gap Report 2013* (Geneva: World Economic Forum, 2013), p. 10.

[299] "Turkey," *Freedom in the World*, Freedom House, Washington, D.C., accessed Oct. 27, 2014.

[300] "Eastern Europe and Central Asia: Authoritarian Regional Models," *World Press Freedom Index 2014*, Reporters Without Borders, Washington, D.C., accessed Oct. 8, 2014.

[301] Cumhuriyet (Istanbul), Sept. 28, 2015.

[302] Hürriyet, Jan. 27, 2016; "Eğilimler Araştırması 2015 Sonuçları Açıklandı," Kadir Has University, Istanbul.

[303] https://besacenter.org/perspectives-papers/Erdoğan-popularity/

[304] http://www.telegraph.co.uk/news/2017/03/17/Erdoğan-calls-turkish-families-have-five-children-bulwark-against/

[305] A. Banu Ergöçmen, presentation, Hacettepe University's Institute of Population Studies, Ankara, May 11, 2015.

306 https://www.theguardian.com/world/2017/dec/25/turkey-fertility-secular-religious-divide-Erdoğan-population-growth

307 Al-Jazeera America (New York), Nov. 5, 2015.

308 BBC News, July 20, 2015.

309 Al-Jazeera (Doha), July 22, 2015.

310 BBC News, Oct. 10, 2015.

311 https://www.haber3.com/guncel/politika/039039turkiye039de-kutuplasma039039-anketi-herkesi-soke-haberi-3771572

312 http://www.hurriyetdailynews.com/turkish-youth-overwhelmingly-against-other-study-says-124595

313 https://www.dailysabah.com/elections/2017/01/28/mhp-chair-to-say-yes-in-referendum-for-the-sake-of-turkey

314 http://www.hurriyetdailynews.com/mhp-will-not-present-presidential-candidate-for-2019-election-bahceli-125379

315
http://www.cumhuriyet.com.tr/haber/siyaset/902158/Meral_Aksener__iYi_Parti_nin_oy_oranini_acikladi.html

316 http://www.hurriyet.com.tr/yarin-sabaha-dair-yeni-bir-utopyaya-ihtiyacimiz-var-40709976

317 http://www.hurriyet.com.tr/yazarlar/abdulkadir-selvi/Erdoğanin-abdullah-gul-hamlesi-40696685

318 https://besacenter.org/perspectives-papers/turkey-america-relationship/

319 https://besacenter.org/perspectives-papers/trumps-security-strategy-messages-turkey/

320 http://edition.cnn.com/2018/01/15/middleeast/Erdoğan-us-terror/index.html

321 https://www.nytimes.com/2018/01/10/opinion/turkey-united-states-Erdoğan.html

322 https://besacenter.org/perspectives-papers/turkey-eu-membership/

323 http://www.hurriyetdailynews.com/german-coalition-draft-suggests-no-steps-for-turkeys-eu-bid-report-125624

324 http://www.bbc.com/news/world-europe-42586108

325 https://clarionproject.org/turkeys-shift-west-Erdoğan-switching-teams/

326 http://time.com/4447996/recep-tayyip-Erdoğan-vladimir-putin-turkey-russia-alliance/

327 http://time.com/4448459/turkey-nato-defense-foreign-affairs-minister/

328 https://www.reuters.com/article/us-russia-turkey-missiles/turkey-russia-sign-deal-on-supply-of-s-400-missiles-idUSKBN1EN0T5

329 https://nzhistory.govt.nz/war/ottoman-empire/arab-revolt

330 http://www.erzurumsayfasi.com/haber/arapca-dersi-yillik-planlari-2017-2018-h4067.html

331
http://www.trt.net.tr/kurumsal/kurumsalyapidetay.aspx?id=TRT+El+Arabia+Kanal+Koordinat%u00f6rl%u00fc%u011f%u00fc

332 http://www.yeniakit.com.tr/video/cumhurbaskani-Erdoğan-araplar-bizi-arkadan-vurdu-yalanini-artik-birakalim-20259.html

333 http://www.mfa.gov.tr/interview-of-mevlut-cavusoglu-to-qatar-tribune-qatar-turkey-business-magazine.en.mfa

334 https://www.theguardian.com/world/2016/feb/14/turkey-and-saudi-arabia-consider-ground-campaign-in-syria-following-border-strikes

335 http://www.arabnews.com/node/1116511/middle-east

336 https://www.reuters.com/article/us-turkey-emirates/in-first-remarks-since-retweet-feud-uae-diplomat-says-arabs-wont-be-led-by-turkey-idUSKBN1EL139

337 https://www.reuters.com/article/us-turkey-emirates/in-first-remarks-since-retweet-feud-uae-diplomat-says-arabs-wont-be-led-by-turkey-idUSKBN1EL139

338 http://www.hurriyet.com.tr/yazarlar/taha-akyol/ortadogu-cikmazi-40502244

339 http://www.middleeasteye.net/news/eu-delegation-warns-democratic-legitimacy-risk-over-turkish-referendum-339505016

340 https://www.politico.eu/article/turkeys-lose-lose-referendum-recep-tayyip-Erdoğan-constitutional-reform/

341 http://www.hurriyetdailynews.com/chp-slams-election-board-for-controversial-decision--112090

342 http://www.hurriyet.com.tr/yazarlar/akif-beki/dikkat-provokasyon-gelebilir-40256389

343 http://www.sozcu.com.tr/2016/gundem/adnan-tanriverdi-kimdir-sadat-nedir-1355672/

344 http://www.abcgazetesi.com/Erdoğanin-ordusunu-kurma-gorevi-sadata-mi-verildi-25679h.htm

345 https://tr.sputniknews.com/turkiye/201801021031645928-aksener-sadat-tokat-konya-silahli-egitim-kamp/

346 http://www.hurriyet.com.tr/iste-tartisilan-halk-ozel-harekat-40693394

347 http://www.foxnews.com/world/2017/12/25/critics-turkish-coup-decree-fear-death-squad-formation.html

348 "Jihad: The New 'Value' in Turkey's Educational System," The Clarion Project, January 19, 2017. https://clarionproject.org/jihad-new-value-turkeys-educational-system/

349 Bulut, Uzay, "In Turkey, the Victims Change but the Regime Remains the Same," Philos Project, April 18, 2017. https://philosproject.org/turkey-victims-change-regime-remains/

350 İnsan Hakları Ortak Platformu, Olağanüstü Hal Tedbir Ve Düzenlemeleri 31 Ağustos 2017, Güncellenmiş Durum Raporu," September. 18, 2017.

351 69,301 Students Behind Bars: Increase by a Factor of 25 in 4 Years," BIA News Desk, September 11, 2017.

352 Kural, Beyza, "Academic Discharges on Map as New Academic Year Begins," Bianet, September 19, 2017. https://bianet.org/english/human-rights/189957-academic-discharges-on-map-as-new-academic-year-begins

353 Carey, Brian Todd, "Battle of Manzikert," Oxford Bibliographies Online, July 26, 2017. http://www.oxfordbibliographies.com/view/document/obo-9780199791279/obo-9780199791279-0063.xml

354 Adler, Franklin Hugh, "Jews in Contemporary Turkey," Macalester International, Volume 15, 2005. http://digitalcommons.macalester.edu/cgi/viewcontent.cgi?article=1395&context=macintl

355 Bulut, Uzay, "Turkey Uncensored: A History of Censorship and Bans," Philos Project, September 20, 2017. https://philosproject.org/turkey-uncensored-printing-press-state-archives-wikipedia-history-censorship-bans/

356 Pavlidis, Theo, "Chapter 14: The Rise of the Ottoman Empire", 2012. http://www.theopavlidis.com/MidEast/part50.htm

357 Ibrahim, Raymond, "A brief historical survey of Christians in Turkey," Jihad Watch, January 22, 2009. https://www.jihadwatch.org/2009/01/a-brief-historical-survey-of-christians-in-turkey

358 Tzanos, Constantine, "The Conquest of Constantinople, Hagia Sofia and Turkey — EU," Huffington Post, June 25, 2014. http://www.huffingtonpost.com/constantine-tzanos/the-conquest-of-constantinople_b_5500136.html

359 Bulut, Uzay, "Turkey: Christian Refugees Live in Fear," the Gatestone Institute, January 24, 2016. https://www.gatestoneinstitute.org/7284/turkey-christian-refugees

360 Bulut, Uzay, "5000-year-old Assyrian Culture Facing Devastation," the Gatestone Institute, November 29, 2015. https://www.gatestoneinstitute.org/6976/assyrians-genocide

361 Bulut, Uzay, "Turkey: Historic Armenian Church Now Used as a Stable," the Clarion Project, April 5, 2017. https://clarionproject.org/turkey-historic-armenian-church-now-used-as-a-stable/

362 Tatz, Colin, Higgins, Winton, "The Magnitude of Genocide," Praeger, March 14, 2016.

363 "The Armenian Genocide: Cultural and Ethical Legacies," edited by Richard G. Hovannisian, Transaction Publishers, December 31, 2011.

364 "Resolution," the International Association of Genocide Scholars (IAGS), 2007. http://www.genocidescholars.org/sites/default/files/document%09%5Bcurrent-page%3A1%5D/documents/IAGS-Resolution-Assyrian%20and%20Greek%20Genocide.pdf

365 Bulut, Uzay, "'Secular' Turkey", the Gatestone Institute, May 27, 2015. https://www.gatestoneinstitute.org/5833/secular-turkey

366 Official website of the Republic of Turkey, Presidency of Religious Affairs (Diyanet). http://diyanet.gov.tr/en/icerik/high-board-of-religious-affairs/12598

367 Bulut, Uzay, "'Secular' Turkey", the Gatestone Institute, May 27, 2015. https://www.gatestoneinstitute.org/5833/secular-turkey

368 Bayar, Yesim, "Formation of the Turkish Nation-State, 1920–1938," Palgrave Macmillan, June 5, 2014.

369 Ibid.

370 Parla, Taha, Davison, Andrew, "Corporatist Ideology in Kemalist Turkey: Progress or Order?," Syracuse University Press, December 1, 2004.

371 "Foreigners don't like Muslims, only their money: Turkish President Erdoğan," Hurriyet Daily News, November 27, 2014. http://www.hurriyetdailynews.com/foreigners-dont-like-muslims-only-their-money-turkish-president-Erdoğan.aspx?PageID=238&NID=74893&NewsCatID=338

372 Bayar, Yesim, "Formation of the Turkish Nation-State, 1920–1938," Palgrave Macmillan, June 5, 2014.

373 "Lausanne Peace Treaty", the official website of the Turkish Ministry of Foreign Affairs, retrieved on April, 15, 2017. http://www.mfa.gov.tr/lausanne-peace-treaty.en.mfa

374 Bayar, Yesim, "Formation of the Turkish Nation-State, 1920–1938," Palgrave Macmillan, June 5, 2014.

375 Ibid.

376 "6 bin 437 azınlık okulundan sadece 23'ü eğitime devam ediyor," Hurriyet, September 19, 2013. http://www.hurriyet.com.tr/6-bin-437-azinlik-okulundan-sadece-23-u-egitime-devam-ediyor-24746437

377 Bedrosyan, Raffi, "Bedrosyan: Searching for Lost Armenian Churches and Schools in Turkey," the Armenian Weekly, August 1, 2011.

http://armenianweekly.com/2011/08/01/searching-for-lost-armenian-churches-and-schools-in-turkey/

378 Bedrosyan, Raffi, "Revisiting the Turkification of Confiscated Armenian Assets," the Armenian Weekly, April 17, 2012. http://armenianweekly.com/2012/04/17/revisiting-the-turkification-of-confiscated-armenian-assets/

379 Hofmann, Tessa, "Armenians In Turkey Today: A Critical Assessment of the Situation of the Armenian Minority in the Turkish Republic," the EU Office of Armenian Associations of Europe, October, 2002. http://www.armenian.ch/gsa/Docs/faae02.pdf

380 Ibid.

381 Bulut, Uzay, "Turkey: Racist Attacks Against Armenians Go Unpunished," the Armenian Weekly, December 5, 2016. http://armenianweekly.com/2016/12/05/racist-attacks-against-armenians-go-unpunished/

382 Bulut, Uzay, "Greeks in Turkey on the Verge of Extinction," the Clarion Project, February 15, 2017. https://clarionproject.org/greeks-in-turkey-on-the-verge-of-extinction-this-population-decline-of-gre/

383 "Helsinki Watch Report: Denying Human Rights and Ethnic Identity: The Greeks Of Turkey," Human Rights Watch, March 1992.
https://www.hrw.org/sites/default/files/reports/TURKEY923.PDF

384 Ibid.

385 Kotam, Aleksia, "Sad condition of Greek schools," Agos, June 13, 2016.
http://www.agos.com.tr/en/article/15638/sad-condition-of-greek-schools

386 De Zayas, Alfred, "The Istanbul Pogrom of 6–7 September 1955 in the Light of International Law," Genocide Studies and Prevention: An International Journal, Volume 2, 2007.
http://scholarcommons.usf.edu/cgi/viewcontent.cgi?article=1206&context=gsp

387 "The Holy Theological School of Halki," the English website of The Ecumenical Patriarchate of Constantinople, retrieved on April 15, 2017. https://www.ec-patr.org/mones/chalki/english.htm

388 Bostom, Andrew, "The Legacy of Islamic Antisemitism: From Sacred Texts to Solemn History," Prometheus Books, May 30, 2008.

389 Bulut, Uzay, "How Turkey's Jewish Alliance Schools Have Become History," the Algemeiner, February 7, 2017. https://www.algemeiner.com/2017/02/07/how-turkeys-jewish-alliance-schools-have-become-history/

390 "Jewish/Israel Organizations: Alliance Israelite Universelle," Jewish virtual Library, retrieved on April 15, 2017. http://www.jewishvirtuallibrary.org/alliance-israelite-universelle,

391 Ibid.

392 Güven, Ahmet Hilmi, "Educational Activities of the Ottoman Jews from the Last Decades of the Empire to the Early Years of the Turkish Republic: The Alliance Israélite Universelle Experience in Light of Turkish and French Archival Documents (1860-1937)", a thesis submitted to the Graduate School of Social Sciences of Middle East Technical University, February, 2013. http://etd.lib.metu.edu.tr/upload/12615771/index.pdf

393 Bayar, Yesim, "Formation of the Turkish Nation-State, 1920–1938," Palgrave Macmillan, June 5, 2014.

394 Travis, Hannibal, "'Native Christians Massacred': The Ottoman Genocide of the Assyrians during World War I," Genocide Studies and Prevention: An International Journal, volume 1, 2006. http://scholarcommons.usf.edu/cgi/viewcontent.cgi?article=1233&context=gsp

395 Bulut, Uzay, "Turkey Removes Assyrian Sculpture, Continues Crackdown on Christians," the Armenian Weekly, February 9, 2017. http://armenianweekly.com/2017/02/09/turkey-removes-assyrian/

396 Bulut, Uzay, "Assyrian Christians Targeted in Turkey, Iraq and Syria," The Philos Project, November 18, 2016. https://philosproject.org/assyrian-christians-targeted-turkey/

397 Orer, Ayca, "Turkey Denies Request for Assyrian-Language Kindergarten," Al-Monitor, December 12, 2012. http://www.al-monitor.com/pulse/tr/culture/2012/12/turkey-denies-assyrian-request-to-open-kindergarten.html

398 Gültekin, Uygur, "Süryaniler eğitim yılına ilkokulsuz başlıyor," Agos, September 18, 2017. http://www.agos.com.tr/tr/yazi/19343/suryaniler-egitim-yilina-ilkokulsuz-basliyor

399 "Chapter: Restrictions on the Use of the Kurdish Language" in "Turkey: Violations of Free Expression in Turkey," Human Rights Watch, 1999. https://www.hrw.org/reports/1999/turkey/turkey993-08.htm

400 Bulut, Uzay, "So how are the Kurds in Turkey doing?," Israel National News, March 2, 2017. http://www.israelnationalnews.com/News/News.aspx/225968

401 Bulut, Uzay, "Poll: Turkish Public Still Oppose Kurdish Rights,"Basnews, June 1, 2015. http://www.basnews.com/index.php/en/news/176276

402 Bulut, Uzay, "Yazidis—A History of Persecution," Philos Project, November 4, 2016. https://philosproject.org/yazidis-history-persecution/

403 Bulut, Uzay, "Choosing between freedom and Islamism," Israel Hayom, August 26, 2014. http://www.israelhayom.com/site/newsletter_opinion.php?id=9759

404 "Turkey," by Malcolm Edward Yapp and John C. Dewdney, Encyclopedia Britannica, updated January 31, 2018, https://www.britannica.com/place/Turkey

405 "Where does Erdoğan Want to Take Turkey?," by Soner Cagaptay, Washington Institute website, June 15, 2016, http://www.washingtoninstitute.org/policy-analysis/view/where-does-Erdoğan-want-to-take-turkey

406 "How Erdoğan Made Tukey Authoritarian Again," by Steven A. Cook, The Atlantic, July 21, 2016, https://www.theatlantic.com/international/archive/2016/07/how-Erdoğan-made-turkey-authoritarian-again/492374/

407 See generally "Turkey's Press Freedom Crisis," Committee to Protect Journalism, https://cpj.org/reports/2012/10/turkeys-press-freedom-crisis-assault-on-the-press.php

408 "Getting Off the Train," Special Report, The Economist, February 4, 2016, https://www.economist.com/news/special-report/21689877-mr-Erdoğans-commitment-democracy-seems-be-fading-getting-train

409 "Amnesty Accuses Turkey of 'brutal' Gezi Park Protest Abuse," BBC News, October 2, 1013, http://www.bbc.com/news/world-europe-24361082

410 "Turkey Divided More than Ever by Erdoğan's Gezi Park Crackdown," by Ian Traynor and Constanze Letsch, The Guardian, June 20, 2013, https://www.theguardian.com/world/2013/jun/20/turkey-divided-Erdoğan-protests-crackdown

411 "Amnesty Accuses Turkey of 'brutal' Gezi Park Protest Abuse," BBC News, October 2, 1013, http://www.bbc.com/news/world-europe-24361082

412 "Turkey's Coup Attempt: What You Need to Know," BBC News, July 17, 2016, http://www.bbc.com/news/world-europe-36816045 The Gülen Movement was originally an ally of the AKP, but at some point had differences, which are not the subject of this paper. Rightly or wrongly, the Turkish government now classifies the Gülen as a terrorist organization. Gülenist publications have been shut down and journalists who report favorably on the Gülen movement are often charged with being part of, or supporting a terrorist group.

413 "Turkey: Freedom in the World," Freedom House, 2017, https://freedomhouse.org/report/freedom-world/2017/turkey

[414] "Turkey Extracts: Emergency Decree Laws" published by the European Commission for Democracy through Law, Venice Commission Website, PDF, February 20, 2017, http://www.venice.coe.int/webforms/documents/default.aspx?pdffile=CDL-REF(2017)011-e

[415] "Turkey: Freedom in the World," Freedom House, 2017, https://freedomhouse.org/report/freedom-world/2017/turkey

[416] "Questions and Answers: Freedom of Expression and Language Rights in Turkey," Human Rights Watch website, April, 2002, http://pantheon.hrw.org/legacy/press/2002/08/turkeyqa041902.htm

[417] See generally, "Turkey Jails More Journalists than Any Other Nation. Those in Detention are All Terrorists, Erdoğan Says." By Zia Weise, PRI, June 28, 2017, https://www.pri.org/stories/2017-06-28/turkey-jails-more-journalists-any-other-nation-those-detention-are-all-terrorists

[418] See generally, "Turkey's Press Freedom Crisis," Committee to Protect Journalism, https://cpj.org/reports/2012/10/turkeys-press-freedom-crisis-assault-on-the-press.php; Also "Turkey: Freedom in the World," Freedom House, 2017, https://freedomhouse.org/report/freedom-world/2017/turkey

[419] See generally, "Turkey: Freedom of the Press," Freedom House, 2016, https://freedomhouse.org/report/freedom-press/2016/turkey.

[420] The stations were precluded from timely reporting by the Supreme Electoral Council which is a body purportedly designed to uphold the Turkish Constitution in elections.

[421] See generally "Turkey: Freedom of the Press," Freedom House, 2016, https://freedomhouse.org/report/freedom-press/2016/turkey; Also "Republic of Turkey, Parliamentary Elections," Final Report by the OSCE/ODIHR Limited Election Observation Mission, OSCE Office for Democratic Institutions and Human Rights, OSCE website download, June 7, 2015, http://www.osce.org/odihr/elections/turkey/177926?download=true

[422] "CNN-Türk Airs Penguin Documentary During Istanbul Riots," by Istanbul riots by Cooper Fleishman, The Daily Dot, June 2, 2013, https://www.dailydot.com/news/cnn-turk-istanbul-riots-penguin-doc-social-media/

[423] "Turkey: 72 Journalists Forced Out for Covering Protests, Union Says," New York Times, July 23, 2013, http://www.nytimes.com/2013/07/24/world/europe/turkey-72-journalists-forced-out-for-covering-protests-union-says.html?_r=1&

[424] "Turkey's Crackdown Propels Number of Journalists in Jail Worldwide to Record High," Report: Turkey: A Prison for Journalists", Committee to Protect Journalists, December 13, 2016, https://cpj.org/reports/2016/12/journalists-jailed-record-high-turkey-crackdown.php

[425] "Turkey: Freedom in the World," Freedom House, 2017, https://freedomhouse.org/report/freedom-world/2017/turkey

[426] "Turkey: Freedom in the World," Freedom House, 2017, https://freedomhouse.org/report/freedom-world/2017/turkey

[427] See generally "Turkey: Freedom of the Press," Freedom House, 2016, https://freedomhouse.org/report/freedom-press/2016/turkey

[428] See Turkey Coup Attempt: Arrest Warrants Issued for Former Newspaper Staff, " by Chris Johnston and agencies in Istanbul, The Guardian, July, 27, 2016, https://www.theguardian.com/world/2016/jul/27/turkey-discharges-1700-officers-from-military-after-coup-attempt

[429] "Turkish Criminal Code (Law No. 5237)," passed September 26, 2004, http://www.wipo.int/edocs/lexdocs/laws/en/tr/tr171en.pdf

[430] See "Turkish Criminal Code (Law No. 5237)," passed September 26, 2004, http://www.wipo.int/edocs/lexdocs/laws/en/tr/tr171en.pdf; See also "The Law on the Fight Against Terrorism of Turkey, Act. No. 3713 (as amended)," http://www.legislationline.org/documents/id/16875

[431] "Turkey: Freedom of the Press," Freedom House, 2015, https://freedomhouse.org/report/freedom-press/2015/turkey

[432] "Turkey Tops Countries Demanding Content Removal: Twitter," by Humeyra Pamuk and Jonny Hogg, Reuters, February 9, 2015, https://www.reuters.com/article/us-turkey-twitter/turkey-tops-countries-demanding-content-removal-twitter-idUSKBN0LD1P620150209

[433] "Turkey Blocks Several Websites Saying They Violate Blasphemy Laws," by Debapriya Chatterjee, Atheist Republic website, March 18, 2015, http://www.atheistrepublic.com/news/turkey-blocks-several-websites-saying-they-violate-blasphemy-laws

[434] "Turkey Blocks Several Websites Saying They Violate Blasphemy Laws," by Debapriya Chatterjee, Atheist Republic website, March 18, 2015, http://www.atheistrepublic.com/news/turkey-blocks-several-websites-saying-they-violate-blasphemy-laws

[435] "Turkey: Freedom on the Net," Freedom House, 2016, https://freedomhouse.org/report/freedom-net/2016/turkey

[436] "Turkey Uncensored: A History of Censorship and Bans," by Uzay Bulut, Philos Project website, September 20, 2017, https://philosproject.org/turkey-uncensored-printing-press-state-archives-wikipedia-history-censorship-bans/

[437] "Turkey," End Blasphemy Laws website, https://end-blasphemy-laws.org/countries/europe/turkey/

[438] "Turkey," End Blasphemy Laws website, https://end-blasphemy-laws.org/countries/europe/turkey/

[439] "Turkey," End Blasphemy Laws website, https://end-blasphemy-laws.org/countries/europe/turkey/

[440] "Turkey Uncensored: A History of Censorship and Bans," by Uzay Bulut, Philos Project website, September 20, 2017, https://philosproject.org/turkey-uncensored-printing-press-state-archives-wikipedia-history-censorship-bans/

[441] "Turkey: Freedom on the Net," Freedom House, 2017, https://freedomhouse.org/report/freedom-net/2017/turkey

[442] "Turkey: Freedom on the Net," Freedom House, 2017,https://freedomhouse.org/report/freedom-net/2017/turkey

[443] "Mass. Judges Express Fears Over Arrests, Firings Of Judges In Turkey," by David Boeri, wbur website, October 06, 2016, http://www.wbur.org/morningedition/2016/10/06/arrests-firings-judges-turkey

[444] See generally "Turkey," Freedom House Report, 2017, https://freedomhouse.org/report/freedom-world/2017/turkey

[445] See generally "Turkey Post-Referendum: Institutions And Human Rights," Joint Briefing of the Helsinki Commission and Lantos Commission, Commission on Security and Cooperation in Europe website, May 2, 2017, https://www.csce.gov/international-impact/events/turkey-post-referendum-institutions-and-human-rights

[446] "The Organization of Islamic Cooperation's Jihad on Free Speech, p. 15," by Deborah Weiss, Esq., The Center for Security Policy Press, 2015, p. 13.

[447] "The Organization of Islamic Cooperation's Jihad on Free Speech, p. 15," by Deborah Weiss, Esq., The Center for Security Policy Press, 2015, p. 34. Also "Criminalizing Islamophobic

Speech," by Deborah Weiss, Esq., article within "Free Speech Under Fire: The Red-Green Axis' Unrestricted Warfare In OSCE and Beyond," PDF published by the Center for Security Policy, November 29, 2017, https://www.centerforsecuritypolicy.org/wp-content/uploads/2017/12/Free_Speech_Under_Fire_12-01-17a.pdf, p. 15.

[448] "Turkey and the Organization of Islamic Cooperation: Part 1," By Armine Muradyan, Armenian Center of Young Analysts website, June 19, 2016, https://acoya.org/language/en/international-relations/turkey-and-the-organization-of-islamic-cooperation-part-1/?print=print

[449] "Turkey and the Organization of Islamic Cooperation: Part 2," By Armine Muradyan, Armenian Center of Young Analysts website, June 20, 2016, https://acoya.org/language/en/international-relations/turkey-and-the-organization-of-islamic-cooperation-part-2/

[450] For more information on the OIC, Resolution 16/18, and the OIC's Ten Year Programme of Action, see generally "The Organization of Islamic Cooperation's Jihad on Free Speech, p. 15," by Deborah Weiss, Esq., The Center for Security Policy Press, 2015.

[451] "Turkish Prime Minister: 'Islamophobia' is a 'Crime Against Humanity'," by Laura Byrne, The Daily Caller, September 18, 2012, http://dailycaller.com/2012/09/18/turkish-prime-minister-islamophobia-is-a-crime-against-humanity/

[452] "Erdoğan: Islamophobia Should be Recognized as Crime," by the World Bulletin News Desk, World Bulletin, September 17, 2012, http://www.worldbulletin.net/?aType=haber&ArticleID=95670

[453] "Turkish Prime Minister: 'Islamophobia' is a 'Crime Against Humanity'," by Laura Byrne, The Daily Caller, September 18, 2012, http://dailycaller.com/2012/09/18/turkish-prime-minister-islamophobia-is-a-crime-against-humanity/

[454] "Shifting into Reverse: Turkish Constitutionalism under the AKP," by Aslı Bâli, Theory & Event Project 19, Issue 1 Supplement, excerpt on Project Muse website, January 2016, https://muse.jhu.edu/article/610221/summary

INDEX

H

I

N

O

P

Pavlidis, Theo · 123
Peace At Home Council, The · 77
People's Liberation Army · 97
People's Special Forces (HOH) · 120
Pew Research Center · 76, 111, 161
Phases of the World Underground
    Movement Plan · 21
Pipes, Daniel · 2, 78, 82, 87, 94, 161,
    163, 167
Piri, Kati · 103
Political Islam · 11, 18, 102, 109
Presidency of Religious Affairs
    (Diyanet) · 28
Prince George's County Muslim
    Council · 37
Putin, Vladimir (Russia's president) ·
    115

Q

Qaddafi, Muammar · 78
Qatar · 13, 23, 67, 87, 97, 112, 117,
    118
Qutb, Sayyid · 21

R

Rabia al-Adawiya Square · 46
Rabia hand sign · 46
Rahman, Muhammad Tariq · 35
Raindrop Houses · 55
Ramallah · 14
Rasmussen, Anders Fogh · 92
Red-Green Axis · 41, 44, 176
Reporters Without Borders · 103
Republican People's Party (CHP) · 107
Resolution 16/18 · 147
Rhode, Harold · 2, 5, 20
Romania · 93
Rumi Forum · 69
Russia · 88, 89, 96, 110, 111, 112, 114,
    115, 116, 118

S

S-400 anti-aircraft missile system · 91
SADAT · 90, 120
Sakal, Ak · 6
Sakina Collective, The · 62
Salman, Mohammed bin (Saudi Crown
    Prince) · 76
Sarajevo, Bosnia · 14
Saudi Arabia · 88, 97, 110, 117, 118,
    168
Say, Fazil · 144
Scheffer, Jaap de Hoop · 92
Shanghai Cooperative Organization ·
    91
Shareef, Imam Talib · 60
Sheridan Circle · 91
Shin Bet · 26
Shoulder to Shoulder program · 44
Sinanovic, Ermin · 37
Sobieski, Jan (John III) · 75, 85
Social media · 140, 141, 143, 144
Soviet Union · 87, 90
Star Spangled Shariah · 23, 39, 46, 151,
    152
Steudtner, Peter · 90
Supreme Board of Elections · 119
Susin, Sait · 133
Swift, Charles · 38
Syeed, Sayyid · 35

T

Taliban · 89
Tarin, Haris · 60
Tatz, Colin · 124
Theological School of Halki · 131
Today's Zaman · 72, 142
Tolu, Mesale · 81
Travis, Hannibal · 133
Treaty of Lausanne · 128, 133